COMPANION

TO

CAESAR

NEW REVISED EDITION
With Latest Regents Vocabulary Lists

By

Joseph Pearl, Ph.D.

Formerly Professor of Classic Languages, Brooklyn College
Author of "Companion to Cicero" and "Companion to Vergil"

COLLEGE ENTRANCE BOOK COMPANY
104 Fifth Avenue   New York City

PREFACE

The purpose of this book is to present in teachable form all the material which should accompany a sound and thorough Latin course based on Caesar.

The outstanding features of this book are:

1. **A Biography of Caesar,** containing the most important and outstanding events of his life.

2. **Roman Military Affairs,** thoroughly treated in outline form. (**Instructive illustrations** have been included to help the pupil understand the text.)

3. **A Summary of Syntax.** The important rules are clearly stated and illustrated by examples from the earlier chapters of the **Gallic War.**

4. **Exercises in Prose Composition,** consisting of 300 sentences for translation into Latin. These sentences have been selected from **Regents and College Entrance Examinations** and arranged according to the main construction they illustrate, e.g., purpose, result, etc. References within the sentences themselves to the rules of syntax will prove a valuable innovation. Also, **Selections for Translation at Sight.**

5. **Idioms and Phrases,** which occur in Caesar, have been collected and alphabetized with the **verb as base.** This enables immediate reference.

6. **Derivation and Word Formation.** These topics have been thoroughly presented. The outline form has been employed and **copious exercises** included.

7. **A List of Latin Words,** arranged in order of the half year in which they are studied, and classified according to parts of speech.

8. **Latest Regents Word List.** The revised vocabulary list includes all the words required by the New York State Board of Regents, as well as many others, together with their Latin translations. All words listed in the latest Regents Syllabus have been marked for easy identification.

9. **An English-Latin Vocabulary** for use in connection with the sentences for translation.

10. **The Recent Examination Papers** of the State Department of Education have been included, to give the student an idea as to the nature of the questions asked.

JOSEPH PEARL, PH.D.

CONTENTS

Examination Papers

CHAPTER I

IMPORTANT EVENTS IN CAESAR'S LIFE

B. C.

100 Gaius Julius Caesar was born July 12, 100 B.C. His father's family traced its history to Iulus, son of Aeneas and grandson of Venus. His mother Aurelia belonged to a prominent plebeian family.

Caesar's early education was that usually received by the sons of wealthy families. Besides Latin and Greek he was taught rhetoric, grammar, philosophy, and oratory. M. Antonius Gnipho, an educated Gaul, was his private teacher.

83 Married Cornelia, the daughter of Cinna, a prominent leader of the popular party; through this marriage and through the influence of his uncle Marius, "the darling of the soldiers and of the crowd," Caesar later became the champion of the popular party.

82 Sulla, the leader of the aristocratic party, which was then in power, ordered Caesar to divorce his wife. Caesar's refusal almost cost him his life.

81 In fear of Sulla, Caesar left for Asia Minor, where he served in the war against Mithridates. Here he was awarded the civic crown (corōna cīvīca)
80 for saving the life of a fellow citizen at the siege of Mytilene.

78 On Sulla's death, Caesar returned to Rome and brought charges of extortion against Dolabella, who had been governor of Macedonia.

76 Went to Rhodes to study oratory under the famous rhetorician Apollonius Molo. On his way thither, he was captured by pirates, whom, after he had been ransomed, he put to death.

74 Returned to Rome and was chosen military tribune.

68 Served as quaestor and accompanied the governor to Spain as his financial secretary.

67 His wife Cornelia having died, Caesar married Pompeia, Sulla's granddaughter and Pompey's cousin.

Helped to carry the Lex Gabinia, giving Pompey command against the Mediterranean pirates.

66 Supported the Lex Manilia, giving Pompey command against Mithridates.

65 Was curule aedile. In order to win the favor of the multitude, Caesar gave them magnificent theatrical entertainments which involved him in heavy debt.

B. C.

63 Became Pontifex Maximus, the head of the Roman state religion.
Spoke in the Senate in the debate on the fellow conspirators of Catiline.

62 Held the office of praetor, whose duties were chiefly judicial. Divorced Pompeia.

61 As propraetor (governor) in Spain he subdued several mountain tribes.

60 Returned to Rome, and formed together with Pompey, the conqueror of Mithridates, and Crassus, the richest man in Rome, a league known as the First Triumvirate, whose object was to secure for the triumvirs the honors of the state.

59 Consul with Bibulus.
Married Calpurnia.
To strengthen the alliance made with Pompey, Caesar gave him his daughter Julia in marriage.
He secured for Pompey's soldiers the land which they had been promised, and in return, he received, through the influence of the Triumvirate, as his prize, the provinces of Cisalpine Gaul, Illyricum, and Transalpine Gaul for five years.

58 Conquered the Helvetians and Ariovistus.

57 Subdued the Belgians.

56 War with the Veneti.
At a conference of the Triumvirate at Luca, Caesar's governorship of Gaul was extended for five years.

55 Expedition to Germany and Britain.

54 Second expedition to Britain.
Revolt of the Nervii.
Death of Julia.

53 Second expedition to Germany.
Rebellion of the Gallic states.
The death of Crassus and Pompey's alliance with the senatorial party, prompted by his jealousy of Caesar's reputation and influence, broke up the Triumvirate.

52 Revolt of almost all Gaul under Vercingetorix. Fall of Alesia.

51 The last embers of revolt in Gaul quenched.
Caesar published his Commentaries.

49 Upon the demand of the Senate that Caesar give up his provinces and dismiss his army, Caesar with a faithful legion crossed the Rubicon, a little stream between his province and Italy, thus precipitating civil war. Soon all Italy was in his power; Pompey and his followers fled to Macedonia.

B. C.

48 Consul for the second time.

Defeated Pompey at Pharsalus in Thessaly. Pompey fled to Egypt, where, upon landing, he was put to death by order of the king.

47 Defeated Ptolemy, King of Egypt, and placed his sister Cleopatra on the throne.

In Pontus, he defeated Pharnaces, the son of Mithridates, and reported that victory to the senate in his three famous words: **vēnī, vīdī, vīcī.**

46 Consul for the third time.

Conquered the adherents of Pompey at Thapsus, in Africa.

Returned to Rome, where he celebrated four triumphs—over Gaul, Egypt, Pontus, and Africa.

Elected dictator for ten years.

Reformed the calendar.

45 Conquered the sons of Pompey at Munda, in Spain.

Made dictator for life.

44 The bitter hatred of his political enemies together with the fear that his growing power might endanger the general good of Rome prompted the conspirators to kill Caesar on the Ides of March.

CAESAR'S ACCOMPLISHMENTS

Caesar is considered by many the foremost character in history.

He distinguished himself in three directions—in statesmanship, in generalship, and in literature.

He showed his statesmanship in dealing with the Gallic tribes and with both his friends and enemies at Rome.

His generalship has never been surpassed.

His Commentaries are "unadorned, straightforward, and elegant, every embellishment being stripped off as a garment."

CHAPTER II

CAESAR'S ARMY

1 *The Infantry (pedites).*

This was composed exclusively of Roman citizens, who were subject to military service between the ages of seventeen and forty-six for a period of twenty years.

The largest unit of this branch of the army was the legion (**legiō**). Its normal strength was 6,000 men, but in the Gallic War its average size was probably about 3,600 men. The members of the legion were called either **mīlitēs legiōnāriī** or **mīlitēs**.

The legion was divided into ten cohorts (**cohortēs**) of 360 men each; each cohort into three maniples (**manipulī**) of 120 men each; each maniple into two centuries (**centuriae, ordinēs**) of 60 men each. Thus, **1** legion = **10** cohorts = **30** maniples = **60** centuries = **3,600** men.

The legions were designated by ordinal numbers given in the order of their formation. Caesar began the Gallic War with six legions; at the close of the War he had eleven. His favorite legion was the Tenth.

2 *The Cavalry (equitēs).*

This was composed chiefly of non-citizens, especially Gauls, Spaniards, and Germans. In the Gallic Wars Caesar used from five to six thousand **equitēs**.

The tactical unit of the cavalry was the squadron (**turma**) of about 30 men.

3 *The Auxiliaries (auxilia).*

These were made up chiefly of non-citizens from allied or subject states. They included:

a. Light-armed foot soldiers (**levis armātūrae peditēs**), used chiefly to make a show of force and in foraging expeditions.

b. Slingers (**funditōrēs**), from the Balearic Islands.

c. Bowmen (**sagittāriī**), from Crete and Numidia.

4 *The Non-combatants.*

- *a.* Camp servants (**cālōnēs**); these performed menial camp duties and acted as servants of the officers.
- *b.* Muleteers (**mūliōnēs**); in charge of the heavy baggage of the army.
- *c.* Traders (**mercātōrēs**); these bought booty from the soldiers and sold them provisions.

OFFICERS

1 *The Commander-in-Chief (dux),* or *(imperātor),* after his first important victory. After his victory over the Helvetians, Caesar received the title **imperātor.**

2 *The Lieutenants (lēgāti).*

These were men of senatorial rank, appointed by the senate and assigned to the Commander-in-chief. They usually commanded one or more legions, and were regularly in charge of the winter quarters. Caesar mentions about twenty different lēgāti, of whom the most famous were: M. Antōnius, L. Aurunculeius Cotta, O. Titūrius Sabinus, D. Iūnius Brūtus, T. Labiēnus, and Q. Tullius Cicerō, the brother of the famous orator.

3 *The Quartermaster (quaestor).*

He, too, was of senatorial rank. He was elected by the people for one year and assigned to a particular province to administer its financial affairs. In connection with the army, the quaestor discharged the duties of a modern quartermaster, such as the charge of the military chest, the pay, food, clothing, and general equipment of the soldiers. In battle, the quaestor sometimes commanded a legion.

4 *The Tribunes (tribuni militum).*

Six military tribunes were attached to each legion. They were usually young men of equestrian rank, without any previous military experience, who owed their appointment to family or political influence. Their duties were therefore of minor importance, such as the levying and the discharge of soldiers, the command of small detachments and participation in the councils of war.

5 *The Prefects (praefecti).*

These were the commanders of the auxiliaries and of the largest unit of the cavalry (**āla**).

6 *The Centurions (centuriones).*

These were men of plebeian origin, promoted from the ranks on account of their faithfulness, bravery, and efficient service.   Each legion had sixty centurions, one for every century.   The first centurion of the first cohort was called **prīmipīlus** or **prīmus pīlus;** in battle, it was he who had special care of the standard of the legion.   Besides training and leading their centuries, the centurions had other duties, such as finding a suitable place for the camp and bringing together the booty.

7 *The Decurions (decuriones).*

These were subordinate cavalry leaders.   Each decurion was in charge of a squadron (**turma**).

Besides these seven classes of officers, there were the privileged soldiers who enjoyed certain exemptions.   Such were the **veteran volunteers** (**ēvocātī**) who enjoyed the rank and pay of the centurions, and the **standard bearers** of the legions (**aquiliferī**) and of the maniples (**sīgniferī**).

CLOTHING AND EQUIPMENT
OF
THE LEGIONARY SOLDIER

1 *Clothing.*

a. A short-sleeved or sleeveless woolen tunic (**tunica**) reaching to the knees.

b. A woolen mantle (**sagum**) for wet or cold weather.

c. Heavy leather shoes (**caligae**), fastened by straps.

GALEA

2 *Armor.*

a. Defensive weapons.

1. A helmet (**galea**) of leather, often adorned with a crest.

2. A coat of mail (**lōrīca**) of leather, strengthened with bands of metal.

3. A shield (**scūtum**), slightly curved, about four feet long and two and a half feet wide, made of wood covered with linen and leather, and bound with metal about the rim. In the middle on the inside, it had a handle, and opposite it on the outside a metal boss (**umbō**).   The shield was carried on the left arm.

SCUTUM

b. Offensive weapons.

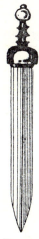

GLADIUS

1. A sword (**gla-dius**), which was about two feet long, straight, pointed, and two-edged. It was kept in a metal-covered wooden scabbard a n d carried on the right side. The officers carried the sword on the left side.

CASSIS

PILUM

2. A javelin (**pīlum**). This consisted of an iron shaft two feet long, which was inserted in a wooden shaft about four feet long. The **pīlum** could be thrown about 75 feet.

ARMOR OF THE AUXILIARY FORCES

1 *The Cavalry.*

a. A long sword.

b. A lance (**trāgula**) provided with a leather thong (**ammentum**).

c. A light round or oval shield (**parma**).

d. A helmet of metal (**cassis**).

2 *The Auxiliary Infantry.*

a. A sword.

b. A missile (**gaesum, matara, trāgula, verūtum**).

c. The Balearic slingers used slings (**fundae**) of leather and bullets of stone or lead (**glandēs**).

ARTILLERY (TORMENTA)

Three kinds of engines of war are mentioned by Caesar:

1. **The catapult** (**catapulta**) for shooting large arrows or javelins in a horizontal direction.

2. **The scorpion** (**scorpiō**), which was a small catapult.

3. **The ballista** (**ballista**) for hurling huge stones or heavy blocks of wood through the air at an angle of 45 degrees.

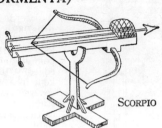

SCORPIO

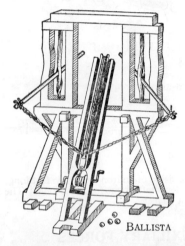

BALLISTA

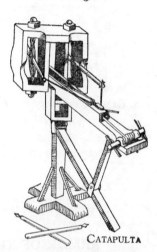

CATAPULTA

STANDARDS

1. The standard of the legion was a silver eagle (**aquila**) mounted on a wooden staff.

2. The standards of the maniples consisted of streamers attached to a cross-bar or a pole, with ornaments of various designs below. A common design was the figure of an animal or an open hand.

3. The standard of the cavalry and of the light-armed troops was the **vēxillum,** a square piece of colored cloth extended on a frame.

VEXILLUM

AQUILA

4. The signal for battle was a large red **vēxillum** displayed over the commander's tent.

THE FLEET

1. The war ship (**nāvis longa**), rather long and narrow, was propelled by both oars and sails. It usually had three banks of oars, which were arranged one above the other (**trireme**). At the prow was a sharp beak (**rōstrum**) of bronze or iron, for ramming the vessels of the enemy. The ship was provided with two rudders, one mast, one large sail, grappling hooks, wooden-towers, and **tormenta**. When not in use, it was drawn up on the shore.

2. The transport (**nāvis onerāria**), shorter and broader than the war ship, was used to convey troops and supplies. It was propelled mainly by sails.

THE PAY, FOOD, AND DISCIPLINE

1. The pay (**stīpendium**) of the legionary soldier was 225 denarii, or about $45 a year. The centurion and the veteran volunteer received twice as much. Higher officers naturally received higher pay.

2. Twice a month, each soldier received thirty pounds of grain (**frūmentum**), usually wheat, which was ground in a hand-mill and prepared for food by boiling into a paste or by making into unleavened bread.

3. For special bravery, the soldiers would receive one or more of the following rewards:

   a. Gifts of money.

   b. Public praise in the presence of the army.

   c. Promotion in rank.

   d. Decorations of honor, such as medals, necklaces, armlets, and the most coveted of all—the **corōna cīvica** for saving the life of a Roman citizen in battle.

   At the close of his period of service, the soldier would receive an honorable discharge together with a sum of money or an allotment of land.

   For insubordination or neglect of duty the following were the usual forms of punishment:

   a. Extra assignment of labor.

   b. Shortening of rations.

   c. Degradation in rank.

   d. Dismissal from the service.

   e. Corporal punishment.

   f. Death (in extreme cases).

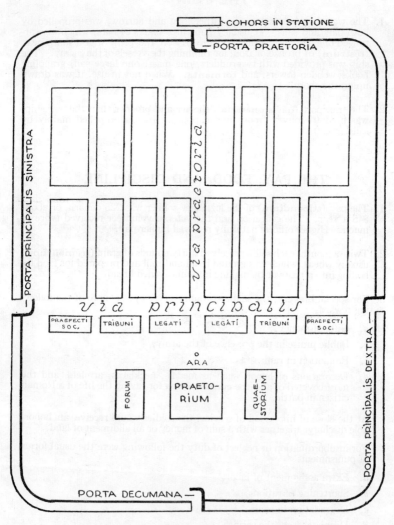

A ROMAN CAMP

THE CAMP

1 Site.

A high, sloping ground in the vicinity of wood and water.

2 Shape.

Quadrilateral, usually in the form of a rectangle or square, with its corners rounded.

3 Dimensions.

Depended on the size of the army; a camp accommodating eight legions covered about 106 acres.

4 Fortifications.

a. Trench (**fossa**), usually nine to twelve feet wide at the top, three feet at the bottom, and seven to nine feet deep.

b. Rampart (**vāllum**), formed of the dirt removed from the trench and thrown up toward the inside of the camp. This was usually six to ten feet high, and wide enough at the top to afford comfortable standing room for the defenders. On the wall was a breastwork of stakes (**vālli**), which was sometimes reënforced by branches, wicker-work, and towers erected at regular intervals.

5 Streets.

a. **Via praetōria.**

b. **Via prīncipālis.**

These crossed each other at right angles and connected the four gates.

6 Gates.

a. **Porta praetōria,** the front gate, facing the enemy.

b. **Porta decumāna,** the rear gate.

c. **Porta prīncipālis dextra,** on the right side.

d. **Porta prīncipālis sinistra,** on the left side.

Each gate was constantly guarded by a cohort (**cohors in statiōne**).

7 Tents (**tabernācula**).

a. The general's tent (**praetōrium**), in the rear of the camp.

b. The officers' tents, near that of the general.

c. The soldiers' tents, in the forward part of the camp. Each tent accommodated ten men.

BAGGAGE

1 **Heavy baggage (impedīmenta).**

   a. Extra supplies of arms.
   b. Provisions.
   c. Clothing.
   d. Tents.
   e. Artillery.
   f. Hand-mills.

This baggage was carried either on the backs of horses and mules (**iūmenta**) or in carts (**carrī**).

2 **The soldier's pack (sarcinæ).**

   a. Tools for digging.
   b. Cooking utensils.
   c. A supply of grain for two weeks.
   d. One or two rampart stakes.

These articles were tied in a bundle and fastened to the end of a forked pole, which was carried over the shoulder.　The weight of the bundle was about sixty pounds.

TRIPLEX ACIES

First line:　Four cohorts, consisting of the most experienced soldiers.　This line began the attack.

Second line:　Three cohorts, so arranged that the cohorts blocked the intervals between those of the first line.　This line stood ready to relieve the first.

Third line:　Three cohorts, consisting of the least experienced soldiers.　This line was used to assist the first two lines or to ward off an attack from the rear.

One legion in triple line formation.

4	3	2	1	prīma aciēs
	7	6	5	secunda aciēs
10		9	8	tertia aciēs

One cohort in formation.

3	2	1
a	a	a
b	b	b

In each cohort the three maniples stood side by side, and in each maniple the centuries stood one behind the other.

THE ARMY ON THE MARCH

1. **The van (prīmum agmen).** consisting of the cavalry and light-armed infantry.

2. **The main force (agmen).** Each legion was followed by its own baggage, but in case of danger of an attack, the baggage of the whole army was placed in the center of the column.

3. **The rear guard (novissimum agmen).**

A regular day's march lasted about seven hours, and the distance covered was about seventeen miles; a forced march (**iter magnum**) was about twenty-five miles.

VARIOUS SIEGE TERMS

1. The **vīnea** was a shed, about 15 feet long, 7 feet wide, and 8 feet high. It was built of heavy timbers covered with hides; it had open ends and was mounted on rollers. Several **vīneae** were placed end to end along the siege-mole to enable attacking forces to come close to the enemy's wall in order to break it down.

2. The **testūdō** was a shed with a sloping roof of strong boards used to protect soldiers near the enemy's walls. (Sometimes the name **testūdō** was applied to a kind of covering formed by the shields of the soldiers who were attacking a wall).

3. The **ariēs** (*battering ram*) was a heavy log, 60 to 100 feet long, capped with solid bronze, which was employed in sieges to break down the enemy's walls.

4. The **turris ambulātōria** (*movable tower*) was pushed forward on rollers toward the enemy's walls. The lowest story usually contained a battering ram, and above were artillery, bowmen, and slingers.

5. The **agger** (*siege-mole*) was a great roadway of logs and earth, 40 to 50 feet wide; it was begun about 500 feet from the wall and was gradually extended and raised until it was even with the top of the wall.

CHAPTER III

IDIOMS AND PHRASES

Arranged Alphabetically with the Verb as Base

(ā) bellō **abesse**	*to take no part in war*
facinus **admittere**	*to commit a crime*
beneficiō **afficere** aliquem	*to treat some one with kindness*
laetitiā **afficere**	*to fill with joy*
suppliciō **afficere**	*to punish*
difficultāte **afficī**	*to experience difficulty*
dolōre **afficī**	*to be greatly distressed (annoyed*
conventūs **agere**	*to hold court*
cum aliquō **agere**	*to plead (confer) with some one*
grātiās **agere** alicuī	*to express gratitude, to thank some one*
praedam **agere**	*to drive off the plunder*
vīneās **agere**	*to bring up the sheds*
in aliquem **animadvertere**	*to inflict punishment upon some one*
nāvis **appellitur**	*the ship lands*
arma **capere**	*to take up arms*
cōnsilium **capere**	*to form a plan*
dolōrem **capere**	*to be grieved*
initium **capere** ab	*to begin at*
īnsulam **capere**	*to reach an island*
portum **capere**	*to make a harbor*
agmen **claudere**	*to bring up the rear*
deōs **colere**	*to worship the gods*
proelium **committere**	*to join battle*
ad arma **concurrere**	*to rush to arms*
sē **cōnferre**	*to betake oneself, turn, proceed*
bellum **cōnficere**	*to finish a war*
in fugam **conicere**	*to put to flight*
in vincula (catēnās) **conicere**	*to imprison*
nāvem **cōnscendere**	*to go on board, embark*
mortem sibi **cōnscīscere**	*to commit suicide*
legiōnēs **cōnscrībere**	*to enroll legions*
exercitum **cōnstituere**	*to draw up the army*

Proelium committte

in fugam **dare**	*to put to flight*
inter sē **dare**	*to exchange*
operam **dare**	*to take pains*
ad ancorās **dēligāre**	*to anchor*
(proeliō) **dēcertāre**	*to fight a decisive battle*
nāvem **dēdūcere**	*to launch a ship*
bellum **dēfendere**	*to wage a defensive war*

[14]

summam bellī ad aliquem **dēferre**	*to confer the management of the war upon some one*
arma **dēpōnere**	*to lay down arms*
memoriam **dēpōnere**	*to forget*
causam **dīcere**	*to plead a case*
iūs **dīcere**	*to administer justice*
ab armīs **discēdere**	*to lay down arms*
praesidia **dispōnere**	*to station detachments of troops at intervals*
bellum **dūcere**	*to prolong a war*
in mātrimōnium **dūcere**	*to marry*
prīmum pīlum **dūcere**	*to hold the rank of first centurion*

in vulgus **efferre**	*to spread abroad among the common people*
oculōs **effodere**	*to gouge out the eyes*
nāvibus **ēgredi**	*to disembark*
sē **ēicere**	*to rush out*
bonō animō **esse** in aliquem	*to be well disposed toward some one*
dictō audiēns **esse** alicuī	*to obey some one*
ex ūsū **esse**	*to be of advantage*
in statiōne **esse**	*to be on guard*
est in animō alicuī	*some one intends*
nihil **est** negōtī	*there is no trouble*
rēs **est** in angustō	*matters have reached a crisis*
impetum **excipere**	*to meet the attack*
turrim **excitāre**	*to erect a tower*
ēventum **experīrī**	*to await the outcome*

bellum **facere** alicuī	*to make war on some one*
certiōrem **facere** aliquem	*to inform some one*
fidem **facere** alicuī	*to convince some one, to give a pledge to some one*
grātum **facere** alicuī	*to do a favor to some one*
imperāta **facere**	*to carry out orders*
impetum **facere** in aliquem	*to make an attack on some one*
iter **facere**	*to march*
perīculum **facere**	*to run a risk; to make an attempt*
potestātem **facere**	*to give opportunity (chance)*
proelium **facere**	*to fight*
verba **facere**	*to speak*
vim **facere**	*to use violence*
aegrē **ferre**	*to take to heart, to be vexed*
graviter (molestē) **ferre**	*to be annoyed, to be vexed*
signa **ferre**	*to advance*
certior **fierī**	*to be informed*

bellum **gerere** cum aliquō	*to wage war with some one.*

cēnsum habēre	to take the census
fidem habēre alicuī	to have confidence in some one
grātiam habēre	to feel thankful
in animō habēre	to intend
in numerō habēre	to consider as
ōrātiōnem habēre	to make a speech
ratiōnem habēre	to keep an account; to take account of
ratiō aliter sē habet ac	the principle is different from what

ancorās iacere	to drop anchor, to anchor
mīlitēs imperāre alicuī	to levy soldiers upon some one
bellum incidit	war breaks out
incidere in aliquem	to fall in the way of some one, to come upon some one
cursum incitāre	to quicken the pace
equum incitāre	to urge on (spur) the horse
bellum īnferre alicuī	to make war upon some one
iniūriam īnferre	to inflict an injury
signa īnferre	to advance
signa conversa īnferre	to face about and advance
vulnera īnferre	to inflict wounds
metum (timōrem) inicere	to strike fear
cōnsilium inīre	to form a plan
pugnae ratiōnem īnsistere	to adopt a plan of battle
sacrificiīs interdīcere	to excommunicate
proeliō interesse	to take part in battle

fugae sē mandāre	to flee
tēla mittere	to hurl darts
castra movēre	to break camp

operam nāvāre	to do one's best

adversīs hostibus occurrere	to meet the enemy face to face

bellum parāre	to prepare for war
poenās pendere	to pay the penalty
stīpendium pendere	to pay tribute
mūrum perdūcere	to construct a wall
poenās persolvere	to pay the penalty
eōdem pertinēre	to point to the same thing, be of the same nature
fugam petere	to flee
fugā salūtem petere	to flee for safety
arma pōnere	to lay down arms
castra pōnere	to pitch camp
multum posse	to have great influence

plūs **posse**	*to have greater influence*
plūrimum **posse**	*to have very great influence*
legiōnī **praeesse**	*to be in command of a legion*
rēbus dīvīnīs **praeesse**	*to have charge of the services of worship*
magistrātuī **praeesse**	*to hold public office*
sē **praeterre** alicuī	*to show oneself superior to some one*
praeficere (**praepōnere**) aliquem castrīs	*to put some one in command of the camp*
officium **praestāre**	*to do one's duty*
sacrificia **prōcūrāre**	*to regulate the sacrifices*
memoriam **prōdere**	*to hand down the memory*
pedibus **proeliārī**	*to fight on foot*

in fidem **recipere**	*to take under one's protection*
sē **recipere**	*to withdraw, retreat*
sē **recipere** ex terrōre	*to recover from a panic*
iūs **reddere**	*to render justice*
grātiam **referre**	*to make return, requite*
pedem **referre**	*to retreat*
obsidiōnem **relinquere**	*to leave off a siege*
proelium **restituere**	*to renew the battle*
ad sānitātem **revertī**	*to come to one's senses*

nāvem **solvere**	*to set sail*
novīs rēbus **studēre**	*to desire a revolution*
supplicium **sūmere** dē aliquō	*to inflict punishment on some one*

castrīs sē **tenēre**	*to remain in camp*
memoriā **tenēre**	*to remember*
ancorās **tollere**	*to weigh anchor*
famem **tolerāre**	*appease hunger, keep from starving*

cōnsiliō **ūtī**	*to adopt a plan*
pāce **ūtī**	*to enjoy peace*

multum **valēre**	*to have great influence*
plūs **valēre**	*to have greater influence*
plūrimum **valēre**	*to have very great influence*
sub corōnā **vēndere**	*to sell into slavery*
in dēditiōnem **venīre**	*to surrender*
in fidem **venīre**	*to put oneself under protection*
in spem **venīre**	*to entertain hope*
in bellō **versārī**	*to engage in war*
terga **vertere**	*to turn and flee, to flee*
āversum hostem **vidēre**	*to see the enemy in flight*
aliquā rē **vīvere**	*to live on something*

MISCELLANEOUS PHRASES

adversō colle	*up the hill*
aequō animō	*with tranquil mind, without **anxiety***
capitis poena	*capital punishment*
ex equīs	*on horseback*
ex itinere	*directly after marching*
magnum iter	*a forced march*
multā nocte	*late at night*
nāvis longa	*battleship*
nāvis onerāria	*transport*
novissimum agmen	*the rear*
prīmā aestāte	*at the beginning of **summer***
prīmā lūce	*at daybreak*
prīmā nocte	*at nightfall*
prīmum agmen	*the van*
proelium secundum	*a successful battle*
rēs adversae	*misfortune, disasters*
rēs frūmentāria	*supplies*
rēs gestae	*exploits, operations*
rēs mīlitāris	*warfare*
rēs novae	*a revolution*
summa imperī	*the supreme command*
summus mōns	*the top of the mountain*

CHAPTER IV

SUMMARY OF SYNTAX

Agreement — *Means 'You don't need to know*

1. A finite verb (i.e., a verb in the indicative or subjunctive) agrees with its subject in person and number.

   Īnsula **est** magna, *the island is large.*

2. In the perfect, pluperfect, and future perfect passive, the participle agrees in gender, number, and case with the subject.

   Dīvicō dux **factus** est, *Divico was made leader.*

3. A predicate noun or predicate adjective agrees with its subject in **case.**

   (*a*) Caesar **imperātor** factus est, *Caesar was made general.*

   (*b*) Sciō Caesarem **imperātōrem** factum esse, *I know that Caesar was made general.*

   (*c*) Īnsula est **magna,** *the island is large.*

   (*d*) Sciō īnsulam esse **magnam,** *I know that the island is large.*

4. An appositive agrees in case with the noun which it explains.

   Labiēnus, **lēgātus** decimae legiōnis, fuit fortis, *Labienus, the lieutenant of the tenth legion, was brave.*

5. An adjective, whether attributive or predicate, agrees with the noun **or** pronoun to which it belongs in gender, number, and case.

   (*a*) Dux nautae **bonō** dōnum dedit, *the leader gave a gift to the good sailor.*

   (*b*) Nautae **nostrī** sunt **bonī,** *our sailors are good.*

6. A relative pronoun agrees with its antecedent in gender and **number,** but its case is determined by its use in its own clause.

   Germānī, **quibuscum** bellum gessimus, trāns Rhēnum incolunt, *the Germans, with whom we waged war, dwell across the Rhine.*

7. The reflexive pronoun (**suī, sibi, sē, sē**) refers either to the subject of the clause in which it stands (direct reflexive) or to the subject of the principal clause (indirect reflexive).

   (*a*) Is **sibi** lēgātiōnem suscēpit, *he took upon himself the office of envoy* (direct reflexive).

   (*b*) Caesar lēgātōs iussit ad **sē** revertī, *Caesar ordered the envoys to return to him* (indirect reflexive).

8. The possessive pronoun of the third person (**suus, -a, -um**) refers either to the subject of the clause in which it stands, or to the subject of the principal clause.

   Helvētiī sē **suaque** omnia Caesarī dēdidērunt, *the Helvetians surrendered themselves and all their possessions to Caesar.*

[19]

SYNTAX OF NOUNS

Nominative

9. The subject of a finite verb (i.e., a verb in the indicative or subjunctive) is in the nominative.

Gallia est dīvīsa in partēs trēs, *Gaul is divided into three parts.*

10. After the copula **sum, fīō,** *become,* **videor,** *seem,* and the passive voice of verbs meaning *call, choose, appoint, make,* and the like, a predicate noun or predicate adjective is in the nominative.

Nōnnūllī Gallī **Celtae** appellābantur, *some Gauls were called Celts.*

Genitive

11. The possessive genitive is used with a noun to indicate the possessor.

Mīlitēs **Caesaris** fortiter pugnābant, *Caesar's soldiers used to fight bravely.*

12. The possessive genitive is used idiomatically with **causā,** *for the sake of,* **prīdiē,** *the day before,* and **postrīdiē,** *the day after.* With **causā** the genitive always precedes.

Bellandī causā, *for the purpose of fighting.*

13. The subjective genitive is used with nouns having verbal ideas to denote the doer of an action.

Memoriā **patrum nostrōrum,** *in the memory of our fathers.*

14. The objective genitive is used with nouns expressing action or feeling to denote the person or thing toward which the action or feeling is directed.

(*a*) **Rēgnī** cupiditāte inductus Orgetorīx coniūrātiōnem fēcit, *led by the desire for kingly power, Orgetorix made a conspiracy.*

(*b*) Spēs **reditiōnis** sublāta est, *the hope of returning was taken away.*

15. The adjectives **cupidus,** *desirous,* **perītus,** *skilled,* **imperītus,** *unskilled,* ~~memor~~, *mindful,* and others of similar character are followed by the objective genitive.

Gallī cupidī **bellandī** erant, *the Gauls were desirous of waging war.*

16. The partitive genitive or the genitive of the whole is used with words denoting a part to indicate the whole to which the part belongs.

(*a*) Pars **urbis** capta est, *a part of the city was taken.*

(*b*) **Hōrum** fortissimī sunt Belgae, *of these the bravest are the Belgians.*

17. With cardinal numerals (except **mīlia**), **quīdam,** *a certain one,* and **paucī,** *a few,* the ablative with **dē** or **ex** is used, instead of the partitive genitive.

(*a*) Unus ē **fīliīs** captus est, *one of the sons was captured.*

(*b*) Paucī dē **nostrīs** cecidērunt, *a few of our men fell.*

18. The genitive of quality or description is used to describe a person or thing, but only when the noun of quality is modified by an adjective.

Belgae erant **magnae virtūtis,** *the Belgians were men of great courage.*

19. When the genitive of quality is modified by a numeral, the genitive is called a genitive of measure.

Mūrum **sēdecim pedum** perdūxit, *he built a sixteen-foot wall.*

Note: There is very little difference between the genitive of quality and the ablative of quality (52), but the genitive **must** be used when the noun is modified by a numeral.

Dative

20. The indirect object of a verb is in the dative. This dative is used especially with verbs of *telling, reporting,* and *giving.*

Mihi pecūniam dedit, *he gave the money to me, he gave me the money.*

21. The dative of the indirect object is used with the intransitive verbs cõnfidō, *trust,* crēdō, *believe* ~~faveō~~, *favor,* imperō, *command,* **noceō,** *harm,* parcō, *spare,* pāreō, *obey,* **persuādeō,** *persuade,* **placeō,** *please,* **resistō,** *resist,* studeō, *be eager for,* and others of like meaning.

(a) Caesar **hostibus** perpercit, *Caesar spared the enemy.*

(b) Mīlitēs **imperātōrī** pārent, *the soldiers obey the general.*

22. The verbs enumerated in **21** are used impersonally in the passive. The dative of the indirect object is retained.

Mīlitī persuāsum est, *the soldier was persuaded.*

23. The dative of the indirect object is used with some verbs compounded with **ad, ante, con, dē, in, inter, ob, post, prae, prō, sub,** and **super.**

(a) Caesar **Gallīs** bellum intulit, *Caesar made war on the Gauls.*

(b) Caesar Labiēnum **legiōnī** praefēcit, *Caesar put Labienus in charge of the legion.*

24. The dative is used with adjectives meaning *near, fit, friendly, pleasing, like,* and their opposites.

Dumnorīx **Helvētiīs** erat amīcus, *Dumnorix was friendly to the Helvetians.*

25. The dative of purpose is used to express the purpose of an action.

Locum **castrīs** dēlēgit, *he chose a place for a camp.*

26. The dative of purpose is often accompanied by a dative denoting the person interested in the action (dative of reference). This construction is called the double dative.

Hōc est magnō impedīmentō **nōbīs**, *this is a great hindrance to us.*

27. The possessor may be expressed by the dative with some part of **sum** (dative of the possessor).

Mihi est in animō īre, *I have it in mind to go, I intend to go.*

28. The dative of agent is used with the passive periphrastic conjugation to denote the person upon whom the obligation rests.

Hōc **nōbīs** faciendum est. *this must be done by us, we must do this.*

Accusative

29. The direct object of a transitive verb is in the accusative.

Helvētiī **Orgetorĭgem** dēlēgērunt, *the Helvetians chose Orgetorix.*

30. Verbs meaning *name, choose, call,* and *make* usually take a predicate accusative along with the direct object.

(*a*) Eum **rēgem** cōnstituit, *he made him king.*

(*b*) Caesarem **certiōrem** faciunt, *they inform Caesar.*

31. The verb **rogō,** *ask,* takes two accusatives, one of the person, the other of the thing.

Mē sententiam rogāvit, *he asked me my opinion.*

32. With the verbs **petō** and **quaerō,** *ask,* the person is expressed by the ablative with **ab, dē,** or **ex** (ablative of source) and the thing by the accusative.

Pācem ab Rōmānīs petīvērunt, *they sought peace from the Romans.*

33. Duration of time is expressed by the accusative without a preposition.

Paucōs diēs morātī sunt, *they delayed a few days.*

34. Extent of space is expressed by the accusative without a preposition.

Tria mīlia passuum prōcessit, *he advanced three miles.*

35. The verb **trādūcō,** *lead across,* takes two accusatives, one the object of **dūcō,** and the other governed by **trā (trāns).**

Mīlitēs flūmen trādūxit, *he led the soldiers across the river.*

36. The place to which is expressed by the accusative with the prepositions **ad** or **in.**

Caesar **in Galliam** contendit, *Caesar hastened into Gaul.*

37. With names of towns and **domus,** the place to which is expressed by the accusative without a preposition.

Caesar **Rōmam** īre contendit, *Caesar hastened to go to Rome.*

38. The subject of the principal clause in an indirect statement is in the accusative.

Caesar dīcit **Belgās** esse fortēs, *Caesar says that the Belgians are brave.*

Ablative

39. Separation is expressed by the ablative, usually with the prepositions **ā (ab), dē, ē (ex).**

Rhodanus prōvinciam **ab Helvētiīs** dīvidit, *the Rhone separates the province from the Helvetians.*

40. The verbs **careō,** *lack,* **dēsistō,** *desist from,* **līberō,** *free from,* and **prohibeō,** *keep from* regularly take the ablative of separation without a preposition.

Suīs fīnibus eōs prohibent, *they keep them from their territory.*

41. The place from which is expressed by the ablative with the prepositions **ā (ab), dē, ē (ex).**

Dē mūrō, *down from the wall.*

42. With names of towns and **domus,** the place from which is expressed by the ablative without a preposition.

Rōmā profectus est, *he set out from Rome.*

43. The place in which is expressed by the ablative with the preposition **in.**

Erant duae factiōnēs **in Galliā,** *there were two parties in Gaul.*

44. With **locus,** in the singular and plural, and several other nouns of place when modified by **tōtus,** the place in which is expressed by the ablative without a preposition.

Multīs locīs, *in many places.*

45. With names of towns and **domus,** the place in which is expressed by the locative.

Rōmae, *at Rome;* domī, *at home.*

46. Means is expressed by the ablative without a preposition.

Partem hostium **gladiīs** interfēcērunt, *they killed a part of the enemy with swords.*

47. The deponents **ūtor,** *use,* and **potior,** *get possession of,* take the ablative of means.   *fruor, vescor, fungor*

Castrīs potītī sunt, *they got possession of the camp.*

48. Cause may be expressed by the ablative, usually without a preposition.

Grātiā plūrimum poterat, *he was very powerful because of his popularity.*

49. With a verb in the passive voice, the personal agent is expressed by the ablative with **ā** or **ab.**

Ab explōrātōribus certior factus est, *he was informed by scouts.*

50. The manner of an action is expressed by the ablative with **cum,** but **cum** may be omitted if the ablative is modified by an adjective.

(a) **Cum studiō** labōrat, *he works with eagerness (eagerly).*

(b) **Magnō cum studiō** labōrat, *he works with great eagerness,* or

(c) **Magnō studiō** labōrat, *he works with great eagerness.*

51. The degree of difference between two objects or actions is expressed by the ablative without a preposition.

(a) Sum **pede** altior quam Mārcus, *I am a foot taller than Marcus.*

(b) **Paucīs** ante **diēbus,** *a few days before.*

52. The ablative of quality or description (without a preposition) is used to describe a person or thing, but only when the noun of quality is modified by an adjective.

Hominēs **inimīcō animō,** *men of unfriendly attitude of mind.*

53. The ablative without a preposition is used to denote in what respect something is true (ablative of specification or respect).

Helvētiī reliquōs Gallōs **virtūte** praecēdunt, *the Helvetians surpass the rest of the Gauls in bravery.*

54. The adjectives **dignus,** *worthy,* and **indignus,** *unworthy,* take the ablative of specification.

Sunt dignī **honōre,** *they are worthy of honor.*

55. Accompaniment is expressed by the ablative with **cum.**

Cum legiōne decimā profectus est, *he set out with the tenth legion.*

56. A noun or a pronoun with a present or perfect participle in agreement may be used in the ablative case to form an ablative absolute.

Rēgnō occupātō, tōtīus Galliae potītī sunt, *having seized the supreme power, they became masters of all Gaul.*

57. In the ablative absolute construction, an adjective, or a second noun may take the place of the participle.

(*a*) **Sēquanīs invītīs,** *against the will of the Sequani.*

(*b*) **Caesare cōnsule,** *in the consulship of Caesar.*

58. Time when or within which is expressed by the ablative without a preposition.

(*a*) **Diē tertiō** pervēnit, *he arrived on the third day.*

(*b*) **Paucīs annīs** omnēs ex Galliā pellentur, *within a few years all will be driven from Gaul.*

59. The ablative of accordance is used to denote that in accordance with which anything is done or is true.

Mōribus suīs Orgetorīgem coēgērunt, *in accordance with their customs they compelled Orgetorix.*

SYNTAX OF VERBS

60. A primary tense of the indicative is followed by a primary tense of the subjunctive; a secondary tense of the indicative is followed by a secondary tense of the subjunctive.

61. (*a*) **Primary tenses**
   Indicative: present, future, future perfect.
   Subjunctive: present (incomplete action), perfect (completed action).

(*b*) **Secondary tenses**
   Indicative: imperfect, perfect, pluperfect.
   Subjunctive: imperfect (incomplete action), pluperfect (completed action).

Table for Sequence of Tenses

Tenses of Verb in Principal Clause		Tenses of Subjunctive in Subordinate Clause	
		Incomplete Action	Completed Action
Primary	Present Future Future Perfect	Present	Perfect
Secondary	Imperfect Perfect Pluperfect	Imperfect	Pluperfect

Note: By incomplete action is meant action not finished before that of the main verb; by completed action is meant action finished before that of the main verb.

62. A clause expressing the purpose of the action of the verb in the principal clause takes the present or imperfect subjunctive introduced by **ut,** *in order that,* or **nē,** *in order that not;* the tense of the subjunctive is determined by the rule for the sequence of tenses (60-61).

(a) Puer cum studiō labōrat **ut laudētur,** *the boy works zealously that he may be praised.*

(b) Fortiter pugnāvērunt **nē** urbs **caperētur,** *they fought bravely in order that the city might not be taken.*

63. If the principal clause contains a definite antecedent, the purpose clause is regularly introduced by a relative pronoun.
Mīlitēs mīsit **quī** hostēs **oppugnārent,** *he sent soldiers to attack the enemy.*

64. If the purpose clause contains a comparative of either an adjective or adverb, *in order that* is translated by **quō.**
Oppidum mūnīvit **quō facilius** hostēs prohibēret, *he fortified the town in order that he might keep off the enemy more easily.*

65. The following verbs are followed by substantive clauses of purpose introduced by **ut** or **nē:**

hortor, *urge*	**persuadeō,** *persuade*
imperō, *command*	**peto,** *ask, beg*
mandō, *command*	**postulō,** *demand*
moneō, *advise*	**rogō,** *ask*

Helvētiīs **persuāsit ut** dē fīnibus **exīrent,** *he persuaded the Helvetians to leave their country.*

66. A clause expressing the result of the action of the verb in the principal clause takes the subjunctive introduced by **ut**, *so that*, or **ut nōn**, *so that not*; the tense of the subjunctive is determined by the rule for the sequence of tenses.

> Puerī tam bonī sunt **ut** ab omnibus **laudentur**, *the boys are so good that they are praised by everybody.*

67. The verbs **accidit**, *it happens*, **fit**, *it happens*, **faciō**, *bring it about*, and **efficiō**, *bring it about*, are followed by substantive clauses of result introduced by **ut** or **ut nōn**.

> **Accidit ut** lūna **esset** plēna, *it happened that there was a full moon.*

68. A causal clause introduced by **quod**, *because*, takes the indicative when the writer or speaker gives his own reason, but the subjunctive when the writer or speaker gives another person's reason.

> (a) Dumnorīx Helvētiīs erat amīcus, **quod** ex eā cīvitāte Orgetorīgis fīliam in mātrimōnium **dūxerat**, *Dumnorix was friendly to the Helvetians because out of that state he had married the daughter of Orgetorix.*
>
> (b) Legiō Caesarī grātiās ēgit, **quod** optimum iūdicium **fēcisset**, *the legion thanked Caesar because he had expressed a very favorable opinion.*

69. A causal clause introduced by **cum**, *since*, always takes the subjunctive.

> **Cum** aeger **sim**, tēcum nōn ībō, *since I am ill, I shall not go with you.*

70. A temporal clause introduced by **cum**, *when*, referring to present time takes the present indicative.

> **Cum** aere aliēnō **premuntur**, *when they are overwhelmed by debt.*

71. A temporal clause introduced by **cum**, *when*, referring to future time takes the future or future perfect indicative.

> **Cum** domum **redierō**, tibi scrībam, *when I return home, I shall write to you.*

72. A temporal clause introduced by **cum**, *when*, takes some past tense of the indicative if it denotes the time at which the action of the principal verb took place.

> **Cum** Caesar in Galliam **vēnit**, prīncipēs erant Aeduī, *when Caesar came into Gaul, the Aedui were leaders.*

73. A temporal clause introduced by **cum**, *when*, takes the imperfect or pluperfect subjunctive to describe the circumstances that accompanied or preceded the action of the principal verb (**cum**-circumstantial clause).

> **Cum** cīvitās iūs suum exsequī **cōnārētur**, Orgetorīx mortuus est, *when the state was attempting to enforce its authority, Orgetorix died.*

74. A temporal clause introduced by **ut** or **ubi**, *when*, **postquam**, *after*, and **simul atque**, *as soon as*, takes the indicative, usually the perfect, sometimes the historical present.

> **Ubi** id **cōnspexit**, signum mīlitibus dedit, *when he noticed this, he gave the signal to the soldiers.*

75. A temporal clause introduced by **antequam** or **priusquam**, *before*, takes the indicative when the subordinate verb denotes an actual fact (usually after a negative), but the subjunctive when the subordinate verb denotes an expected event.

    (*a*) **Neque** fugere dēstitērunt **priusquam** ad flūmen **pervēnērunt,** *and they did not cease to flee before (until) they reached the river.*

    (*b*) **Priusquam** quicquam cōnārētur, Dīviciācum ad sē vocārī iubet, *before he should attempt anything, he ordered Diviciacus to be called to him.*

76. A temporal clause introduced by **dum**, *while*, takes the present indicative usually translated by the English past progressive.

    Dum haec **geruntur,** Caesarī nūntiātum est, *while these things were going on, word was brought to Caesar.*

77. A temporal clause introduced by **dum**, *until*, takes the indicative when the subordinate verb denotes an actual fact, but the subjunctive when the subordinate verb denotes an expected event.

    (*a*) Domī manēbam **dum** pater **rediit,** *I stayed at home until my father returned.*

    (*b*) Domī manēbam **dum** pater **redīret,** *I stayed at home until my father should return.*

78. A concessive clause introduced by **cum**, *although*, takes the subjunctive.

    Cum ad vesperum **pugnātum sit,** āversum hostem vidēre nēmō potuit, *although the battle lasted till evening, no one could see the enemy turned to flight.*

79. A relative clause which merely tells what person or thing is meant by the antecedent or which merely states an additional fact about the antecedent takes the indicative.

    Tertiam partem Galliae eī incolunt **quī** ipsōrum linguā Celtae **appellantur,** *the third part of Gaul is inhabited by those who in their own language are called Celts.*

80. A relative clause which describes the antecedent by stating some characteristic takes the subjunctive (relative clause of characteristic or description).

    Unus erat **quī** addūcī nōn **posset,** *he was the only one who could not be persuaded.*

81. Relative clauses of characteristic are especially common after the following expressions:

            Ūnus est quī, *he is the only one who*
            Sōlus est quī, *he is the only one who*
            Est quī, *there is some one who*
            Sunt quī, *there are some who*
            Quis est quī, *who is there who*
            Nēmo est quī, *there is no one who*

82. Verbs of *fearing* are followed by substantive clauses with the subjunctive introduced by **nē**, *that, lest*, or **ut**, *that . . . . not*.

    (*a*) Hostēs **verēbantur nē** exercitus noster ad eōs **addūcerētur,** *the enemy feared that our army would be led against them.*

    (*b*) **Veritus sum ut venīret,** *I feared that he would not come.*

83. Verbs of *hindering*, *preventing*, and *refusing* are followed by substantive clauses with the subjunctive introduced by **nē** or **quōminus** if the principal verb is positive, but by **quīn** if the principal verb is negative.

(*a*) **Dēterrēre** possunt **nē** maior multitūdō **trādūcātur,** *they can prevent a greater host from being brought over.*

(*b*) Nāvēs ventō **tenēbantur quōminus** in eundem portum venīre **possent,** *the ships were prevented by the wind from being able to reach the same harbor.*

(*c*) Germānī **retinērī nōn poterant quīn** tēla **conicerent,** *the Germans could not be restrained from hurling javelins.*

84. The verb **prohibeō** regularly takes the accusative and the infinitive. Belgae **Teutonōs** intrā suōs fīnēs **ingredī prohibuērunt,** *the Belgians prevented the Teutons from entering their country.*

85. *Negative* expressions of *doubting* are followed by substantive clauses with the subjunctive introduced by **quīn.**

Nōn dubium erat **quīn** Helvētiī plūrimum **possent,** *there was no doubt that the Helvetians were the most powerful.*

86. Conditions which may be either true or false (simple conditions) take the indicative. The tense is the same as that found in the English sentence, except that in a simple condition referring to future time (sometimes called future more vivid) the Latin uses the future or even the future perfect where the English uses the present tense.

(*a*) **Sī adest,** eum **vidēmus,** *if he is present, we see him.*

(*b*) **Sī aderat,** eum **vidēbāmus,** *if he was present, we saw him.*

(*c*) **Sī aderit,** eum **vidēbimus,** *if he is present, we shall see him.*

87. Future less vivid (*should-would*) conditions take the present subjunctive in both clauses.

Sī adsit, eum **videāmus,** *if he* **should** *be present, we* **would** (*should*) *see him.*

88. Contrary to fact (unreal) conditions in present time take the imperfect subjunctive in both clauses.

Sī adesset, eum **vidērēmus,** *if he were present, we should see him.*

89. Contrary to fact (unreal) conditions in past time take the pluperfect subjunctive in both clauses.

Sī adfuisset, eum **vīdissēmus,** *if he had been present, we should have seen him.*

90. The verb of a direct question is in the indicative.
Quis eum interficī **iussit?** *Who ordered him to be put to death?*

91. The verb of an indirect question is in the subjunctive; the tense of the subjunctive is determined by the rule for the sequence of tenses (60-61).

Rogat **quis** captīvum interficī **iusserit,** *he asks who has ordered the captive to be put to death.*

92. The verb of a subordinate clause in indirect discourse is in the subjunctive: the tense of the subjunctive is determined by the rule for the sequence of tenses, depending on the introductory verb (60-61).

Dīxit sē lēgātum vīdisse **quem** Caesar **mīsisset,** *he said that he had seen the envoy whom Caesar had sent.*

93. The verb of a principal clause in indirect discourse is in the present infinitive if its action is contemporaneous with that of the introductory verb.

(a) **Dīcit eōs pugnāre,** *he says that they are fighting.*
(b) **Dīxit eōs pugnāre,** *he said that they were fighting.*

94. The verb of a principal clause in indirect discourse is in the perfect infinitive if its action occurred before that of the introductory verb.

(a) **Dīcit eōs pugnāvisse,** *he says that they have fought.*
(b) **Dīxit eōs pugnāvisse,** *he said that they had fought.*

Note: The participle forming part of the perfect infinitive passive must agree with the subject in gender, number, and case.

95. The verb of a principal clause in indirect discourse is in the future infinitive if its action is subsequent to that of the introductory verb.

(a) **Dīcit eōs pugnātūrōs esse,** *he says that they will fight.*
(b) **Dīxit eōs pugnātūrōs esse,** *he said that they would fight.*

Note: The participle forming part of the future infinitive active must agree with the subject in gender, number, and case.

96. The verbs **cōgō,** *compel,* **iubeō,** *order,* **patior,** *allow,* are followed by the object infinitive and subject accusative.

Mīlitēs hostēs oppugnāre iussit, *he ordered the soldiers to attack the enemy.*

97. The following verbs are followed by the complementary infinitive:

audeō, *dare*	**dēbeō,** *ought*
coepī, *began*	**dubitō,** *hesitate*
cōnor, *try*	**mātūrō,** *hasten*
cōnstituō, *determine*	**possum,** *be able*
contendō, *hasten*	**videor,** *seem*

98. The genitive of the gerund or gerundive followed by **causā,** *for the sake of.* expresses purpose.

(a) **Videndī causā vēnit,** *he came to see.*
(b) **Oppidī videndī causā vēnit,** *he came to see the town.*

99. The accusative of the gerund or gerundive with **ad** expresses purpose.

(a) **Ad videndum vēnit,** *he came to see.*
(b) **Ad oppidum videndum vēnit,** *he came to see the town.*

100. The future active participle is used with the forms of **sum** to express a future or intended action (active periphrastic conjugation).

(a) **Sciō quid factūrus sit,** *I know what he will do.*
(b) **Tē crās vīsūrus sum,** *I intend to see you to-morrow.*

101. The future passive participle is used with the forms of **sum** to express necessity or obligation (passive periphrastic conjugation).

Mīlitēs nōbīs mittendī sunt, *we must send the soldiers.*

102. The supine in —**um** is used with verbs of motion to express purpose.

Lēgātōs ad Caesarem mittunt rogātum auxilium, *they send ambassadors to Caesar to ask for aid.*

103. The supine in —**ū** is used with certain adjectives as an ablative of specification.

Facile factū, *easy to do.*

CHAPTER V

SENTENCES FOR TRANSLATION

*Compiled from Regents, College
Entrance, and other Standard Examination Papers*

(Students preparing for the **Regents Examinations** should cover the sentences contained in parts **A, B, C, D, E, F,** and **J.** Students preparing for other examinations should, in addition, cover sentences contained in parts **G, H, I.**)

Note: Numbers within parentheses refer to sections of Syntax, pp. 19 to 29.

A. PURPOSE CLAUSES

1. The German horsemen had come to give *(62; 60)* aid to the Roman legions *(20)*.
2. The commander led his army across the river to attack the Gauls.
3. Allies came from many towns of Italy to bring grain to the army.
4. The lieutenants came together for one hour to hear Caesar's plan of battle.
5. My brother departed from the city to fight with the Romans in the province.
6. Our scouts hastened across the river in order that they might not be captured *(62b)* by the Gauls *(49)*.
7. The Gauls were moving across the river in order to occupy the territory of our allies.
8. Two new legions were sent from Italy in order that the Romans might conquer the Helvetians.
9. At that time, our men marched from Italy in order to attack the Helvetians.
10. For a few days *(33)* Caesar remained in that place *(44)* in order that he might see the leaders of his allies.
11. The ambassadors remained for many hours *(33)* in order that they might hear Caesar's plans.
12. The commander came with great speed *(50)* in order that he might lead the tenth legion across the mountains.

13. Caesar gave weapons to his friends in order that they might be able to defend (97) themselves.

14. The leader sent one legion across the river to defend the large town.

15. The Helvetians are crossing the river in order to make a march through our province.

16. Caesar left his tenth legion in Gaul in order that they might fortify the town.

17. Messengers quickly set out to Caesar in order to announce the victory.

18. Ambassadors came to Caesar to complain in regard to this.

19. Caesar hastens with all his forces to capture this large town.

20. On that day (58) Caesar will send very brave soldiers to take (61a) the town.

21. He went to the general to give a message to him (20).

22. Caesar sent two lieutenants to find out the easiest route to the town (36).

23. We shall remain at Rome (45) a few days (33) in order that these things may not happen.

24. Caesar marched all day (33) in order that he might reach his camp before night.

25. On the same day he hastened to return (97) home (37) with two legions to encourage the people with a speech (46).

26. That he might not be cut off (**prohibeō**) from supplies (40), he set out for the nearest winter quarters (36) by forced marches (46).

27. The leader ordered the soldiers (21) to fortify (65; 60) the camp with speed (50).

28. After the camp had been fortified (56), Caesar ordered the cohorts (21) to attack (65) the enemy.

29. On the third night (58), the Gauls sent messengers from the neighboring province to seek peace.

30. Caesar ordered his lieutenant (21) to lead (65) two legions out of winter quarters.

31. The commander ordered his horsemen (21) to remain (65) in camp for ten days.

32. These tribes will not permit their neighbors (21) to go (65) through their lands.

33. Caesar urged his soldiers to join (65) battle with the enemy.

34. He ordered the lieutenants (*21*) to hasten (*65*) to the river before daybreak.

35. Caesar persuaded the Gauls (*21*) to furnish (*65*) boats.

36. Those whom he had with him (*7*) begged him not to fight (*65*) with this multitude of the enemy.

37. Mithridates had been sent by Caesar into Syria to ask (*63*) the allies to send (*65*) aid.

38. On that day Caesar sent messengers who (*63*) should choose a place for the camp (*26*).

39. Ambassadors will be chosen by the Germans (*49*) to go (*63; 60*) to Caesar with hostages (*55*).

40. Labienus sent a messenger to tell Caesar (*20*) that the enemy (*38*) were crossing (*93*) the river.

41. This he did in order that (*64*) he might see more quickly what he ought (*91*) to do (*97*).

42. Caesar ordered the cohorts (*96*) to come (*96*) together in order to speak to them about his plans.

43. After the soldiers had been defeated (*56*), ambassadors came with great speed to seek (*62; 99*) peace.

44. When Caesar was (*73*) in Gaul, the Germans sent envoys to him in order to seek peace.

45. Labienus ordered his men (*96*) to fortify (*96*) the camp in order that he might withstand the attack of the enemy.

46. Caesar placed these lieutenants (*29*) in charge of his legions (*23*) that they might be witnesses (**testis**) of the bravery of the soldiers.

47. Scouts were sent to find out into whose territory the enemy were making (*91; 60*) a march.

48. Having made peace (*56*), Caesar marched into this town to get grain.

49. After the Gauls were conquered (*56; 74*), Caesar went to Rome (*37*) to see (*62; 98; 99; 102*) his friends.

50. Crassus led his army out of the camp in order that he might attack the Sontiates.

B. RESULT CLAUSES

51. The scouts were so terrified (*2*) that they were not able (*66; 60*) to find out (*97*) the number of the enemy.

52. The time was so short (*5*) that the signal could not be given.

53. They were so eager (*5*) for war (*15*) that they neglected everything else.

54. So quickly was the attack made that the soldiers were unable to draw up the line of battle.

55. The Germans resisted the Romans (*21*) so fiercely that they could not advance.

56. The danger is so great that no one dares to go (*97*).

57. Caesar attacked the Germans so bravely that they fled into the woods.

58. The Gauls fought so fiercely that the enemy could not drive them back.

59. The soldiers fought so bravely that they captured the city within five hours (*58*).

60. The danger was so great that our men did not dare to resist them (*21*).

61. There was no state (*9*) so small that it did not send envoys to this council.

62. The Romans were so brave (*3*) that they captured (*66; 60*) the large town in three days (*58*).

63. The Romans fought so bravely for five days (*33*) that the Gauls could not (*66*) capture the town.

64. The soldiers marched so swiftly that they were able to cross (*97*) the river on the same day.

65. The Gauls were so brave that Caesar's horsemen were not able to capture the camp.

66. Our (*men*) fought so fiercely that the enemy were not able to conquer them.

67. Our (*men*) came out of the camp so quickly that the enemy were not able to defend themselves.

68. The fear of the Germans is so great that they are sending hostages to Caesar.

69. The army of the enemy was so large that Caesar's legions were in great danger.

70. The soldiers marched so swiftly that they crossed the river on the same day.

71. The tenth legion fought so bravely that the city was captured by the general (*49*) within a few hours (*58*).

72. The courage of our men was so great that the enemy wished to retreat quickly.

73. So great a number of the enemy had been killed that new messengers came to Caesar.

74. So swift was the arrival of our men that they were able to seize the town without a battle.

75. The fear of the enemy was so great that they decided to surrender their weapons.

76. The danger was so great that the troops wished to depart with speed (50).

77. The soldiers marched with so great speed (50) that they came to the river before night.

78. The army of the lieutenant was so large that the enemy was quickly overcome.

79. The garrison was so brave that the soldiers were not able to capture (97) it.

80. The war was so long that many brave soldiers were killed.

81. The men fought so fiercely that many were killed in battle.

82. There was so great a multitude (9) of the enemy drawn up in line of battle that our forces were not able to withstand the attack.

83. The Helvetians were so terrified by Caesar's (13) arrival (48) that they did not depart from the territory of the Lingones.

84. Caesar was so alarmed by these reports that he determined to wage war at once.

85. The Boii were so brave that the Aedui wished to use (97) their aid (47) in war.

86. The Veneti were so strong in ships (53) that they resisted the Romans (21) a long time.

87. This plan had seemed to them (20) so good that they followed it for seven years (33).

C. TEMPORAL CLAUSES

88. After the arrival of the Romans was announced (74), the enemy departed from the province with great speed (50).

89. After the enemy had been conquered (74; 56), the general ordered hostages (96) to be sent (96) to his camp.

90. When Caesar's enemies had departed (73) from the city, (his) legions seized Rome.

91. When the messengers had seen (73) the army of the enemy, they went back quickly to Caesar.

92. After the allies had been conquered, the Germans attempted to cross (*97*) the river.

93. When Ariovistus and Caesar had come together (*73*), the Germans attempted to kill the Roman horsemen.

94. When Considius had seen the horsemen of the enemy, he hastened to Caesar's camp.

95. When the soldiers had seen Caesar himself in the battle, they made a fierce attack on the enemy.

96. After the horsemen of the enemy had been defeated (*74*), the Romans remained in the province for three days (*33*).

97. When the leader had drawn up a line of battle, he ordered the soldiers (*96*) to fight (*96*) bravely.

98. When the Germans had come into the province, they were able to remain (*97*) for many years (*33*).

99. When the soldiers were coming together, it was announced that the Germans (*38*) were leading (*93*) horsemen across the river.

100. When the Germans had been seen across the river, the horsemen hastened into camp with great speed (*50*).

101. When the leaders had surrendered part of the hostages, they heard that few Roman ships (*38*) remained.

102. When the messenger had come, the soldiers knew that they would move (*95*) camp.

103. When the enemy had learned that Caesar had come (*94*), they quickly withdrew.

104. After the arrival of the army had been announced (*74*), ambassadors of the Gauls hastened to Caesar.

105. When the messenger of the Romans had come, the allies learned that Caesar (*38*) had crossed the river.

106. After the town had been captured (*74; 56*), the enemy sent ambassadors to Caesar concerning peace.

107. When the Germans were hastening into the territory of the allies, Caesar ordered his men (*21*) to collect (*65; 61*) a large army.

108. After the enemy had been defeated, Caesar sent ambassadors to the leaders of the Germans.

109. When the allies had attacked the town, Caesar, with large forces, hastened out of the province.

110. When they heard the enemy, the soldiers seized their weapons quickly.

111. After the king had been killed, the people departed from the city with great speed.

112. After the town had been captured, the soldiers killed all the citizens with swords (*46*).

113. When Caesar had conquered (*73*) the Gauls, he led his men into winter quarters.

114. After the Gauls had been conquered (*74; 56*), their towns were quickly occupied by the Romans (*49*).

115. When the Gauls had seen the multitude of the enemy, they sent envoys to Caesar (*36*).

116. When Labienus was fortifying (*73*) the camp, the Gauls attacked the neighboring towns.

117. After the lieutenant had been captured, the leader ordered his soldiers (*96*) to retreat (*96*) from the city.

118. When the army was led (*73*) by Caesar (*49*) into those territories, the enemy did not dare to make (*97*) war on him.

119. When the Germans had arrived (*73*) at the river, they were not able to cross on account of its depth.

120. When Caesar learned (*74*) through whose territory the Helvetians had gone (*91*), he sent instructions (**mandātum**) to those states in great haste.

121. When Caesar had heard this, he hurried with all his troops (*55*) to attack (*62*) the Nervii.

122. When the enemy had been conquered, the messenger ran with great speed (*50*) to the camp.

123. When Ariovistus came (*74*) to the place appointed for the conference, he took possession of the mound (*47*).

124. When Caesar had crossed the river, he fortified his camp and sent ambassadors to the nearest states.

125. When the fleet came (*74*), Brutus announced to Caesar that he (*7; 38*) was willing (*93*) to attack the enemy.

126. When they had thrown a multitude of soldiers around the wall (*23*), they brought forward the towers.

127. When the army had pitched camp, they saw the enemy on the top of the mountain.

128. When the Helvetians came to him, he ordered them (*96*) to surrender their (*8*) arms.

129. While these things were being done (76), Caesar ordered Vatinius (96) to come to Brundisium (37) with a fleet.

130. As soon as the bridge was completed (74), Caesar led his army over with the greatest possible speed.

D. CAUSAL CLAUSES

131. Since (69) the lieutenant was not able to defend (97) the camp, he sent a messenger to Caesar.

132. Since the Gauls were not able to defend the town, the leader ordered them (96) to retreat (96) into the forest.

133. At Caesar's arrival (58) the enemy fought bravely, since they were defending their own territory.

134. Since the leader was not able to defend the city, he quickly led his army out of the territory.

135. Since the river was very deep, the troops decided to remain (97) in camp for a few days (33).

136. Since the soldiers had fought bravely, the commander ordered them (96) to remain (96) in camp.

137. Since a Roman camp was being attacked, Caesar, with two legions, came with great speed.

138. Since the danger is great, the Romans quickly seize their swords.

139. Since our soldiers did not know (69) the fords, they were thrown into confusion by the enemy (49).

140. Since the Helvetians (27) had nothing (9) at home (45), Caesar ordered the Allobroges (96) to give (96) them a supply of grain.

141. Since they have persuaded you (21), the town must not be seized (101).

142. Since they could not find their friends, they returned in great haste to us (36).

143. Since your brother is fighting for (**prō**) his country, you ought to write (97) a letter to him.

144. Since the Helvetians were very powerful, they fought with their neighbors (55) in daily battles (46).

145. Since there was no danger, the men went off to pillage (62) the neighboring farms.

146. Since a very small part of the summer remained, Caesar was unwilling to wage war on this tribe.

147. I could not make war on the Germans because the consul was unwilling (68) to aid me.

148. The Suebi began to return home (37) because this battle had been reported (68) across the Rhine.

149. Orgetorix made a conspiracy against the Roman people because he desired (68) to seize the throne in his own country.

150. The hostages fled into the woods that day (58) because they feared the Belgians.

151. The soldiers were unwilling to advance on that day (58) because there was a new moon.

152. They cannot march through our city because it is well fortified.

E. INDIRECT QUESTIONS

153. Caesar learned from the messenger what was being done (91; 60) among the Belgians.

154. Ariovistus asked why Caesar had not led (91; 60) his forces across the river.

155. The soldiers asked why Caesar's allies had not given grain to them (7).

156. The Romans in the city asked why Caesar had fought with the Gauls for ten years (33).

157. The commander asked why the legions had not fought on that day (58).

158. Cicero knew why the Gauls had come from the town so quickly.

159. Labienus knew why Caesar had not captured the town at that time.

160. The allies knew why the general had not defended the city for many days.

161. Labienus knew why our (men) were not able to attack the town at that time.

162. Caesar asked why the allies had not carried the grain to the town.

163. The lieutenant asked why the allies had not brought (91; 60) grain for many days (33).

164. The troops marched without heavy baggage for many hours and asked why aid had not come (91; 60).

165. For many years he had wished to know what the men of that state were doing.

166. The troops understood why grain had been carried from the fields into the city.
167. On the same day Caesar asked why the Gauls were not giving grain to his soldiers (*20*).
168. The leader asked why the Gauls had not given grain to the Roman soldiers.
169. At that time the senate did not understand why Caesar did not send help.
170. The lieutenants asked why the general wished to attack the bridge that night.
171. Labienus was not able to learn what the enemy did at that time.
172. The general knew why the soldiers had not defended the city at that time.
173. Caesar inquired of the ambassadors (*32*) whom (*6*) he saw in the senate why they had come (*91; 60*) to Rome (*37*).
174. The enemy quickly learned why the Romans had attacked (*91; 60*) this strongly fortified hill.
175. Did not (**nōnne**) Ariovistus ask (*90*) Caesar (*31*) why he had come (*91*) with an army into that part of Gaul?
176. It was not easy (*neuter*) to say (*subject infinitive*) what men the enemy had killed in battle.
177. After receiving this letter (*56*), I knew why my friend had not come home (*37*).
178. We asked the boy (*31*) whom we saw in the city why he had not returned with his brother.
179. Caesar asked them why they wished to march through his province.
180. The general inquired how large (*3*) the enemy's forces were.
181. He himself asked why larger forces had not been given to him (*7; 20*).
182. Who will inform us in what direction the enemy marched (*60*)?
183. He asked what Volusenus had ascertained (**reperiō**) about the harbors and coasts of Britain.

F. INDIRECT DISCOURSE

184. The messenger said that the allies (*38*) had sent (*94*) grain to the enemy.

185. On the same day Labienus heard that aid had been sent (*94*) by Caesar.

186. Caesar knew that these men would not send (*95 and Note*) aid to him (*7*).

187. Ariovistus knew that the Romans had led many troops into Gaul.

188. The general said that he (*7*) would lead (*95 and Note*) the army across the river.

189. Caesar heard that the Germans had led a large army across the river.

190. The messengers said that the Roman forces had fought with great courage (*50*).

191. The messenger said that the general would send envoys about peace to Caesar.

192. The Gauls thought that they (*7*) would defeat Caesar's army very quickly.

193. Caesar said that the cavalry would remain, and ordered one legion (*96*) to bring (*96*) grain.

194. Caesar thought that aid (*38*) had been sent (*94 and Note*) from Britain to his enemies in Gaul.

195. The leaders knew that they (*7; 38*) could not conquer the powerful legions.

196. The messenger announced that many horsemen had departed quickly at daybreak.

197. The messenger thought that the Roman army had departed in the fourth watch (*58*).

198. Labienus said that the mountain had been occupied by the Roman army for two days (*33*).

199. The leader said that he could easily defend (*97*) the city with his large army.

200. The leader said that he would not defend (*95 and Note*) the city since there were (*69*) so few soldiers (*9*).

201. The general thought that his army had fought very bravely.

202. Caesar said that he could not surrender the hostages to the enemy.

203. He says that he (*38; 7*) is (*93*) ready (*3*) to begin.

204. He says that the chiefs of the Belgians have sought (*94*) safety in flight (*46*).

205. They thought that these machines could (*93*) not be moved (*97*).
206. He did not know that for many years (*33*) there had been a confederacy (*38*) of the nations of Gaul.
207. The messenger said that the next night (*58*) the general would set out (*95 and Note*) from Rome (*42*) with all his troops.
208. The soldiers knew that they (*7*) were led (*93*) by a man of very great courage (*18; 52*).
209. The Belgians had learned that the enemy had moved their (*8*) camp.
210. The ambassadors replied to Caesar (*20*) that within three days (*58*) they would do (*95*) that which they had promised (*92; 60*).
211. The lieutenant said he would not surrender (*95 and Note*) his forces to the leaders (*20*) of the state.
212. He says that he has been wounded (*94 and Note*) and asks where the camp is (*91*).
213. We know that the forces of Caesar, because of their great courage, are in the midst of the fight.
214. Labienus reported that the enemy had crossed (*94*) the river and were holding (*93*) the mountain.
215. The soldiers knew they were waging war in the territory where many years (*51*) before the Roman armies had fought (*92*).
216. They say that they will not arrive home (*37*) before dawn.
217. Caesar says that he will bring aid to his brave soldiers as soon as possible.
218. Some said that Caesar had moved his camp to another place after the enemy had been defeated (*56*).
219. At sunset, Caesar was informed that aid was coming from Rome (*42*).
220. After these things had been accomplished (*56*), we thought we ought to await the arrival of the cavalry.
221. Caesar had heard that ambassadors had been sent by the Gauls to seek (*63; 98; 99; 102*) peace.
222. The Germans said that they would not give up the territory that they had won (*92*) by their valor.
223. The same messenger said that the Belgians had made peace

with their neighbors and that they had driven the Germans across the Rhine.

224. The Helvetians said that they (7) would not give Caesar (20) the hostages that he demanded (92).

225. The prisoners said that they had sent a messenger to Caesar on that day.

226. The Remi said that they were ready (3) to give hostages and that they would surrender (95 and Note) their arms.

227. They said ambassadors had been sent because they feared (92) the barbarians.

228. They answered him (20) that they were unable to use any other road (47).

229. Ambassadors sent by the Gauls said that they wished to confer with Caesar.

230. The Helvetians say that the enemy will send ambassadors to seek peace (see sentence 221).

231. The commander thought that in number (53) of men the Helvetians were the most powerful in Gaul.

232. One of the soldiers (17) reported that the king was retreating with all his forces.

233. Commius said that Caesar's legions would come (95 and Note) on the third day.

234. Caesar said that he was able to send their legions into Gaul.

235. The Helvetians promised to go out (95) of their territory.

236. The lieutenant reported that the camp of the enemy had been captured at sunset.

237. The Bellovaci heard that Caesar was coming into their country with three legions.

G. CONCESSIVE CLAUSES

238. Though Caesar ordered (78) the Helvetians (96) to bring all their weapons to him (7), yet they were unwilling to do it.

239. Although Labienus had been killed (78) by the enemy, his army was not put to flight.

240. Although he was a brave soldier (10), he did not wish to go with the others to the top of the mountain.

241. Although Caesar wished to take the town, nevertheless he did not make an attack.

242. Although this was his plan, his army marched so slowly

that many of the gates of the town were captured (*66*) before his arrival.

243. Although the soldiers were eager for battle (*15*), Caesar ordered them (*96*) not to make an attack.

244. Although Caesar did not know of the plans of the enemy, he decided to wait (*97*) until they should return (*77*).

245. Although the king used the river (*47*), nevertheless Caesar sailed so swiftly that he arrived (*66*) there within a few hours (*58*).

H. SUBSTANTIVE CLAUSES WITH VERBS OF FEARING

246. Our allies did not fear that they would be defeated (*82; 60*) by the enemy.

247. He feared that he could (*82; 60*) not easily resist (*97*) both the old and the new forces (*21*) of Ariovistus.

248. Caesar feared that the Germans would cross (*82*) from their own territory into the territory of the Helvetians on account of the fertility (**bonitās**) of the fields.

249. They feared that the Romans would not pass through their territory without violence.

250. I fear that the enemy may get possession of our baggage (*47*).

251. Our soldiers feared that Caesar could not supply grain because of the winter.

252. Are you afraid (*90*) that the enemy will attack (*82*) us during the night (*58*)?

253. We fear that he will not come.

254. I fear that Ariovistus will not seek (*82; 60*) Caesar's friendship.

255. Crassus feared that the auxiliaries would desert him (*7*).

256. The legions feared that they would be surrounded (*82*).

257. They were afraid that aid would not be sent to the town.

I. CONDITIONAL SENTENCES

258. If they send (*86*) legates to Caesar, he will make peace with them.

259. If the consul had not been (*89*) brave (*5*), the whole city would have been taken (*89*) by the enemy.

260. If a battle is fought (*86*), we shall conquer on account of the great number of our soldiers.

261. If the soldiers do not have enough food (*16*), they can not fight for many hours (*33*) against the enemy.
262. If Caesar had not set out (*89*) at this time, they would have collected larger forces.
263. Caesar would have been able to conquer the enemy, if he had had a larger number of ships.
264. If the foot soldiers should fight (*87*) more bravely, the enemy would not be able to defeat the cavalry.
265. If Labienus should hear (*87*) the signal, he would lead out all his troops to battle.
266. Had they been willing (*89*) to make peace, they would have been willing to give hostages.
267. I would have ordered (*89*) you to return (*96*) home (*37*), if I had been with you.
268. If they send (*86*) hostages, we will spare them (*21*).
269. If he had remained in Gaul (*43*), he would have captured the city.
270. If the Gauls had marched more swiftly, they would have surprised (**opprimere**) their foes.

J. MISCELLANEOUS SENTENCES

271. After their general had been killed (*56*), the Gauls were defeated by Caesar's army.
272. After the Gauls had been defeated (*56*), the lieutenant ordered them (*96*) to give hostages to Caesar.
273. After the army of the enemy had been defeated, the leader ordered his (*men*) to come into camp.
274. After the battle had been fought, the great courage of the tenth legion was announced by the general.
275. After (*their*) army had been conquered, the enemy quickly sent ambassadors to the Roman camp.
276. After the army of the enemy had been captured, the soldiers pitched camp in the territory of our allies.
277. After peace had been made, many hostages were handed over to Caesar by the enemy.
278. For many hours the Roman troops marched into the camp with heavy baggage.
279. "I am going to return (*100*) to my house," replied the man; and having said this (*56*), he set forth.

280. Why did not the enemy cross (*90*) the marsh that is very near their town (*24*)?

281. Why do you not recall the soldiers and form your line of battle?

282. Caesar said, "Soldiers, resist the attack (*21*) of the enemy."

283. He ordered his whole army (*96*) to be brought together, since he wished (*69*) to besiege the city.

284. Fortify the camp with a very deep ditch (*46*).

285. Why do you not attack their ships?

286. This battle was fought very fiercely by the Gauls and the Romans.

287. Caesar placed Labienus in charge of the legions (*23*) that (*6*) he had sent from Rome (*42*).

288. Was it not (**nōnne**) more difficult to make a bridge than to cross this river by boats?

289. The soldiers who were coming as a guard (*25*) from the camp were able to reach the place quickly by forced marches.

290. This river is three feet (*51*) wider than the river that he crossed.

291. The wagons that brought the supplies to us halted outside the camp.

292. At sunset (*58*), Caesar is said to have ordered his soldiers (*96*) to give thanks for their victory.

293. Procillus went with Metius as an envoy (*4*) to the camp of the Germans.

294. The Roman people made war on all who were attempting to go through the province.

295. Soldiers are not always willing to listen to the commands of their leaders.

296. The legion whose leader was slain by the cavalry (*49*) of the Gauls returned to the fight and drove the enemy into the woods.

297. Having delayed many days (*33*), our legions built a bridge and tried to return home (*37*).

298. The general led his army across the river with the captives whom he had taken.

299. After the new plans had been announced (*56*), the lieutenants ordered the soldiers to go into Italy.

300. The man whose letter you saw became a very loyal citizen (*10*) a few days (*51*) afterward.

CHAPTER VI

WORD FORMATION

Prefixes

Learn the meaning of each of the following prefixes and use each in two ways: first to form new Latin verbs from simple verbs; second, to form English derivatives. For example: **dūcō,** *lead* + **ab,** *away* = **abdūcō,** *lead away.* English derivative: **abduct.**

1.	**ā, ab, abs,**	*away, from.*
2.	**ad,**	*to, toward*
3.	**ante,**	*before*
4.	**circum,**	*around, about*
5.	**con,**	*with, together; entirely, thoroughly*
6.	**dē,**	*down from*
7.	**dis-,**	*apart; not, un-*
8.	**ē, ex,**	*out of, from; thoroughly, completely*
9.	**in,**	*in, into*
10.	**in-,**	*not, un-*
11.	**inter,**	*between*
12.	**ob,**	*against, toward*
13.	**per,**	*through; thoroughly, very*
14.	**post,**	*after*
15.	**prae,**	*before, at the head of*
16.	**prō,**	*before, forth, forward*
17.	**re-, red-,**	*back, again*
18.	**sē-, sēd-,**	*aside, apart*
19.	**sub,**	*under, from under*
20.	**super,**	*over, above*
21.	**trāns, trā-,**	*across*

Some prefixes change their final consonants to make them like the initial consonants of the words to which they are prefixed. Such a change is called assimilation. For example:

$$\text{ad} + \text{capiō} = \text{accipiō}$$
$$\text{con} + \text{locō} = \text{collocō}$$
$$\text{in} + \text{pōnō} = \text{impōnō}$$
$$\text{ob} + \text{ferō} = \text{offerō}$$
$$\text{sub} + \text{cēdō} = \text{succēdō}$$

When a Latin verb is compounded with a prefix, short **ă** or short **ĕ** in the root of the verb is usually changed to short **ĭ** before a single consonant. For example:

in + capiō = incipiō	re + teneō = retineō
re + capiō = recipiō	dē + faciō = dēficiō
ad + teneō = attineō	re + faciō = reficiō

Exercise 1

Divide each of the following compound words into its component parts, and show how the force of the prefix affects the meaning of each:

1. dēligō	26. prōiciō	51. colloquor
2. sēditiō	27. abstineō	52. subeō
3. commoveō	28. praetor	53. permultus
4. īnfluō	29. intercēdō	54. exclūdō
5. trāiciō	30. efferō	55. praecēdō
6. succīdō	31. commūniō	56. anteferō
7. cōgō	32. suscipiō	57. redigō
8. ēvocō	33. praeficiō	58. occurrō
9. dīripiō	34. excēdō	59. inīquus
10. attingō	35. āmittō	60. trādō
11. circumdūcō	36. dēcidō	61. adhibeō
12. inimīcitia	37. reddō	62. perficiō
13. perfacilis	38. prohibeō	63. antecēdō
14. dissimilis	39. conveniō	64. perfringō
15. trānsmittō	40. obtineō	65. sustineō
16. sēparō	41. incertus	66. accurrō
17. antepōnō	42. respiciō	67. circumdō
18. redeō	43. abiciō	68. permagnus
19. obiciō	44. afferō	69. dīmittō
20. perterreō	45. subdūcō	70. īnfīnītus
21. contineō	46. repellō	71. sēcēdō
22. prōvideō	47. oppōnō	72. āvertō
23. sustineō	48. convocō	73. dēdūcō
24. difficilis	49. ēdūcō	74. cōnferō
25. abstrahō	50. interpōnō	75. referō

Prefixes are also used in English to form compounds from simple words; as in Latin, some change their final consonants to make them like the initial consonants of the words to which they are prefixed. For example: **in + legible = illegible.**

Exercise 2

Give the prefix and root word of each of the following, and show how the force of the prefix affects the meaning of each:

1. translate	16. affix	31. educe	46. illegal
2. abstract	17. illuminate	32. antecedent	47. commotion
3. precede	18. accede	33. collect	48. transfer
4. depend	19. depose	34. abundance	49. occur
5. correct	20. announce	35. seclude	50. evoke
6. inactive	21. secede	36. preside	51. pervade
7. return	22. attend	37. disarm	52. exclude
8. offer	23. proceed	38. recede	53. absent
9. dislocate	24. subscribe	39. effect	54. deter
10. suspend	25. abrupt	40. suggest	55. dishonest
11. acquire	26. circumference	41. perfect	56. impose
12. separate	27. irruption	42. abstain	57. cohere
13. immigrant	28. support	43. deduce	58. ascribe
14. propel	29. differ	44. avocation	59. oppose
15. dispel	30. ignoble	45. egress	60. concur

Suffixes

A. Suffixes Used to Form Nouns from Verbs

Suffix	Meaning	Illustration
1. **-tor** (**-sor**)	one who	ōrā-tor, *one who speaks*, i.e., a speaker dēfēn-sor, *one who defends*, i.e. a defender
2. **-a**	one who	scrīb-a, *one who writes*, i.e., a clerk
3. **-or**	activity, condition, state	am-or, *love*
4. **-iō** 5. **-tiō** (**-siō**) 6. **-tus** (**-sus**) 7. **-ēs** 8. **-tūra** 9. **-ium**	action, result of an action	leg-iō, *the result of choosing*, i.e. a legion dēdi-tiō, *a surrender* dēfēn-siō, *defense* conven-tus, *assembly, meeting* cūr-sus, *running, course* caed-ēs, *slaughter* cul-tūra, *tilling, cultivation* aedific-ium, *building*
10. **-men** 11. **-mentum** 12. **-bulum** 13. **-ulum** 14. **-trum**	means, result of an action	nō-men, *means of knowing*, i.e., an name ōrnā-mentum, *decoration* pā-bulum, *fodder* vinc-ulum, *chain* arā-trum, *a plow*

B. Suffixes Used to Form Nouns from Nouns

Suffix	Meaning	Illustration
1. **-ia** 2. **-tās** 3. **-tūs**	condition, characteristic	victòr-ia, *victory* cīvi-tās, *citizenship* servi-tūs, *slavery*
4. **-ātus**	office	cōnsul-ātus, *consulship*

C. Suffixes Used to Form Nouns from Adjectives

Suffix	Meaning	Illustration
1. **-ia** 2. **-tia** 3. **-tās** 4. **-tūdō**	quality, condition	audāc-ia, *boldness* trīsti-tia, *sadness* celeri-tās, *swiftness* magni-tūdō, *greatness*

Exercise 3

Define each of the following words according to its etymology:

Model: ōrātor = ōrā (from ōrō, *speak*) + **tor** (*one who*) = *one who speaks,* i.e., a speaker.

1. adventus	17. excursiō	33. monumentum
2. aegritūdō	18. exercitus	34. mūnīmentum
3. agmen	19. exitus	35. mūnītiō
4. agricultūra	20. explōrātor	36. nōbilitās
5. amīcitia	21. fortitūdō	37. offēnsiō
6. armātūra	22. iaculum	38. perfuga
7. auctōritās	23. impedīmentum	39. praetor
8. beneficium	24. imperātor	40. profectiō
9. clāmor	25. imperium	41. prūdentia
10. concursus	26. incola	42. reditiō
11. crūdēlitās	27. iūmentum	43. rōstrum
12. cupiditās	28. lībertās	44. scientia
13. dīligentia	29. longitūdō	45. sepultūra
14. discessus	30. magistrātus	46. timor
15. ēgressus	31. maleficium	47. victor
16. ēruptiō	32. memoria	48. virtūs

Exercise 4

Define each of the following words according to its etymology:

Model: description = de, *down* + **scrip** (from **scribo,** *write*) + **tion** (*denotes act or result*) = the act or result of writing down or describing.

1. advent	11. expulsion	21. opposition
2. agency	12. injury	22. prediction
3. attitude	13. inspection	23. premonition
4. avocation	14. inspector	24. protection
5. benefactor	15. intention	25. punishment
6. circumlocution	16. intervention	26. purity
7. circumnavigation	17. inventor	27. recurrence
8. collector	18. magnitude	28. spectator
9. docility	19. malediction	29. submission
10. excitement	20. navigator	30. suspicion

D. Suffixes Used to Form Adjectives from Verbs

	Suffix	Meaning	Illustration
1.	**-ilis**	able to be	**fac-ilis,** *able to be done,* i.e., easy
2.	**-bilis**	able to be	**mō-bilis,** *able to be moved,* i.e., movable, fickle
3.	**-idus**	condition	**tim-idus,** *being in a condition of fearing* i.e., timid

E. Suffixes Used to Form Adjectives from Nouns

Suffix	Meaning	Illustration
1. -ōsus	full of	perīcul-ōsus, *full of danger*, i.e., dangerous
2. -eus	made of	ferr-eus, *made of iron*
3. -ālis		nāv-ālis, *pertaining to a ship*, i.e., naval
4. -ānus		Rōm-ānus, *pertaining to Rome*, i.e., Roman
5. -āris		cōnsul-āris, *pertaining to a consul*, i.e., consular
6. -ārius	pertaining to	legiōn-ārius, *pertaining to a legion*, i.e., legionary
7. -icus		bell-icus, *pertaining to war*, i.e., martial
8. -īlis		serv-īlis, *pertaining to a slave*, i.e., servile
9. -īnus		Lat-īnus, *pertaining to Latium*, i.e., Latin
10. -īvus		aest-īvus, *pertaining to summer*
11. -ius		patr-ius, *pertaining to a father*, i.e., ancestral

Exercise 5

Define each of the following adjectives according to its etymology:

Model 1: urbānus = urb (from urbs, *city*) + ānus (*pertaining to*) = *pertaining to the city*, i.e., of the city.

Model 2: legible = leg (from legō, *read*) + ible (*able to be*) = *able to be read*.

A

1.	aureus	6.	frūmentārius	11.	mīlitāris
2.	bellicōsus	7.	Gallicus	12.	mūrālis
3.	captīvus	8.	incrēdibilis	13.	oppidānus
4.	cupidus	9.	laudābilis	14.	ōtiōsus
5.	familiāris	10.	marīnus	15.	rapidus

B

1.	civic	6.	fertile	11.	mental
2.	copious	7.	fluid	12.	noble
3.	divine	8.	inaudible	13.	ocular
4.	domestic	9.	irrevocable	14.	puerile
5.	feminine	10.	laborious	15.	soluble

F. Verbs Derived from Verbs

1. Frequentatives, expressing repeated or intensive action, are formed by adding the suffixes: -tō (-itō), or -sō to the stems of other verbs; as,

   clām (from clāmō, *shout*) + itō (*intensive suffix*) = clāmitō, *cry out loudly*

   iac (from iaciō, *throw*) + tō (*intensive suffix*) = iactō, *throw about, toss*

   cur (from currō, *run*) + sō (*intensive suffix*) = cursō, *run about*

2. Inceptives, expressing the beginning of an action, are formed by adding the suffix -scō to the stems of other verbs; as,

   timē (from timeō, *be afraid of*) + scō (*inceptive suffix*) = timēscō, *begin to be afraid of, become afraid of*

CHAPTER VII

DERIVATION

Since a very large number of English words has come, directly or indirectly, from Latin, special attention should be given to the derivation of such words. Accordingly, ten Latin verbs are assigned for each half year as a basis for study in derivation. From each of these verbs the pupil should be required to make a list of all the more important English derivatives. An optional list of ten verbs has been added for each half year in the belief that many teachers will wish to emphasize even more strongly this feature of the study of Latin.

The Required and Optional Lists for the First Half Year are as follows:

Required		*Optional*	
1.	servō	1.	iūdicō
2.	locō	2.	pācō
3.	vocō	3.	parō
4.	putō	4.	pugnō
5.	videō	5.	spectō
6.	moveō	6.	habeō
7.	dūcō	7.	moneō
8.	mittō	8.	teneō
9.	dīcō	9.	agō
10.	capiō	10.	cognōscō

Note—A suggested form of arrangement in this work follows:

Derivation Notebook (specimen page)

Type 1 (without definitions)

locō, locāre, locāvī, locātus— *place*

locate, local, locality, location, locus, collocate, collocation, dislocate, localization, localize, locally, locative, locomotive, locomotor

Type 2 (with definitions)

vocō, vocāre, vocāvī, vocātus— —*call*

vocation—a *calling*, occupation
vocational—pertaining to a vocation or *calling*
vocal—pertaining to *voice*
evoke—*call* out
convoke—*call* together
vocative—case of *calling*, case of address
revoke—*call* back, remand
invoke—*call* upon, ask for
invocation—a *calling* upon, a prayer

Type 3 (with examples of use in English)

mittō, mittere, mīsī, missus—
send

mission—He was sent on a mission to Europe

missionary—He was sent as a missionary to China

missive—The letter was a formidable missive

missile—Stones were the missiles of early warfare

transmit—They will transmit the message to us

remission—He preached the remission of sins

commit—She was committed to his care

submit—They submitted to the inevitable

submissive—The slave was not submissive

omit—Omit the nonessential

The Required and Optional Lists for the Second Half Year are as follows:

Required	Optional
1. nāvigō	1. dō
2. doceō	2. veniō
3. timeō	3. fīdō
4. sedeō	4. pōnō
5. scrībō •	5. terreō
6. vincō	6. trahō
7. sūmiō	7. pellō
8. faciō	8. cōnsulō
9. iaciō	9. audeō
10. audiō	10. mūniō

The Required and Optional Lists for the Third Half Year are as follows:

Required	Optional
1. ōrō	1. mandō
2. portō	2. arbitror
3. stō	3. valeō
4. ferō	4. cadō
5. (in) colō	5. currō
6. regō	6. tribuō
7. legō	7. (ad) iungō
8. solvō	8. sequor
9. fugiō	9. tollō
10. expediō	10. vertō

EXAMPLES OF LATIN ROOTS AND THEIR LATIN AND ENGLISH DERIVATIVES

Certain easily intelligible Latin words not found in the vocabulary prescribed for a particular half year have been included.

The list of English words derived from them is not exhaustive; only the most important have been selected.

The following abbreviations are used:

n = noun   a = adjective   v = verb   av = adverb

Latin roots	*Latin derivatives*		*English derivatives*	
	(v)	spectō	(n)	aspect
	(n)	spectātor	(v)	inspect
	(n)	spectāculum	(n)	inspection
	(v)	aspiciō (ad-spiciō)	(n)	spectator
	(n)	aspectus	(n)	spectacle
	(v)	circumspiciō	(a)	spectacular
	(v)	cōnspiciō	(a)	circumspect
	(v)	perspiciō	(n)	circumspection
	(v)	prōspiciō	(n)	species
	(v)	respiciō	(a)	conspicuous
			(a)	suspicious
			(v) (n)	suspect
			(n)	perspective
			(n)	prospect
			(a)	prospective
			(n)	prospector
			(v) (n)	respect
			(a)	respectable
	(v)	retrōspiciō	(av)	respectably
			(n)	respectability
	(v)	speculor (dep.)	(n)	retrospect
			(n)	retrospection
			(a)	retrospective
			(v)	speculate
			(n)	speculator
			(n)	speculation

2 ten	(v)	teneō	(a)		tenable
	(a)	tenāx	(a)		tenacious
	(n)	tenācitās	(a)		pertinacious
	(v)	abstineō	(n)		tenacity
	(n)	abstinentia	(v)		abstain
	(v)	contineō	(n)		abstinence
	(v)	continuō	(v)		contain
	(v)	dētineō	(n)	(a)	content
	(v)	obtineō	(v)		continue
	(v)	pertineō	(a)		continual
	(v)	retineō	(a)		continuous
	(v)	sustineō	(v)		detain
			(n)		detention
			(v)		obtain
			(v)		pertain
			(v)		retain
			(v)		sustain
			(n)		sustenance
			(v)		maintain
			(v)		entertain
			(a)		pertinent
			(a)		impertinent
			(n)		tenant
3 cap	(v)	capiō	(v)	(n)	capture
	(n)	captīvus	(n)		captive
	(n)	captīvitās	(n)		captivity
	(v)	accipiō	(v)		accept
	(v)	excipiō	(a)		acceptable
	(v)	recipiō	(n)		acceptability
	(v)	incipiō	(v)		except
	(v)	dēcipiō	(n)		exception
	(a)	capāx	(n)		receptacle
	(v)	suspiciō	(n)		recipient
	(v)	praecipiō	(a)		incipient
	(v)	percipiō	(v)		participate
	(n)	praeceptor	(a)	(n)	principal
	(v)	intercipiō	(n)		principle
			(n)		recipe
			(n)		deception
			(n)		capacity
			(n)		incapacity
			(a)		capacious
			(n)		precept
			(n)		preceptor
			(n)		perception
			(av)		(ĭm) perceptibly
			(v)		emancipate
			(n)		emancipation
			(a)		susceptible
			(n)		susceptibility

4 vid

(v)	videō	(n)		vision
(v)	prōvideō	(a)		visible
(a)	prūdēns	(n)		visibility
(n)	prūdentia	(v)	(n)	visit
		(a)		visual
		(v)		provide
		(n)		providence
		(n)		provision
		(a)		providential
		(a)		evident
		(n)		evidence
		(a)		visionary
		(n)		proviso
		(a)		prudent
		(n)		prudence
		(n)		vista

In accordance with the above models, give the Latin roots and their **Latin** and English derivatives of the following verbs:

1.	cēdō	7.	sedeō
2.	cadō	8.	habeō
3.	caedō	9.	sentiō
4.	moveō	10.	vertō
5.	pellō	11.	trahō
6.	vehō	12.	rogō

VOCABULARIES

CHAPTER VIII

LATIN WORD LIST

The following list is divided into groups of words recommended for learning during each half year of the first two years of Latin study. The words in each half-year group are classified according to parts of speech.

FIRST HALF YEAR

Verbs

amō	love	agō	drive, do, plead
appellō	name, call	cōgō	drive together, gather, compel
cōnfīrmō	strengthen, assert		
dō	give	redigō	drive back, reduce
exspectō	look out for, wait for	cēdō	move, go away, yield
labōrō	toil, suffer	discēdō	go away
līberō	set free	excēdō	go out, withdraw
nāvigō	sail	dēfēndō	ward off, defend
nūntiō	give news, announce	dūcō	lead
occupō	seize	addūcō	lead to, influence
parō	make ready, prepare	indūcō	lead on, influence
comparō	make ready, buy, compare	perdūcō	lead through, construct
portō	carry	prōdūcō	lead forward, protract
pugnō	fight	gerō	carry on
servō	keep, save	lūdō	play
spectō	look at	mittō	send
superō	overcome, surpass, defeat	āmittō	send away, let go, lose
		committō	send together, entrust, join
vocō	call		
habeō	have, hold	dīmittō	send away, dispatch
moneō	warn, advise	inter-	
moveō	move	mittō	interrupt, stop
commoveō	move thoroughly, alarm	permittō	allow
		praemittō	send ahead
permoveō	move strongly, excite	remittō	send back, let go. relax
removeō	move back, withdraw		
respondeō	answer	petō	seek, attack, ask
teneō	hold	relinquō	leave behind
contineō	hold together, bound	scrībō	write
obtineō	hold fast, obtain	cōnscrībō	write together, enroll
pertineō	extend, belong to	vincō	conquer
sustineō	uphold, resist	sum	be
timeō	be afraid, fear	absum	be away, be absent
videō	see	adsum	be near, be present

Nouns

agricola	farmer	gladius	sword
amīcitia	friendship	liber	book
aqua	water	locus	place
fāma	reputation, rumor	magister	master, teacher, helmsman
fēmina	woman		
fīlia	daughter	negōtium	business, task
fortūna	chance, fortune	numerus	number
fuga	flight	oculus	eye
iniūria	wrong	officium	duty
īnsula	island	oppidum	town
lingua	tongue, language	perīculum	trial, danger
lūna	moon	populus	people, nation
memoria	memory	praemium	reward
mēnsa	table, dish	praesidium	garrison, protection
nātūra	nature, character	proelium	battle
nauta	sailor	puer	boy
patria	one's country	rēgnum	kingdom, royal power
pecūnia	money	servus	slave
poena	penalty, punishment	signum	sign, signal, standard
poēta	poet	socius	ally
porta	gate	vesper	evening
prōvincia	province	vir	man
puella	girl		
pugna	fight	aestās	summer
rēgīna	queen	altitūdō	height
silva	forest	arbor	tree
terra	earth, land	auctōritās	authority, influence
via	way, road	caput	head
victōria	victory	celeritās	swiftness, speed
vīta	life	cōnsul	consul
		corpus	body
ager	field, country	dux	leader
animus	spirit, courage, mind	flūmen	river
annus	year	frāter	brother
arma	arms, implements	hiems	winter
auxilium	aid, assistance	homō	man, human being
bellum	war	lātitūdō	width
castra	camp	lēx	law
cōnsilium	plan, counsel	lībertās	freedom
deus	god	lūx	light
dominus	master	magnitūdō	greatness, size
equus	horse	māter	mother
factum	deed	mīles	soldier
fīlius	son	multitūdō	large number, crowd
frūmentum	grain	nōmen	name

pater	father	soror	sister
pāx	peace	tempus	time
pēs	foot	victor	conqueror
prīnceps	leading man, chief	virtūs	manliness, bravery
rēx	king	vōx	voice, word
sōl	sun		

Adjectives, Pronouns

aequus	level, equal, kindly	pūblicus	belonging to the people, public
altus	high, deep		
amīcus	friendly	quārtus	fourth
amplus	large, splendid	quīntus	fifth
barbarus	foreign, rude	reliquus	left behind, remaining, rest of
bonus	good		
certus	sure, certain	secundus	following, second, favorable
crēber	thick, close, frequent		
decimus	tenth	septimus	seventh
ēgregius	outstanding, distinguished	sextus	sixth
		tertius	third
fīnitimus	neighboring	timidus	fearful, cowardly
ignōtus	unknown	tuus	thy, thine, your, yours
inimīcus	unfriendly	ūnus	one
inīquus	uneven, unfair	vērus	true
integer	whole	vester	your, yours
lātus	wide		
līber	free	centum	hundred
longus	long	decem	ten
magnus	great	duo	two
malus	bad	novem	nine
meus	my, mine	octō	eight
miser	wretched	quattuor	four
multus	much; (pl. many)	quīnque	five
nōnus	ninth	septem	seven
noster	our, ours	sex	six
nōtus	known	trēs	three
novus	new	vīgintī	twenty
octāvus	eighth		
parvus	small	is	this, that, he
paucī	a few, few	quī	who, which, that
prīmus	first		

Prepositions, Adverbs, Conjunctions

ā (ab)	from, away from, by	ē (ex)	out of
ad	to, toward, near	in	in, into
ante	before	per	through
cum	with	post	after, behind
dē	down from, concerning	prō	in front of, in behalf of

sine	*without*	cūr	*why*
sub	*under, close to*	et	*and*
trāns	*across*	et . . . et	*both . . . and*
anteā	*before that, previously*	etiam	*also, even*
iam	*now, already, presently*	-ne	interrogative particle
nōn	*not*	nec (neque)	*and not, nor, neither*
nunc	*now*	neque . . .	
posteā	*after that, afterwards*	neque	*neither . . . nor*
tum (tunc)	*at that time*	quam	*how, as, than*
ubi	*where, when*	-que	*and*
ac (atque)	*and also, and*	quod	*because*
aut	*or*	sed	*but*
aut . . aut	*either . . . or*		

SECOND HALF YEAR

Verbs

appropin-quō	*approach*	iubeō	*order, command*
clāmō	*shout, cry*	licet	*it is permitted*
commūnicō	*share, communicate*	maneō	*stay, remain*
dēmōnstrō	*point out*	permaneō	*stay through, abide*
(dō—1st & 3d conjugation compounds)		noceō	*harm*
		obsideō	*sit against, besiege*
circumdō	*put around, surround* (1)	oportet	*it behooves, ought*
		perterreō	*frighten thoroughly*
		possideō	*possess, acquire*
abdō	*put away, hide* (3)	prohibeō	*keep away*
reddō	*give back, return* (3)	studeō	*be eager, desire*
trādō	*hand over, entrust, surrender* (3)		
		antecēdō	*go before, surpass*
dubitō	*hesitate, doubt*	succēdō	*approach, come next*
ēnūntiō	*disclose, announce*	claudō	*close, shut*
exīstimō	*think, believe*	coepī	*have begun*
prōnūntiō	*declare*	cognōscō	*learn;* (perfect: *know*)
putō	*think*	cōnfīdō	*trust*
renūntiō	*announce, proclaim*	cōnsistō	*take position, halt, stop*
ignōrō	*be unacquainted with*		
laudō	*praise*	dēsistō	*desist, cease*
occultō	*hide, conceal*	resistō	*take a stand, resist*
recuperō	*regain, get back*	contendō	*struggle, hasten*
temptō	*try, attempt*	ostendō	*hold out, show*
vītō	*avoid*	dīcō	*say, speak*
vulnerō	*wound*	exstruō	*pile up, build*
		īnstruō	*arrange, marshal*
audeō	*dare*	legō	*pick, choose, read*
dēbeō	*owe, ought*	dēligō	*pick out, choose*
doceō	*teach, inform*	pellō	*strike, beat, drive*

compellō	*drive together, collect, force*	**iaciō**	*hurl, throw*
impellō	*drive on, urge on*	**adiciō**	*add to*
pōnō	*put, place*	**coniciō**	*hurl, throw*
dēpōnō	*put down, put aside*	**obiciō**	*throw against*
expōnō	*put forth, set forth*	**prōciō**	*hurl (forward)*
impōnō	*put on*	**audiō**	*hear*
prōpōnō	*set forth, propose*	**fīniō**	*limit, bound, end*
premō	*press*	**mūniō**	*do a task, build, fortify*
submittō	*send under, send to assist, yield*	**sciō**	*know*
		sentiō	*feel, think, judge*
trahō	*drag, draw*	**cōnsentiō**	*think together, agree*
capiō	*take, seize*	**veniō**	*come*
accipiō	*take to, receive, accept*	**circumveniō**	*come around, surround, cut off*
excipiō	*take out, succeed to*	**conveniō**	*come together, assemble*
incipiō	*begin*		
cupiō	*desire, wish*	**inveniō**	*come upon, find*
faciō	*do, make*	**perveniō**	*come through, arrive*
cōnficiō	*accomplish, complete*	**dēsum**	*be lacking*
dēficiō	*fail, revolt from*	**possum**	*be able, can*
interficiō	*kill*	**praesum**	*be ahead, be in charge of*
perficiō	*accomplish*		
praeficiō	*put at the head of*		
prōficiō	*accomplish, gain*	**supersum**	*be over, remain, survive*
satisfaciō	*do enough, do one's duty, apologize*		

Nouns

cōpia	*supply, abundance (pl. forces)*	**trīduum**	*three days*
		aetās	*age, time of life*
hōra	*hour*	**cīvitās**	*citizenship, community, state*
inopia	*want, lack*		
rīpa	*bank, shore*	**condiciō**	*agreement, terms, condition*
sagitta	*arrow*		
toga	*toga*	**cōnsuētūdō**	*custom, habit*
tuba	*trumpet*	**cupiditās**	*desire, longing*
vīlla	*farm house*	**difficultās**	*difficulty*
beneficium	*kind deed, service*	**dignitās**	*worth, rank*
bīduum	*two days*	**facultās**	*power of doing, ability, chance*
campus	*plain, field*		
digitus	*finger, toe*	**genus**	*origin, kind, race*
imperātum	*command*	**iūs**	*right, law*
imperium	*command, power*	**laus**	*praise, glory*
maleficium	*evil deed*	**ōrātiō**	*speech*
modus	*measure, manner*	**ōrdō**	*order, rank*
spatium	*space*	**potestās**	*power*

ratiō	reckoning, plan, reason	vīs	violence, force
timor	fear	adventus	approach, arrival
vulnus	wound	cornū	horn, wing (of an army)
iter	road, march	domus	home, house
cīvis	citizen	equitātus	body of horsemen, cavalry
dēns	tooth		
fīnis	end, boundary; (pl. territory)	exercitus	trained body, army
		exitus	outcome, end
hostis	enemy	manus	hand, band, troop
mare	sea	passus	pace, (double) step
mēns	mind	senātus	body of elders, senate
mēnsis	month	aciēs	edge, line of battle
mōns	mountain	diēs	day
mors	death	fidēs	trust, pledge, reli·· ability
nāvis	ship		
nox	night	merīdiēs	midday
pars	part	rēs	thing
pōns	bridge	rēs pūblica	commonwealth
urbs	city	spēs	hope

Adjectives, Pronouns

cupidus	desirous	levis	light, fickle
dexter	right (of direction)	mīlle	thousand
idōneus	suitable	nōbilis	well-known
maritimus	of the sea, maritime	omnis	all, whole (sing. every)
necessārius	necessary	pār	equal
occultus	hidden, secret	potēns	able, powerful
perītus	experienced, skilled	praesēns	present, in person
propinquus	nearby, kinsman	prūdēns	foreseeing, discreet, wise
sinister	left (of direction)		
suus	his, her, its, their (own)	recēns	fresh, new
		similis	like, resembling
vīcīnus	neighboring	singulāris	one by one, extraordi· nary
ācer	sharp, keen, eager		
alacer	eager, cheerful	ego	I
celer	swift	hīc	this
commūnis	common, general	īdem	the same
difficilis	difficult	ille	that
dīligēns	careful	ipse	self, very
facilis	easy	quis	who, any
fidēlis	faithful	suī	(of) himself, herself, itself, themselves
fortis	brave		
gravis	heavy, serious	tū	thou, you
humilis	low, lowly		

Prepositions, Adverbs, Conjunctions

apud	near, in the presence of, among	interim	meanwhile
		magis	more greatly, more
inter	between, among	magnopere	greatly
ob	against, on account of	nē . . .	
propter	near, on account of	quidem	not even
aegrē	with difficulty	parum	(too) little
amplius	more	quidem	certainly, at least
bene	well	quō	whither
bis	twice	satis	enough
eō	thither, to that place	unde	whence
eōdem	to the same place	vehementer	strongly
facile	easily	vērō	in truth, but
hīc (adv.)	here, at this point	autem	moreover, but
hūc	hither	enim	for, indeed
iam prīdem	long ago	nam	for
ibi	there	sī	if
inde	thence		

THIRD HALF YEAR

Verbs

armō	arm, equip	accēdō	go to, approach, be added
commemorō	mention		
cūrō	care for, provide	concēdō	go with, withdraw, yield
dīmicō	fight		
explōrō	reconnoiter	colligō	gather, collect
expugnō	take by storm	intellegō	understand
oppugnō	attack, assault	cōnsuēscō	become accustomed
imperō	command, impose	cōnsulō	plan, consult, deliberate
impetrō	obtain (a request)		
incitō	urge on, arouse	currō	run
mandō	hand over, commission	occurrō	run against, meet
ōrō	pray, plead	dispergō	scatter
postulō	demand	dīvidō	separate, divide
recūsō	object, refuse	emō	buy, take
rogō	ask, ask for	incendō	set on fire
interrogō	ask (a question)	occidō	fall, set
spērō	hope	quaerō	seek, ask
supportō	carry up	conquīrō	seek together, collect
tardō	make slow, check	solvō	untie, release, perform, pay
adhibeō	have on hand, supply	tangō	touch
augeō	make grow, increase	attingō	touch upon, attain
pateō	lie open, extend	tollō	lift, remove
persuādeō	persuade, convince	tribuō	assign, grant
valeō	be strong	distribuō	distribute

afficiō	do to, affect	tueor	gaze at, protect
cōnspiciō	behold	vereor	fear, respect
dēspiciō	look down upon, despise	loquor	talk
		colloquor	talk together, confer
perspiciō	look through, understand	nāscor	be born
		proficīscor	set forth, start
ēripiō	snatch out, free	queror	complain
fugiō	flee	sequor	follow
effugiō	escape	cōnsequor	follow up, overtake, attain
perfugiō	flee to, desert		
recipiō	take back, receive	īnsequor	follow on, pursue
suscipiō	take up, undertake	persequor	follow through, pursue
comperiō	find out, ascertain	prōsequor	follow on, pursue, escort
reperiō	gain back, discover, find	subsequor	follow closely
		ūtor	use, employ
expediō	extricate, free	adgredior	step up, approach, attack
arbitror	consider, think		
cōnor	try, attempt	congredior	step together, meet
cōnspicor	behold	prōgredior	step forward, proceed
suspicor	suspect	patior	suffer, allow
hortor	urge, advise		
moror	delay, tarry	orior	rise
commoror	remain	adorior	rise against, attack
vagor	roam	experior	try out, test
versor	turn about, dwell	potior	get power over, gain possession of
polliceor	promise		

Nouns

causa	reason	iugum	yoke, ridge
familia	household	lēgātus	envoy, deputy
fossa	ditch	līberī	(freeborn) children
grātia	favor, influence, gratitude	nihil	nothing
		pāgus	district, clan
opera	work, effort	subsidium	reserve, reënforcement, assistance
sententia	feeling, opinion		
summa	highest sum, total	supplicium	punishment
		tēlum	missile, weapon
aedificium	building	tergum	back, rear
carrus	wagon, cart	vadum	shoal, ford
castellum	fort, redoubt	vāllum	rampart
impedīmentum	hindrance; (pl. baggage)	verbum	word
		vīcus	village
initium	beginning	vulgus	common crowd
īnstitūtum	custom		

agmen	*marching column*	terror	*fright, panic*
calamitās	*disaster*		
centuriō	*centurion*	adulēscēns	*youth, young man*
clāmor	*outcry, shout*	caedēs	*slaughter*
grātulātiō	*congratulation*	cliēns	*dependent, retainer,*
honor	*honor, glory, office*		*vassal*
hūmānitās	*kindliness, culture*	cohors	*cohort, troop*
labor	*toil*	collis	*hill*
lēgātiō	*mission, embassy*	gēns	*family, clan, tribe*
legiō	*legion*	aditus	*approach*
maiōrēs	*ancestors*	cāsus	*fall, chance, accident*
mōs	*manner, habit*	commeātus	*supplies*
mūnītiō	*fortification*	cōnspectus	*view, sight*
nātiō	*race, people*	cursus	*running, course*
nēmō	*nobody*	impetus	*attack, charge, rush*
nōbilitās	*rank, nobility*	magistrātus	*office, official*
obses	*hostage*	metus	*fear*
opīniō	*belief, view*	occāsus	*falling, setting*
ops	*aid, resources*	portus	*harbor*
opus	*work*	ūsus	*use, advantage, experi-*
plēbs	*common people*		*ence*
quaestor	*quaestor*		
regiō	*boundary line, district*	plānitiēs	*plain*
salūs	*health, safety*	rēs frūmen-	
suspīciō	*suspicion*	tāria	*grain supply*

Adjectives, Pronouns

aeger	*sick*	tantus	*so great*
aliēnus	*belonging to another,*	tūtus	*protected, safe*
	strange, unfavorable	ūniversus	*all together*
angustus	*narrow*	vetustus	*old, ancient*
apertus	*open*	audāx	*bold, daring*
cēterī	*the others, the rest*	brevis	*short, brief*
commodus	*suitable, convenient*	complūrēs	*several, very many*
dīversus	*turned away, different*	familiāris	*belonging to the house-*
fīrmus	*strong*		*hold, intimate*
frūmentār-		mīlitāris	*of a soldier*
ius	*belonging to grain*	necesse	*necessary*
iūstus	*just, fair*	prior	*preceding, former*
medius	*middle*	turpis	*base, disgraceful*
nocturnus	*nightly*	ūtilis	*useful*
perpetuus	*unbroken, lasting*	vetus	*old, longstanding*
posterus	*next, later*		
prīvātus	*apart, private*	alius	*another*
quantus	*how great, as great*	alter	*the other (of two),*
singulī	*one at a time*		*second*
superus	*upper*	neuter	*neither*

nōnnūllus	*some*	ūllus	*any*
nūllus	*none, no*	uter	*which, of two*
sōlus	*alone, only*	uterque	*each of two, both*
tōtus	*whole*		

Prepositions, Adverbs, Conjunctions

circum	*around*	plērumque	*for the greater part.*
extrā	*outside of, beyond*		*generally*
īnfrā	*below*	potius	*rather, preferably*
intrā	*inside, within*	proptereā	*on account of this,*
prope	*near, nearby*		*therefore*
suprā	*above, beyond*	quā	*by what way, where*
ultrā	*beyond*	saepe	*often*
aliter	*otherwise*	semper	*always*
audācter	*boldly*	sīc	*thus, so*
causā	*by reason of, for the*	sōlum	*only*
	sake of	tam	*thus, so*
circiter	*about*	cum	*when, since, although*
diū	*a long time*	cum . . .	
ita	*thus, so*	tum	*both . . . and, not*
itaque	*and thus, therefore*		*only . . . but also*
item	*likewise*	dum	*while, as long as, pro-*
modo	*only, just now*		*vided, until*
noctū	*at night*	etsī	*and if, although*
nōn modo		nē	*lest, that not*
. . . sed		nisi	*if not, unless, except*
etiam	*not only . . . but*	quoniam	*in as much as, since*
	also	tamen	*however, nevertheless*
numquam	*never*	ut	*in order that, so that*

FOURTH HALF YEAR

Verbs

administrō	*govern, manage*	īnstō	*stand on, press on, be*
collocō	*place together, estab-*		*at hand*
	lish	praestō	*stand before, excel,*
commendō	*entrust*		*guarantee*
dēcertō	*fight a decisive battle*	sublevō	*assist*
dēspērō	*give up hope*	vāstō	*lay waste*
hiemō	*spend the winter*		
iūrō	*make oath, swear*	compleō	*fill up*
coniūrō	*conspire, plot*	mereō	
nūdō	*make bare, empty*	mereor	*earn, deserve*
pācō	*make peace, subdue*	praeheō	*hold in front, afford,*
perturbō	*throw into confusion*		*furnish*
significō	*announce*	adigō	*drive to, haul, move*
sollicitō	*stir up, tempt*	admittō	*let go, admit*
stō	*stand*	arcessō	*summon, invite*
cōnstō	*stand with, agree*	cadō	*fall*

accidō	*befall, happen*	advertō	*turn to, proceed against*
incidō	*befall, happen*		
caedō	*fell, cut, kill*	animad-vertō	*turn the mind to, observe*
concīdō	*kill*		
cernō	*distinguish*		
dēcernō	*decide, decree*	convertō	*turn around, change*
circumsistō	*hem in, surround*	revertō	*turn back, return*
compre-hendō	*seize, grasp, understand*	efficiō	*work out, accomplish, bring about*
cōnflīgō	*strike together, fight*	reficiō	*make over, repair*
cōnsīdō	*settle, take position*	praecipiō	*advise, give directions*
dēdō	*give over, devote, surrender*	aperiō	*open*
		impediō	*hinder*
ēdō	*put out, put forth*	eō	*go*
dēdūcō	*lead away, launch*	adeō	*go to, visit*
subdūcō	*lead under, lead up to, draw up, beach*	ineō	*go into, undertake*
		intereō	*perish*
dēserō	*give up, abandon*	pereō	*go through, perish*
incolō	*dwell in*	redeō	*go back, return*
intercēdō	*go between, forbid, veto*	trānseō	*go across, cross*
		ferō	*bear, bring, carry*
prōcēdō	*go forward, advance*	afferō	*bring to*
interclūdō	*shut off, cut off*	cōnferō	*bring together, collect, transport*
iungō	*join*		
coniungō	*join together, unite*	dēferō	*carry away, report*
minuō	*lessen*	differō	*be different, differ, postpone*
nōscō	*learn, recognize*		
opprimō	*crush, overwhelm*	īnferō	*bring in, bring against*
pendō	*hang, suspend, pay*	offerō	*bring against, offer*
poscō	*demand, claim*	perferō	*bear through, endure, announce*
regō	*direct, rule*		
dīrigō	*direct, guide*	referō	*bring back, report*
statuō	*set up, fix, determine*	fīō	*be made, happen, become*
cōnstituō	*put together, establish decide*		
		mālō	*prefer*
īnstituō	*set up, establish, undertake*	nōlō	*be unwilling*
		volō	*be willing, wish*
restituō	*place back, restore*	admīror	*wonder at*
sūmō	*take*	pābulor	*forage*
cōnsūmō	*use up*	populor	*lay waste, ravage*
tegō	*cover, conceal*	nancīscor	*obtain*
vertō	*turn*	mētior	*measure out, distribute*

Nouns

ancora	*anchor*	contrō-versia	*dispute, quarrel*
angustiae	*narrowness, defile, pass*		
		contumēlia	*insult*
aquila	*eagle*	disciplīna	*training, discipline*

fīdūcia	confidence
īnsidiae	ambush, treachery
littera	letter (of the alphabet); pl. a letter, letters
māteria	timber
mora	delay
perfidia	treachery
praeda	prey, booty
vigilia	night watch, guard
cibus	food
colloquium	conference
concilium	calling together, meeting
dētrīmentum	loss
hīberna	winter quarters
intervāllum	space between walls, interval
mandātum	commission
mūrus	(town) wall
nūntius	news, message, messenger
pābulum	fodder
pīlum	spear
praefectus	captain, commander
respōnsum	answer
sagittārius	archer
saxum	rock
scūtum	shield
stīpendium	payment, tax, campaign
studium	eagerness
tormentum	military engine
tribūnus	tribune
tumulus	small hill, mound
ventus	wind
vinculum	bond, fetter
aes	copper, bronze, money
agger	mount, rampart, causeway
dēditiō	surrender
dēfēnsor	defender

eques	horseman, knight; pl. cavalry
ēruptiō	breaking out, sally
exercitātiō	training
explōrātor	scout
factiō	party, faction
funditor	slinger
iūs iūrandum	oath
lapis	stone
latus	side
lītus	coast, shore, beach
mercātor	trader
mulier	woman
mūnus	task, duty, service, offering
obsidiō	siege
occāsiō	opportunity
onus	burden
oppugnātiō	assault
palūs	swamp, marsh
pecus (-oris)	cattle
pedes	foot soldier
prex	prayer
profectiō	departure
pulvis	dust
servitūs	slavery
sponte suā	of one's own will, voluntarily
statiō	outpost, picket
tempestās	period of time, weather, storm
voluntās	willingness, good will
classis	fleet
famēs	hunger, starvation
frōns (-tis)	forehead, front
īgnis	fire
turris	tower
vallēs	valley
aestus	heat, tide
ēventus	outcome, result
prīncipātus	leadership
rēs mīlitāris	warfare
speciēs	appearance

Adjectives, Pronouns

| captīvus | captive, prisoner |
| cōnfertus | crowded together, dense |

continuus	unbroken
cotīdiānus	daily
dēfessus	tired out

exiguus	*limited, little*	citerior	*this side of, hither*
ferus	*wild, fierce*	dēclīvis	*sloping down*
invītus	*against one's will*	equester	*of a horseman, eques-*
onerārius	*suitable for burden,*		*trian*
	of a transport (ship)	incolumis	*unharmed*
oppidānus	*of the town, towns-*	inermis	*unarmed*
	man	interior	*inner*
opportūnus	*at the right time, suit-*	pedester	*of a footsoldier, on*
	able		*foot*
plērīque	*the greater part,*	tot	*so many*
	majority	totidem	*just as many*
prīstinus	*former, of old*	aliquis	*some, any*
quiētus	*at rest, peaceful*	quīcumque	*whoever*
repentīnus	*sudden*	quīdam	*a certain one, some*
tardus	*slow*		*one*
vacuus	*empty*	quisquam	*any one at all*
		quisque	*each one*

Prepositions, Adverbs, Conjunctions

contrā	*against, opposite*	quoque	*also, too*
praeter	*along past, beside*	repente	*suddenly*
admodum	*very, very much.*	rūrsus	*(turned back) again*
adversus	*(turned toward), fac-*	sīcut	
	ing, opposite	(sīcutī)	*just as*
clam	*secretly*	simul	*together, at the same*
cōnfestim	*promptly*		*time*
cotīdiē	*every day, daily*	statim	*at once, immediately*
deinde	*thereupon, next*	subitō	*suddenly*
ferē	*almost, about, gen-*	ultrō	*beyond, unasked,*
	erally		*voluntarily*
frūstrā	*in vain*	ūnā	*together*
grātīs	*for nothing*	undique	*from (on) all sides*
intereā	*meanwhile*	ūsque	*up to*
nōndum	*not yet*	vix	*barely, scarcely*
omnīnō	*altogether, at all*	an	*or (in a question)*
paene	*almost*	at	*but*
partim	*partly*	nēve (neu)	*and that not*
paulātim	*little by little*	postquam	*(later than), after*
paulisper	*for a little while*	(posteā-	
paulō	*(by) a little*	quam)	
paulum	*(for) a little*	priusquam	*(sooner than), before,*
postrīdiē	*the day after, next day*		*until*
praesertim	*particularly*	quīn	*indeed, (but) that*
praetereā	*besides this, more-*		*(with negative ex-*
	over		*pressions of doubt)*
prīdiē	*on the day before*	quod sī	*but if, and if*
prīmō	*at first*	quōminus	*(that less), lest*
prīmum	*first*	sī quis	*if any, whoever*
procul	*afar*	vel	*or*

CHAPTER IX

LATIN WORD LIST
(With Translations)

Words marked with an asterisk (*) are listed in the latest New Yor
State Syllabus as the words required to be taught in second-year Latir
classes.

Words marked with a dagger (†) are listed in this syllabus as a mini-
mum list for mastery by second-year students.

†ā, ab, prep. w.
   abl.   *from, away from, by*
abdō, -dere, -didī,
   -ditus   *put away, hide*
*abeō, -īre, -iī,
   -itūrus   *go away, depart*
*absum, -esse, āfuī,
   āfutūrus   *be away, be absent*
*ac, conj.   *and also, and*
*accēdō, -ere,
   -cessī, -cessūrus   *go to, approach, be added*
*accidō, -ere, -cidī   *befall, happen*
†accipiō, -ere,
   -cēpī, -ceptus   *take to, receive, accept*
†ācer, ācris, ācre,
   adj.   *sharp, keen, eager*
†aciēs, -ēī, f.   *edge, line of battle*

ācriter, ācrius,
   ācerrimē, adv.   *sharply, fiercely*
†ad, prep. w. acc.   *to, toward, near*
addō, -ere, -didī,
   -ditus   *add*
*addūcō, -ere,
   -dūxī, -ductus   *lead to, influence*
*adeō, -īre, -iī,
   -itus   *go to, visit*
adficiō, -ere,
   -fēcī, -fectus   *do to, affect*
adhibeō, -ēre,
   -hibuī, -hibitus   *have on hand, supply*
adiciō, -ere, -iēcī,
   -iectus   *add to*
adigō, -ere, -ēgī,
   -āctus   *drive to, haul, move*

*aditus, -ūs, m.   *approach*
administrō, -āre,
   -āvī, -ātus   *govern, manage*
admīror, -ārī,
   -ātus   *wonder at*
admittō, -ere,
   -mīsī, -missus   *let go, admit*
admodum, adv.   *very, very much*
adorior, -īrī,
   -ortus   *rise against, attack*
*adsum, -esse, -fuī   *be near, be present*
*adulēscēns, -entis,
   m.   *youth, young man*
*adulēscentia, -ae, f. *youth*
†adventus, -ūs, m.   *approach, arrival*
adversus, prep.
   w. acc.   *turned toward, facing, opposite*

advertō, -ere,
   -vertī, -versus   *turn to, proceed against*
*aedificium, -ī, n.   *building*
*aedificō, -āre,
   -āvī, -ātus   *build, construct*
*aeger, aegra,
   aegrum, adj.   *sick*
aegrē, adv.   *with difficulty*
*aequus, -a, -um,
   adj.   *level, even, kindly*
aes, aeris, n.   *copper, bronze, money*
†aestās, -tātis, f.   *summer*
*aetās, -tātis, f.   *age, time of life*
aestus, -ūs, m.   *heat, tide*
afferō, -ferre,
   attulī, allātus   *bring to*
†ager, agrī, m.   *field, country*

agger, aggeris,
m.   *mound, rampart,
causeway*

*aggredior, -ī,
-gressus   step up,
approach,
attack*

agmen, -minis, n. marching column
†agō, -ere, ēgī,
āctus   drive, do, plead
†agricola, -ae, m. farmer
alacer, -cris, -cre,
adj.   eager, cheerful
aliēnus, -a, -um,
adj.   belonging to
another,
strange,
unfavorable

*aliquis, aliqua,
aliquid, indef.
pron.   some, any
aliter, adv.   otherwise
*alius, alia, aliud,
adj.   another
*alter, altera,
alterum, adj. the other (of
two), second
*altitūdō, inis, f. height
†altus, -a, -um, adj. high, deep
*ambulō, -āre,
-āvī, -ātus   walk about, take
a walk
†amīcitia, -ae, f. friendship
†amīcus, -a, -um,
adj.   friendly
†amīcus, -ī, m. friend
*āmittō, -ere,
-mīsī, -missus send away, let go,
lose

†amo, -āre, -āvī,
-ātus   love
*amor, -ōris, m. affection, love
amplius, adv. more
*amplus, -a, -um,
adj.   large, splendid
an, conj.   or (in question)
ancora, -ae, f. anchor
angustiae,
-ārum, f.   narrowness,
defile, pass
angustus, -a, -um,
adj.   narrow

*animadvertō,
-ere, -vertī,
-versus   turn the mind to,
observe
†animus, -ī, m. spirit, courage,
mind
†annus, -ī, m. year
†ante, adv. and
prep. w. acc. before
*antequam, conj. sooner than, be-
fore
anteā, adv.   before that,
previously
antecēdō, -ere,
-cessī   go before,
surpass
aperiō, -īre,
aperuī, apertus open
*apertus, -a, -um,
adj.   open
†appellō, -āre, -āvī,
-ātus   name, call
*appropinquō,
-āre, -āvī,
-ātum   approach
*apud, prep. w.
acc.   near, in the
presence of.
among
†aqua, ae, f. water
*aquila, -ae, f. eagle
†arbitror, -ārī,
-ātus   consider, think
*arbor, -oris, f. tree
arcessō, -ere, īvī,
-ītus   summon, invite
†arma, -ōrum, n. arms, implements
*armō, -āre, -āvī,
-ātus   arm
*at, conj.   but
*atque, conj. and also, and
*ātrium, -ī, n. court, hall, room
attingō, -ere,
attigī, attāctus touch upon,
attain
auctōritās, -tātis,
f.   authority,
influence
*audācia, -ae, f. boldness, daring,
recklessness
*audācter, adv. boldly
*audāx, -ācis, adj. bold, daring
*audeō, -ēre, ausus dare

†audiō, -īre, -īvī,
-ītus — *hear*
*augeō, -ēre, auxī,
auctus — *make grow, increase*
*aut, conj. — *or*
*aut . . aut — *either . . or*
*autem, postpositive
conj. — *moreover, but*
†auxilium, -ī, n. — *aid, assistance*

*barbarus, -a, -um,
adj. — *foreign, rude*
†bellum, -ī, n. — *war*
*bene, adv. — *well*
*beneficium, -ī, n. — *kind deed, service*
bīduum, -ī, n. — *two days*
*bis, adv. — *twice*
†bonus, -a, -um,
adj. — *good*
†brevis, -e, adj. — *short, brief*

cadō, -ere, cecidī,
cāsūrus — *fall*
*caedēs, -is, f. — *slaughter*
caedō, -ere, cecīdī,
caesus — *fell, cut, kill*
*caelum, -ī, n. — *heaven, the sky*
*calamitās, -tātis,
f. — *disaster*
*campus, -ī, m. — *plain, field*
†capiō, -ere, cēpī,
captus — *take, seize*
*captīvus, ī, m. — *captive, prisoner*
†caput, -itis, n. — *head*
carrus, -ī, m. — *wagon, cart*
*casa, -ae, f. — *hut, cottage*
castellum, -ī, n. — *fort, redoubt*
†castra, -ōrum,
n. pl. — *camp*
*cāsus, -ūs, m. — *fall, chance, accident*
†causa, -ae, f. — *reason*
*causā, with gen. — *by reason of, for the sake of*
*cēdo, -ere, cessī,
cessūrus — *move, go away, yield*
†celer, -eris, -ere,
adj. — *swift*

†celeritās, -tātis, f. — *swiftness, speed*
*centum, num.
adj. — *hundred*
*centuriō, -ōnis, m. — *centurion*
cernō, -ere, crēvī,
crētus — *distinguish*
†certus, -a, -um,
adj. — *sure, certain*
*cēterī, -ae, -a, adj. — *the others, the rest*
*cibus, -ī, m. — *food*
*circiter, adv. and
prep. w. acc. — *about*
†circum, adv. and
prep. w. acc. — *around*
*circumdō, -dare,
-dedī, -datus — *put around, surround*
circumsistō,
-sistere, -stetī — *hem in, surround*
*circumveniō, -īre,
-vēnī, -ventus — *come around, surround cut off*
*citerior, -ius, adj. — *this side of, hither*
†cīvis, -is, m. and f. — *citizen*
†cīvitās, -tātis, f. — *citizenship, community state*
clam, adv. — *secretly*
*clāmō, -āre, -āvī,
-ātus — *shout, cry*
*clāmor, -ōris, m. — *outcry, shout*
†clārus, -a, -um,
adj. — *bright illustrious*
*classis, -is, f. — *fleet*
*claudō, -ere,
clausī, clausus — *close, shut*
cliēns, -entis, m. — *dependent, retainer, vassal*
*coepī, -isse,
coeptus — *have begun*
†cognōscō, -ere,
-gnōvī, -gnitus — *learn (in the perf., know)*
*cōgō, -ere, coēgī,
coāctus — *drive together, gather, compel*
†cohors, -hortis, f. — *cohort, troop*

*cohortor, -ārī,
  -ātus   *encourage,*
             exhort

colligō, -ere,
  -lēgī, -lēctus *gather, collect*
*collis, -is, m.   *hill*
*collocō, -āre, -āvī,
  -ātus   *place together,*
             establish

*colloquium, -ī, n. *conference*

colloquor, -ī,
  -locūtus   *talk together,*
             confer

commeātus,
  -ūs, m.   *supplies*

commemorō,
  -āre, -āvī, -ātus *mention*

commendō, -āre,
  -āvī, -ātus   *entrust*

*committō, -ere,
  -mīsī, -missus *send together,*
             entrust, join

commodus, -a,
  -um, adj.   *suitable,*
             convenient

commoror, -ārī,
  -ātus   *remain*

*commoveō, -ēre,
  -mōvī, -mōtus *move thoroughly,*
             alarm

commūnicō, -āre,
  -āvī, -ātus   *share,*
             communicate

*commūnis, -e, adj. *common, general*

*comparō, -āre,
  -āvī, -ātus   *make ready,*
             buy, compare

compellō, -ere,
  -pulī, -pulsus *drive together,*
             collect, force

comperiō, -īre,
  -perī, -pertus *find out, ascertain*

*compleō, -ēre,
  -plēvī, -plētus *fill up*

*complūrēs, -a, adj. *several, very*
             many

*comportō, -āre,
  -āvī, -ātus   *bring in, carry,*
             convey

comprehendō, -ere,
  -hendī, -hēnsus *seize, grasp,*
             understand

*concēdō, -ere,
  -cessī, -cessūrus *go with,*
             withdraw,
             yield

concīdō, -ere,
  -cīdī, -cīsus   *kill*

*concilium, -ī, n. *calling together,*
             meeting

*condiciō, -ōnis, f. *agreement, terms,*
             condition

*cōnferō, -ferre,
  -tulī, collātus *bring together,*
             collect,
             transport

cōnfertus, -a, -um,
  adj.   *crowded*
             together, dense

cōnfēstim, adv. *promptly*

†cōnficiō, -ere,
  -fēcī, -fectus *accomplish,*
             complete

cōnfīdō, -ere,
  -fīsus   *trust*

*cōnfīrmō, -āre,
  -āvī, -ātus   *strengthen,*
             assert

cōnflīgō, -ere,
  -flīxī, -flīctus *strike together,*
             fight

congredior, -ī,
  -gressus   *step together,*
             meet

*coniciō, -ere,
  -iēcī, -iectus *hurl, throw*

*coniungō, -ere,
  -iūnxī, -iūnctus *join together,*
             unite

coniūrō, -āre,
  -āvī, -ātus   *conspire, plot*

*cōnor, -ārī, -ātus *try, attempt*

conquīrō, -ere,
  -quīsīvī,
  -quīsītus   *search together,*
             collect

cōnscrībō, -ere,
  -scrīpsī,
  -scrīptus   *write together,*
             enroll

cōnsentiō, -īre,
  -sēnsī, -sēnsus *think together,*
             agree

*cōnsequor, -ī,
  -secūtus — *follow up, attain, overtake*

*cōnservō, -āre,
  -āvī, -ātus — *keep, maintain, save, spare*

*cōnsīdō, -ere,
  -sēdī, -sessūrus — *settle, take position*

†cōnsilium, -ī, n. — *plan, counsel*

*cōnsistō, -ere,
  -stitī — *take position, halt, stop*

*cōnspectus, -ūs, m. — *view, sight*

*cōnspiciō, -ere,
  -spexī, -spectus — *behold*

cōnspicor, -ārī,
  -ātus — *behold*

†cōnstituō, -ere,
  -stituī, -stitūtus — *put together, establish, decide*

cōnstō, -āre, -stitī,
  -stātūrus — *stand with, agree*

cōnsuēscō, -ere,
  -suēvī, -suētus — *become accustomed*

cōnsuētūdō,
  -inis, f. — *custom, habit*

*cōnsul, -ulis, m. — *consul*

cōnsulātus, -ūs, m. — *consulship*

cōnsulō, -ere,
  -suluī, -sultus — *plan, consult, deliberate*

*cōnsūmō, -ere,
  -sūmpsī,
  -sūmptus — *use up*

†contendō, -ere,
  -tendī, -tentus — *struggle, hasten*

*contineō, -ēre,
  -tinuī, -tentus — *hold together, bound*

*continuus, -a,
  -um, adj. — *unbroken*

†contrā, adv. and
  prep. w. acc. — *against, opposite*

contrōversia, -ae, f. *dispute, quarrel*

contumēlia, -ae, f. *insult*

†conveniō, -īre,
  -vēnī, -ventum — *come together, assemble*

convertō, -ere,
  -vertī, -versus — *turn around, change*

†convocō, -āre, -āvī,
  -ātus — *call together, summon*

†cōpia, -ae, f. — *supply, abundance, pl., forces*

*cornū, -ūs, n. — *horn, wing (of an army)*

†corpus, -oris, n. — *body*

cotīdiānus, -a,
  -um, adj. — *daily*

cotīdiē, adv. — *every day, daily*

crēber, crēbra,
  crēbrum, adj. — *thick, close, frequent*

*crēdō, -ere, -didī,
  -ditus — *give trust, believe, trust*

†cum, prep. w. abl. *with*

†cum, conj. — *when, since, although*

cum . . tum,
  correl. conj. — *both . . and, not only . . but also*

cupiditās, -tātis, f. *desire, longing*

*cupidus, -a, -um,
  adj. — *desirous*

†cupiō, -ere,
  cupīvī, cupītus — *desire, wish*

†cūr, adv. — *why*

*cūra, -ae, f. — *care, anxiety, trouble*

*cūrō, -āre, -āvī,
  -ātus — *care for, provide*

*currō, -ere,
  cucurrī, cursum *run*

*currus, -ūs, m. — *chariot, car*

*cursus, -ūs, m. — *running, course*

†dē, prep. w. abl. — *down from, concerning*

†dēbeō, -ēre,
  dēbuī, dēbitus — *owe, ought*

*decem, num. adj. *ten*

dēcernō, -ere,
  -crēvī, -crētus — *decide, decree*

dēcertō, -āre, -āvī,
  -ātus — *decide, fight a decisive battle*

*decimus, -a, -um,
  num. adj. — *tenth*
dēclīvis, -e, adj. — *sloping down*
*dēditiō, -ōnis, f. — *surrender*
*dēdō, -ere, -didī,
  -ditus — *give up, devote,
  surrender*
*dēdūcō, -ere,
  -dūxī, -ductus — *lead away,
  launch*
†dēfendō, -ere,
  -fendī, -fēnsus — *ward off, defend*
*dēfēnsor, -ōris, m. — *defender*
dēferō, -ferre,
  -tulī, -lātus — *carry away,
  report*
dēfessus, -a, -um,
  adj. — *tired out*
dēficiō, -ere, -fēcī,
  -fectus — *fail, revolt from*
*dēiciō, -ere, -iēcī,
  -iectus — *throw down,
  destroy,
  disappoint*
deinde, adv. — *thereupon, next*
†dēligō, -ere, -lēgī,
  -lēctus — *pick out, choose*
*dēmōnstrō, -āre,
  -āvī, -ātus — *point out*
*dēns, dentis, m. — *tooth*
dēpōnō, -ere,
  -posuī, -positus — *put down,
  put aside*
dēserō, -ere,
  -seruī, -sertus — *give up, abandon*
dēsistō, -ere,
  -stitī, -stitūrus — *desist, cease*
*dēspērō, -āre, -āvī,
  -ātus — *give up hope,
  despair*
dēspiciō, -ere,
  -spexī, -spectus — *look down upon,
  despise*
dēsum, -esse,
  -fuī, -futūrus — *be lacking*
dētrīmentum, -ī, n. — *loss*
*deus, -ī, m. — *god*
*dexter, -tra, -trum,
  adj. — *right*
  (of direction)
†dīcō, -ere, dīxī,
  dictus — *say, speak*
†diēs, diēī, m. and f. — *day*

differō, -ferre,
  distulī, dīlātus — *be different,
  differ, postpone*
*difficilis, -e, adj. — *difficult*
*difficultās, -tātis,
  f. — *difficulty*
*digitus, -ī, m. — *finger, toe*
dignitās, -tātis, f. — *worth, rank*
*dīligēns, -entis,
  adj. — *careful*
*dīligentia, -ae, f. — *carefulness*
dīmicō, -āre, -āvī,
  -ātum — *fight*
*dīmittō, -ere,
  -mīsī, -missus — *send away,
  dispatch*
dīrigō, -ere, -rēxī,
  -rēctus — *direct, guide*
†discēdō, -ere,
  -cessī, -cessūrus — *go away*
*disciplīna, -ae, f. — *training,
  discipline*
dispergō, -ere,
  -spersī, -spersus — *scatter*
*dissimilis, -e, adj. — *unlike, dissimi-
  lar*
distribuō, -ere,
  -tribuī, -tribūtus — *distribute*
†diū, adv. — *a long time*
dīversus, -a, -um,
  adj. — *turned away,
  different*
*dīvidō, -ere, -vīsī,
  -vīsus — *separate, divide*
†dō, dare, dedī,
  datus — *give*
*doceō, -ēre,
  docuī, doctus — *teach, inform*
*dolor, -ōris, m. — *pain, suffering,
  grief*
*domicilium, -ī, n. — *dwelling, abode,
  residence*
*domina, -ae, f. — *mistress of a
  household,
  lady*
*dominus, -ī, m. — *master*
†domus, -ūs, f. — *home, house*
*dōnō, -āre, -āvī,
  -ātus — *make a gift,
  present*
*dōnum, -ī, n. — *gift, present*
*dormiō, -īre, -īvī,
  -ītum — *sleep, be idle*

dubitō, -āre, -āvī,
-ātus — *hesitate, doubt*
†dūcō, -ere, dūxī,
ductus — *lead*
*dum, conj. — *while, as long as,
provided, until*
*duo, duae, duo,
num. adj. — *two*
†dux, ducis, m. — *leader*

†ē, ex, prep. w. abl. — *out of*
ēdō, -ere, ēdidī,
ēditus — *put out, put
forth*
*ēdūcō, -ere, -dūxī,
-ductus — *lead out, draw
(a sword)*
*efficiō, -ere, -fēcī,
-fectus — *work out,
accomplish,
bring about*
effugiō, -ere, -fūgī — *escape*
†ego, person. pron. — *I*
*ēgredior, -ī,
-gressus — *go out, disembark*
ēgregius, -a, -um,
adj. — *outstanding,
distinguished*
*ēiciō, -ere, ēiēcī,
ēiectus — *throw out, drive
out*
emō, -ere, ēmī,
ēmptus — *buy, take*
*enim, postpositive
conj. — *for, indeed*
*ēnūntiō, -āre,
-āvī, -ātus — *disclose,
announce*
†eō, īre, īvī(iī),
itūrus — *go*
*eō, adv. — *thither, to that
place*
*eōdem, adv. — *to the same place*
*epistula, -ae, f. — *letter, dispatch*
†eques, -itis, m. — *horseman,
knight; pl.,
cavalry*
equester, -tris,
-tre, adj. — *of a horseman,
equestrian*
*equitātus, -ūs, m. — *body of horse-
men, cavalry*
*equus, -ī, m. — *horse*

ēripiō, -ere, -ripuī,
-reptus — *snatch out, free*
ēruptiō, -ōnis, f. — *breaking out,
sally*
†et, conj. — *and*
*et . . et — *both . . and*
*etiam, adv. — *also, even*
*etsī, conj. — *and if, although*
ēventus, -ūs, m. — *outcome, result*
†ex, prep. w. abl. — *out of*
*excēdō, -ere,
-cessī, -cessūrus — *go out, withdraw*
*excipiō, -ere, -cēpī,
-ceptus — *take out,
succeed to*
*exeō, -īre, -iī(-īvī),
-itūrus — *go out, withdraw,
leave*
*exerceō, -ēre, -uī,
-itus — *train, exercise,
practice*
exercitātiō, -ōnis,
f. — *training*
†exercitus, -ūs, m. — *trained body,
army*
exiguus, -a, -um,
adj. — *limited, little*
†exīstimō, -āre,
-āvī, -ātus — *think, believe*
*exitus, -ūs, m. — *outcome, end*
expediō, -īre, -īvī,
-ītus — *extricate, free*
expedītus, -a, -um,
adj. — *unencumbered,
light-armed*
*expellō, -ere, -pulī,
-pulsus — *drive out, expel*
experior, -īrī,
-pertus — *try out, test*
*explōrātor,
-ōris, m. — *scout*
*explōrō, -āre, -āvī,
-ātus — *reconnoiter*
*expōnō, -ere,
-posuī, -positus — *put forth, set
forth*
*expugnō, -āre,
-āvī, -ātus — *take by storm*
*exspectō, -āre,
-āvī, -ātus — *look out for,
wait for*
exstruō, -ere,
-strūxī, -strūctus — *pile up, build*

*extrā, prep. w. acc. *outside of, beyond*

*extrēmus, -a, -um, adj. *farthest, last, the end of*

*fābula, -ae, f. *tale, story, fable*
*facile, adv. *easily*
†facilis, -e, adj. *easy*
†faciō, -ere, fēcī, factus *do, make*
*factum, -ī, n. *deed*
*facultās, -tātis, f. *power of doing, ability, chance*
*fāma, -ae, f. *reputation, rumor*
fāmēs, -is, f. *hunger, starvation*
*familia, -ae, f. *household*
familiāris, -e, adj. *belonging to the household, intimate*
*fēlīx, -īcis, adj. *fertile, happy, fortunate*
†fēmina, -ae, f. *woman*
ferē, adv. *almost, about*
†ferō, ferre, tulī, lātus *bear, bring, carry*
ferus, -a, -um, adj. *wild, fierce*
fidēlis, -e, adj. *faithful*
†fidēs, -eī, f. *trust, pledge, reliability*
fidūcia, -ae, f. *confidence*
†fīlia, -ae, f. *daughter*
†fīlius, -ī, m. *son*
*fīnēs, -ium, m. *territory*
*fīniō, -īre, fīnīvī, fīnītus *limit, bound, end*
†fīnis, -is, m. *end, boundary*
†fīnitimus, -a, -um, adj. *neighboring*
*fīō, fierī, factus *be made, happen, become*
*fīrmus, -a, -um, adj. *strong*
†flūmen, -minis, n. *river*
*fōrma, -ae, f. *shape, form*
†fortis, -e, adj. *brave*
*fortitūdō, -inis, f. *courage, bravery*
*fortūna, -ae, f. *chance, fortune*
*forum, -ī, n. *market place*
*fossa, -ae, f. *ditch*

†frāter, -tris, m. *brother*
frōns, frontis, f. *forehead, front*
*frūmentārius, -a, -um, adj. *pertaining to grain*
†frūmentum, -ī, n. *grain*
*frūstrā, adv. *in vain*
†fuga, -ae, f. *flight*
†fugiō, -ere, fūgī, fugitūrus *flee*
funditor, -ōris, m. *slinger*

*gēns, gentis, f. *family, clan, tribe*
*genus, generis, n. *origin, kind, race*
†gerō, -ere, gessī, gestus *carry on*
*gladiātor, -ōris, m. *gladiator*
†gladius, -ī, m. *sword*
†glōria, -ae, f. *renown, glory*
*grātia, -ae, f. *favor, influence, gratitude*
grātis, adv. *for nothing*
grātulātiō, -ōnis, f. *congratulation*
*grātus, -a, -um, adj. *pleasing, acceptable*
*gravis, -e, adj. *heavy, serious*

†habeō, -ēre, -uī, -itus *have, hold*
*habitō, -āre, -āvī, -ātus *occupy, dwell in*
*hīberna, -ōrum, n. *winter quarters*
†hic, haec, hoc, dem. adj. *this*
dem. pron. *he, she, it*
*hīc, adv. *here, at this point*
*hiemō, -āre, -āvī, -ātūrus *spend the winter*
†hiems, hiemis, f. *winter*
*hodiē, adv. *today*
†homō, hominis, m. and f. *man, human being*
*honor, -ōris, m. *honor, glory, office*
†hōra, -ae, f. *hour*
*hortor, -ārī, -ātus *urge, advise*
†hostis, -is, m. and f. *enemy*
hūc, adv. *hither*

hūmānitās,
-tātis, f. — *kindness, culture*
humilis, -e, adj. — *low, lowly*

†iaciō, -ere, iēcī,
iactus — *hurl, throw*
*iam, adv. — *now, already, presently*
iam prīdem, adv. — *long ago*
†ibi, adv. — *there*
†īdem, eadem,
idem, dem.
pron. and adj. — *the same*
*idōneus, -a, -um,
adj. — *suitable*
*igitur, conj. — *therefore, accordingly*
*īgnis, -is, m. — *fire*
ignōrō, -āre, -āvī,
-ātus — *be unacquainted with*
*ignōtus, -a, -um,
adj. — *unknown*
†ille, illa, illud,
dem. adj. — *that*
*immortālis, -e,
adj. — *immortal*
†impedīmentum,
-ī, n. — *hindrance; pl., baggage*
*impediō, -īre, -īvī,
-ītus — *hinder*
*impellō, -ere,
-pulī, -pulsus — *drive on, urge on*
†imperātor, -ōris,
m. — *commander-in-chief, general*
imperātum, -ī, n. — *command*
†imperium, -ī, n. — *command, power*
†imperō, -āre, -āvī,
-ātus — *command, impose*
impetrō, -āre,
-āvī, -ātus — *obtain (a request)*
†impetus, -ūs, m. — *attack, charge, rush*
impōnō, -ere,
-posuī, -positus — *put on*
†in, prep. w. abl.
and acc. — *in (w. abl.); into (w. acc.)*

*incendō, -ere,
-cendī, -cēnsus — *set on fire*
*incertus, -a, -um,
adj. — *uncertain, doubtful*
incidō, -ere, -cidī — *befall, happen*
†incipiō, -ere, -cēpī,
-ceptus — *begin*
*incitō, -āre, -āvī,
-ātus — *urge on, arouse*
*incola, -ae, m. and
f. — *inhabitant*
incolō, -ere, -coluī — *dwell in*
*incolumis, -e, adj. — *unharmed*
inde, adv. — *thence*
indūcō, -ere,
-dūxī, -ductus — *lead on, influence*
*ineō, -īre, -iī, -itus — *go into, undertake*
inermis, -e, adj. — *unarmed*
*īnfēlīx, -īcis, adj. — *unfruitful, unhappy, unlucky*
†īnferō, -ferre,
-tulī, illātus — *bring in, bring against*
īnfrā, adv. and
prep. w. acc. — *below*
*inimīcus, -a,
-um, adj. — *unfriendly*
*inīquus, -a, -um,
adj. — *uneven, unfair*
*initium, -ī, n. — *beginning*
*iniūria, -ae, f. — *wrong*
*inopia, -ae, f. — *want, lack*
*īnsequor, -ī,
-secūtus — *follow on, pursue*
*īnsidiae, -ārum, f. — *ambush, treachery*
*īnstituō, -ere,
-stituī, -stitūtus — *set up, establish, undertake*
īnstitūtum, -ī, n. — *custom*
īnstō, -āre, -stitī,
-stātūrus — *stand on, press on, be at hand*
*īnstruō, -ere,
-strūxī,
-strūctus — *arrange, marshal*
†īnsula, -ae, f. — *island*
*integer, -gra,
-grum, adj. — *whole*

†intellegō, -ere,
-lēxī, -lēctus — *understand*

†inter, prep. w. acc. — *between, among*

intercēdō, -ere,
-cessī, -cessūrus — *go between,
forbid, veto*

interclūdō, -ere,
-clūsī, -clūsus — *shut off, cut off*

*intereā, adv. — *meanwhile*

intereō, -īre, -iī,
-itūrus — *perish*

†interficiō, -ere,
-fēcī, -fectus — *kill*

*interim, adv. — *meanwhile*

interior, -ius, adj. — *inner*

*intermittō, -ere,
-mīsī, -missus — *interrupt, stop*

*interrogō, -āre,
-āvī, -ātus — *ask (a question)*

*intervāllum, -ī, n. — *space between
walls, interval*

*intrā, prep. w. acc. — *inside, within*

*inveniō, -īre,
-vēnī, -ventus — *come upon, find*

invītus, -a, -um,
adj. — *against one's will*

†ipse, ipsa, ipsum,
dem. pron. — *self, very*

*īra, -ae, f. — *anger, wrath*

†is, ea, id, dem. adj. — *this, that;* pron.,
he, she, it

†ita, adv. — *thus, so*

†itaque, adv. — *and thus,
therefore*

*item, adv. — *likewise*

†iter, itineris, n. — *road, march*

†iubeō, -ēre,
iussī, iussus — *order, command*

*iūdicō, -āre,
-āvī, -ātus — *judge, decide*

*iugum, -ī, n. — *yoke, ridge*

*iungō, -ere,
iūnxī, iūnctus — *join*

*iūrō, -āre, -āvī,
-ātus — *take an oath,
swear*

*iūs, iūris, n. — *right, law*

iūs iūrandum,
iūris iūrandī, n. — *oath*

iūstus, -a, -um,
adj. — *just, fair*

*labor, -ōris, m. — *toil*

†labōrō, -āre, -āvī,
-ātus — *toil, suffer*

lapis, -pidis, m. — *stone*

*lātitūdō, -dinis, f. — *width*

*lātus, -a, -um, adj. — *wide*

*latus, lateris, n. — *side*

†laudō, -āre, -āvī,
-ātus — *praise*

*laus, laudis, f. — *praise, glory*

lēgātiō, -ōnis, f. — *mission,
embassy*

*lēgātus, -ī, m. — *envoy, deputy*

*legiō, -ōnis, f. — *legion*

*legō, -ere, lēgī,
lēctus — *pick, choose,
read*

*levis, -e, adj. — *light, fickle*

*lēx, lēgis, f. — *law*

*liber, librī, m. — *book*

†līber, -era, -erum,
adj. — *free*

*līberī, -ōrum, m. — *(freeborn)
children*

†līberō, -āre, -āvī,
-ātus — *set free*

*lībertās, -tātis, f. — *freedom*

*licet, -ēre, licuit
or licitum est — *it is permitted*

*lingua, -ae, f. — *tongue, language*

†littera, -ae, f. — *letter (of the
alphabet);* pl.,
a letter, letters

*lītus, -oris, n. — *coast, shore,
beach*

†locō, -āre, -āvī,
-ātus — *place, put,
arrange*

†locus, -ī, m.; pl.,
loca, -ōrum, n. — *place*

longē, adv. — *far, by far*

†longus, -a, -um,
adj. — *long*

*loquor, -ī, locūtus — *talk*

lūdō, -ere, lūsī,
lūsus — *play*

*lūdus, -ī, m. — *play, school;* pl.,
games

*lūna, -ae, f. — *moon*

†lūx, lūcis, f. — *light*

*magis, adv. — *more greatly,
more*

*magister, -trī, m.   *master, teacher, helmsman*

*magistrātus, -ūs, m.   *office, official*

*magnitūdō, -inis, f. *greatness, size*

*magnopere, adv.   *greatly*

†magnus, -a, -um, adj.   *great*

*maiōrēs, -um, m.   *ancestors*

maleficium, -ī, n.   *evil deed*

mālō, mālle, māluī   *prefer*

†malus, -a, -um, adj.   *bad, evil*

mandātum, -ī, n.   *commission*

*mandō, -āre, -āvī, -ātus   *hand over, commission*

†maneō, -ēre, mānsī, mānsūrus   *stay, remain*

†manus, -ūs, f.   *hand, band, troop*

†mare, -is, n.   *sea*

*maritimus, -a, -um, adj.   *of the sea, maritime*

†māter, -tris, f.   *mother*

*māteria, -ae, f.   *timber*

†medius, -a, -um, adj.   *middle*

†memoria, -ae, f.   *memory*

*mēns, mentis, f.   *mind*

*mēnsa, -ae, f.   *table, dish*

*mēnsis, -is, m.   *month*

*mercātor, -ōris, m. *trader*

mereō, -ēre, -uī, -itus   *earn, deserve*

mereor, -ērī, -itus   *earn, deserve*

*merīdiēs, -ēī, m.   *midday*

mētior, -īrī, mēnsus   *measure out, distribute*

metus, -ūs, m.   *fear*

†meus, -a, -um, adj.   *my, mine*

†mīles, -itis, m.   *soldier*

†mīlia, -um, n., pl.   *thousand, thousands*

mīlitāris, -e, adj.   *of a soldier*

*mīlle, num. adj.   *thousand*

minuō, -ere, -uī, -ūtus   *lessen*

†miser, -era, -erum, adj.   *wretched*

†mittō, -ere, mīsī, missus   *send*

*modo, adv.   *only, just now*

†modus, -ī, m.   *measure, manner*

†moneō, -ēre, monuī, monitus   *advise, warn*

†mōns, montis, m.   *mountain*

*mora, -ae, f.   *delay*

*morior, -ī, mortuus   *die*

*moror, -ārī, -ātus   *delay, tarry*

†mors, mortis, f.   *death*

*mōs, mōris, m.   *manner, habit*

†moveō, -ēre, mōvī, mōtus   *move*

*mox, adv.   *soon, presently*

mulier, -eris, f.   *woman*

†multitūdō, -dinis, f.   *large number, crowd*

†multus, -a, -um, adj.   *much; pl., many*

†mūniō, -īre, -īvī, -ītus   *do a task, build, fortify*

*mūnītiō, -ōnis, f.   *fortification*

mūnus, -eris, n.   *task, duty, service, offering*

†mūrus, -ī, m.   *(town) wall*

*nam, conj.   *for*

nancīscor, -ī, nactus   *obtain*

*narrō, -āre, -āvī, -ātus   *tell, relate*

*nāscor, -ī, nātus   *be born*

†nātiō, -ōnis, f.   *race, people*

†nātūra, -ae, f.   *nature, character*

†nauta, -ae, m.   *sailor*

†nāvigō, -āre, -āvī, -ātus   *sail*

†nāvis, -is, f.   *ship*

†-ne, enclitic   *interrogative particle*

†nē, conj.   *lest, that not*

*nec, conj.   *and not, nor, neither*

*nec . . nec   *neither . . nor*

*necessārius, -a, -um, adj.   *necessary*

*necesse, indecl.
  adj. — *necessary*
*negōtium, -ī, n. — *business, task*
*nēmō, nūllīus,
  nēminī, m. — *nobody*
*nē . . quidem — *not even*
*neque . . neque — *neither . . nor*
*nescio, -īre, -īvī — *know not, be
    unaware*
*neuter, -tra,
  -trum, pron. adj. — *neither (of two)*
nēve (neu), conj. — *and that not*
*nihil, n. indecl. — *nothing*
*nisi, conj. — *if not, unless,
    except*
*nōbilis, -e, adj. — *well-known*
*nōbilitās, -tātis, f. — *rank, nobility*
*noceō, -ēre, nocuī,
  nocitūrus — *harm*
noctū, adv. — *at night*
nocturnus, -a,
  -um, adj. — *nightly*
*nōlō, nōlle, nōluī — *be unwilling*
†nōmen, -minis, n. — *name*
†nōn, adv. — *not*
*nōndum, adv. — *not yet*
nōn iam, adv. — *no longer*
nōn modo . . sed
  etiam — *not only . . but
    also*
*nōnne, adv.
  interrog. — *not?* (expecting
    an affirmative
    answer), *if
    not, whether
    not*
*nōn nūllus, -a,
  -um, adj. — *some*
nōn numquam,
  adv. — *sometimes*
*nōnus, -a, -um,
  num. adj. — *ninth*
nōscō, -ere, nōvī,
  nōtus — *recognize*
†noster, -tra, -trum,
  adj. — *our, ours*
†nōtus, -a, -um,
  adj. — *known*
*novem, num. adj. — *nine*
†novus, -a, -um,
  adj. — *new*
†nox, noctis, f. — *night*

nūdō, -āre, -āvī,
  -ātus — *make bare,
    empty*
†nūllus, -a, -um,
  adj. — *none, no*
†numerus, -ī, m. — *number*
*numquam, adv. — *never*
†nunc, adv. — *now*
†nūntiō, -āre, -āvī,
  -ātus — *give news,
    announce*
†nūntius, -ī, m. — *news, message,
    messenger*

†ob, prep. w. acc. — *against, on
    account of*
obiciō, -ere, -iēcī,
  -iectus — *throw against*
*obses, -sidis, m.
  and f. — *hostage*
*obsideō, -ēre,
  -sēdī, -sessus — *sit against,
    besiege*
obsidiō, -ōnis, f. — *siege*
*obtineō, -ēre,
  -tinuī, -tentus — *hold fast, obtain*
occāsiō, -ōnis, f. — *opportunity*
*occāsus, -ūs, m. — *falling, setting*
*occidō, -ere, -cidī — *fall, set*
occīdō, -ere, -cīdī,
  -cīsus — *cut down, kill*
occultō, -āre, -āvī,
  -ātus — *hide, conceal*
occultus, -a, -um,
  adj. — *hidden, secret*
†occupō, -āre, -āvī,
  -ātus — *seize*
occurrō, -ere,
  -currī,
  -cursūrus — *run against,
    meet*
*ōceanus, -ī, m. — *ocean, sea*
*octāvus, -a, -um,
  num. adj. — *eighth*
*octō, num. adj. — *eight*
*oculus, -ī, m. — *eye*
offerō, -ferre,
  obtulī, oblātus — *bring against,
    offer*
*officium, -ī, n. — *duty*
*ōlim, adv. — *formerly, some
    time ago*
omnīnō, adv. — *altogether, at all*

†omnis, -e, adj.   *every, all, whole*
onerārius, -a, -um,
  adj.   *suitable for burden, transport (ship)*
onus, oneris, n.   *burden*
opera, -ae, f.   *work, effort*
opīniō, -ōnis, f.   *belief, view*
*oportet, -ēre,
  oportuit   *it behooves, ought*
oppidānus, -ī, m.   *townsman; adj., of the town*
†óppidum, -ī, n.   *town*
*opportūnus, -a,
  -um, adj.   *at the right time, suitable*
*opprimō, -ere,
  -pressī, -pressus   *crush, overwhelm*
oppugnātiō,
  -ōnis, f.   *assault*
†oppugnō, -āre,
  -āvī, -ātus   *attack, assault*
ops, opis, f.   *aid; pl., opēs, -um, resources*
*opus, operis, n.   *work*
*ōrātiō, -ōnis, f.   *speech*
*ōrdō, -dinis, m.   *order, rank*
*orior, -īrī, ortus   *rise*
*ōrō, -āre, -āvī,
  -ātus   *pray, plead*
*ostendō, -ere,
  -tendī, -tentus   *hold out, show*

pābulor, -ārī,
  -ātus   *forage*
pābulum, -ī, n.   *fodder*
*pācō, -āre, -āvī,
  -ātus   *make peace, subdue*
*paene, adv.   *almost*
pāgus, -ī, m.   *district, clan*
palūs, -ūdis, f.   *swamp, marsh*
*pār, paris, adj.   *equal*
*pāreō, -ēre, -uī   *obey*
†parō, -āre, -āvī,
  -ātus   *make ready, prepare*
†pars, partis, f.   *part*
partim, adv.   *partly*

parum, adv.   *(too) little, not at all*
†parvus, -a, -um,
  adj.   *small*
†passus, -ūs, m.   *pace, double step*
*pateō, -ēre, patuī   *lie open, extend*
†pater, -tris, m.   *father*
*patior, -ī, passus   *suffer, allow*
†patria, -ae, f.   *one's country*
†paucī, -ae, -a, adj.   *a few, few*
paulātim, adv.   *little by little*
paulisper, adv.   *for a little while*
*paulō, adv.   *(by) a little*
*paulum, adv.   *(for) a little*
†pāx, pācis, f.   *peace*
†pecūnia, -ae, f.   *money*
pecus, -coris, n.   *cattle*
*pedes, -ditis, m.   *foot-soldier*
pedester, -tris,
  -tre, adj.   *of a foot-soldier, on foot*
*pellō, -ere, pepulī,
  pulsus   *strike, beat*
pendō, -ere,
  pependī, pēnsus   *hang, suspend, pay*
†per, prep. w. acc.   *through*
perdūcō, -ere,
  -dūxī, -ductus   *lead through, construct*
pereō, -īre, -iī,
  -itūrus   *go through, perish*
perferō, -ferre,
  -tulī, -lātus   *bear through, endure, announce*
*perficiō, -ere,
  -fēcī, -fectus   *accomplish*
perfidia, -ae, f.   *treachery*
perfugiō, -ere,
  -fūgī   *flee through, desert*
†perīculum, -ī, n.   *trial, danger*
perītus, -a, -um,
  adj.   *experienced, skilled*
permaneō, -ēre,
  -mānsī,
  -mānsūrus   *stay through, abide*
permittō, -ere,
  -mīsī, -missus   *allow*

*permoveō, -ēre,
　-mōvī, -mōtus　　*move strongly,
　　　　　　　　　　excite

perpetuus, -a, -um,
　adj.　　　　　　　*unbroken,
　　　　　　　　　　lasting

*persequor, -ī,
　-secūtus　　　　　*follow through,
　　　　　　　　　　pursue

*perspiciō, -ere,
　-spexī, -spectus　*see through,
　　　　　　　　　　understand

†persuādeō, -ēre,
　-suāsī, -suāsus　 *persuade,
　　　　　　　　　　convince

*perterreō, -ēre,
　-terruī, -territus *frighten
　　　　　　　　　　thoroughly

*pertineō, -ēre,
　-tinuī　　　　　　*extend, belong to*

*perturbō, -āre,
　-āvī, -ātus　　　 *throw into
　　　　　　　　　　confusion

†perveniō, -īre,
　-vēnī, -ventūrus *come through,
　　　　　　　　　　arrive

†pēs, pedis, m.　　*foot*

†petō, -ere, petīvī
　(petiī), petītus　*seek, attack, ask*

pīlum, -ī, n.　　　 *spear*

plānitiēs, -ēī, f.　*plain*

*plēbs, plēbis, f.　*common people*

plērīque, -aeque,
　-aque, adj.　　　*the greater part,
　　　　　　　　　　the majority

plērumque, adv.　*for the most part,
　　　　　　　　　　generally

†poena, -ae, f.　　*penalty,
　　　　　　　　　　punishment

*poēta, -ae, m.　　*poet*

*polliceor, -ērī,
　pollicitus　　　　*promise*

†pōnō, -ere, posuī,
　positus　　　　　*put, place*

†pōns, pontis, m.　*bridge*

populor, -ārī,
　-ātus　　　　　　*lay waste,
　　　　　　　　　　ravage

†populus, -ī, m.　 *people, nation*

†porta, -ae, f.　　*gate*

†portō, -āre, -āvī,
　-ātus　　　　　　*carry*

portus, -ūs, m.　　*harbor*

poscō, -ere,
　poposcī　　　　　*demand, claim*

possideō, -ēre,
　-sēdī, -sessus　　*possess, acquire*

†possum, posse,
　potuī　　　　　　*be able, can*

†post, prep. w. acc. *after, behind*

*posteā, adv.　　　*after that,
　　　　　　　　　　afterwards

*posterus, -a, -um,
　adj.　　　　　　　*next, later*

†postquam
　(posteāquam),
　conj.　　　　　　 *later than, after*

*postrīdiē, adv.　　*the day after,
　　　　　　　　　　next day

*postulō, -āre,
　-āvī, -ātus　　　 *demand*

†potēns, -entis,
　adj.　　　　　　　*able, powerful*

*potestās, -tātis, f. *power*

potior, -īrī,
　potītus　　　　　*get power over,
　　　　　　　　　　*gain possession
　　　　　　　　　　of

potius, adv.　　　 *rather,
　　　　　　　　　　preferably

praebeō, -ēre,
　-buī, -bitus　　　*hold in front,
　　　　　　　　　　afford, furnish

praecipiō, -ere,
　-cēpī, -ceptus　　*advise, give
　　　　　　　　　　directions

praeda, -ae, f.　　*prey, booty*

praefectus, -ī, m.　*captain,
　　　　　　　　　　commander

*praeficiō, -ere,
　-fēcī, -fectus　　*put at the head of*

*praemittō, -ere,
　-mīsī, -missus　　*send ahead*

†praemium, -ī, n.　*reward*

praesēns, -entis,
　adj.　　　　　　　*present, in
　　　　　　　　　　person

praesertim, adv.　*particularly*

†praesidium, -ī, n. *garrison,
　　　　　　　　　　protection

*praestō, -āre,
　-stitī, -stitus　　*stand before,
　　　　　　　　　　*excel,
　　　　　　　　　　guarantee

*praesum, -esse,
-fuī — *be ahead, be in charge of*

*praeter, prep. w. acc. — *along, past, besides*

*praetereā, adv. — *besides this, moreover*

*praetor, -ōris, m. — *praetor*

*premō, -ere, pressī, pressus — *press*

*pretium, -ī, n. — *price*

prex, precis, f. — *prayer*

*prīdiē, adv. — *on the day before*

*prīmō, adv. — *at first*

*prīmum, adv. — *first*

*prīmus, -a, -um, num. adj. — *first*

†prīnceps, -cipis, m. — *leading man, chief*

*prīncipātus, -ūs, m. — *leadership*

*prior, prius, adj. — *preceding, former*

prīstinus, -a, -um, adj. — *former, of old*

*priusquam, conj. — *(sooner than), before, until*

prīvātus, -a, -um, adj. — *apart, private*

†prō, prep. w. abl. — *in front of, in behalf of*

*prōcēdō, -ere, -cessī, -cessūrus — *go forward, advance*

procul, adv. — *afar*

*prōcurrō, -currere, -cucurrī or -currī — *run forward*

*prōdūcō, -ere, -dūxī, -ductus — *lead forward, protract*

†proelium, -ī, n. — *battle*

profectiō, -ōnis, f. — *departure*

prōficiō, -ere, -fēcī, -fectus — *accomplish, gain*

†proficīscor, -ī, profectus — *set forth, start*

profiteor, -ērī, -fessus — *declare publicly, profess*

†prōgredior, -ī, -gressus — *step forward, proceed*

†prohibeō, -ēre, -uī, -itus — *keep away*

prōiciō, -ere, -iēcī, -iectus — *hurl (forward)*

prōnūntiō, -āre, -āvī, -ātus — *declare*

†prope, adv. and prep. w. acc. — *near, nearby*

†properō, -āre, -āvī, -ātus — *hurry, hasten*

*propinquus, -a, -um, adj. — *nearby; as a noun, kinsman*

*prōpōnō, -ere, -posuī, -positus — *set forth, propose*

†propter, adv. and prep. w. acc. — *near, on account of*

*proptereā, adv. — *on account of this, therefore*

prōsequor, -ī, -secūtus — *follow on, pursue, escort*

†prōvincia, -ae, f. — *province*

*proximus, -a, -um, adj. — *nearest, next, last*

prūdēns, -entis, adj. — *foreseeing, discreet, wise*

*pūblicus, -a, -um, adj. — *belonging to the people, public*

†puella, -ae, f. — *girl*

†puer, puerī, m. — *boy*

*pugna, -ae, f. — *fight*

†pugnō, -āre, -āvī, -ātus — *fight*

*pulcher, -chra, -chrum, adj. — *beautiful*

pulvis, pulveris, m. — *dust*

†putō, -āre, -āvī, -ātus — *think*

quā, adv. — *by what way, where*

*quaerō, -ere,
　quaesīvī,
　quaesītus　　　*seek, ask*
*quaestor, -ōris, m.　*quaestor*
*quam, conj. and
　adv.　　　　　*how, as, than*
†quantus, -a, -um,
　adj.　　　　　*how great, as
　　　　　　　　great*
*quārtus, -a, -um,
　num. adj.　　　*fourth*
*quattuor,
　num. adj.　　　*four*
†-que, enclitic conj.　*and*
　queror, -ī, questus　*complain*
†quī, quae, quod,
　rel. and inter.
　pron.　　　　　*who, which, that*
　quīcumque,
　quaecumque,
　quodcumque,
　indef. pron.　　*whoever*
*quīdam, quaedam,
　quiddam, indef.
　pron.　　　　　*a certain one,
　　　　　　　　some one*
*quidem, (postposi-
　tive) adv.　　　*certainly, at
　　　　　　　　least*
　quiētus, -a, -um,
　adj.　　　　　*at rest, peaceful*
　quīn, conj.　　　*indeed, that
　　　　　　　　(w. negative
　　　　　　　　expressions of
　　　　　　　　doubt)*
*quīnque, num. adj.　*five*
*quīntus, -a, -um,
　num. adj.　　　*fifth*
†quis, quid, inter.
　and indef. pron.　*who, any*
　quisquam,
　quicquam,
　indef. pron.　　*any one at all*
*quisque, quaeque,
　quidque, indef.
　pron.　　　　　*each one*
*quō, adv. and conj.　*whither*
†quod, conj.　　　*because*
　quod sī, conj.　　*but if, and if*
　quōminus, conj.　*(that less), lest*
　quoniam, conj.　*inasmuch as,
　　　　　　　　since*
　quōque, adv.　　*also, too*

*ratiō, -ōnis, f.　　*reckoning, plan,
　　　　　　　　reason*
*recēns, -entis, adj.　*fresh, new*
†recipiō, -ere,
　-cēpī, -ceptus　*take back,
　　　　　　　　receive*
　recuperō, -āre,
　-āvī, -ātus　　*regain, get back*
　recūsō, -āre, -āvī,
　-ātus　　　　*object, refuse*
*reddō, -ere, -didī,
　-ditus　　　　*give back, return*
†redeō, -īre, -iī,
　-itūrus　　　*go back, return*
*reditus, -ūs, m.　　*return*
　redigō, -ere, -ēgī,
　-āctus .　　　*drive back,
　　　　　　　　reduce*
*redūcō, -ere,
　-dūxī, -ductus　*lead back,
　　　　　　　　bring back*
　referō, -ferre,
　rettulī, relātus　*bring back,
　　　　　　　　report*
　reficiō, -ere, -fēcī,
　-fectus　　　*make over, repair*
*rēgīna, -ae, f.　　*queen*
†regiō, -ōnis, f.　　*boundary line,
　　　　　　　　district*
†rēgnum, -ī, n.　　*kingdom, royal
　　　　　　　　power*
†regō, -ere, rēxī,
　rēctus　　　　*direct, rule*
†relinquō, -ere,
　-līquī, -lictus　*leave behind*
*reliquus, -a, -um,
　adj.　　　　　*left behind,
　　　　　　　　remaining,
　　　　　　　　rest of*
*remaneō, -ēre,
　-mānsī,
　-mānsūrus　　*stay behind,
　　　　　　　　remain*
*remittō, -ere,
　-mīsī, -missus　*send back, let go,
　　　　　　　　relax*
*removeō, -ēre,
　-mōvī, -mōtus　*move back,
　　　　　　　　withdraw*
　renūntiō, -āre,
　-āvī, -ātus　　*announce,
　　　　　　　　proclaim*

*repellō, -ere,
   reppulī, -pulsus *drive back,*
               repulse
repente, adv. *suddenly*
repentīnus, -a,
   -um, adj. *sudden*
reperiō, -īre,
   repperī, repertus *gain back,*
            discover, find
†rēs, reī, f. *thing*
rēs frūmentāria,
   reī frūmentāriae,
   f. *grain supply*
*resistō, -ere,
   restitī *take a stand,*
            resist
rēs mīlitāris, reī
   mīlitāris, f. *warfare*
†respondeō, -ēre,
   -spondī,
   -spōnsus *answer*
respōnsum, -ī, n. *answer*
rēs pūblica, reī
   pūblicae, f. *commonwealth*
restituō, -ere, -uī,
   -ūtus *place back,*
            restore
†retineō, -ēre,
   -tinuī, -tentus *hold back,*
            restrain,
            detain, retain
revertō, -ere,
   -vertī, -versus *turn back, return*
revertor, -ī, revertī *turn back, return*
†rēx, rēgis, m. *king*
*rīpa, -ae, f. *bank, shore*
†rogō, -āre, -āvī,
   -ātus *ask, ask for*
*rūrsus, adv. *(turned back),*
            again

†saepe, adv. *often*
*sagitta, -ae, f. *arrow*
sagittārius, -ī, m. *archer*
†salūs, -ūtis, f. *health, safety*
*salvus, -a, -um,
   adj. *safe*
*satis, adv. *enough*
satisfaciō, -ere,
   -fēcī, -factus *do enough, do*
            one's duty,
            apologize

saxum, -ī, n. *rock*
*scientia, -ae, f. *knowledge*
†sciō, -īre, scīvī,
   scītus *know*
†scrībō, -ere,
   scrīpsī, scrīptus *write*
*scūtum, -ī, n. *shield*
*secundus, -a, -um,
   adj. *following,*
            second,
            favorable
†sed, conj. *but*
*sedeō, -ēre, sēdī,
   sessum *sit*
†semper, adv. *always*
†senātor, -ōris, m. *senator*
†senātus, -ūs, m. *body of elders,*
            senate
*sententia, -ae, f. *feeling, opinion*
*sentiō, -īre, sēnsī,
   sēnsus *feel, think, judge*
*septem, num. adj. *seven*
*septimus, -a, -um,
   num. adj. *seventh*
†sequor, -ī,
   secūtus *follow*
servitūs, -tūtis, f. *slavery*
†servō, -āre, -āvī,
   -ātus *keep, save*
†servus, -ī, m. *slave*
*sex, num. adj. *six*
*sextus, -a, -um,
   num. adj. *sixth*
*sī, conj. *if*
*sīc, adv. *thus, so*
sīcut (sīcutī), conj. *just as*
significō, -āre,
   -āvī, -ātus *announce*
†signum, -ī, n. *sign, signal,*
            standard
*silentium, -ī, n. *silence*
†silva, -ae, f. *forest*
*similis, -e, adj. *like, resembling*
*simul, adv. *together, at the*
            same time
simul ac (atque),
   conj. *as soon as*
†sine, prep. w. abl. *without*
singulāris, -e, adj. *one by one,*
            extraordinary
*singulī, -ae, -a,
   distr. adj. *one at a time*

*sinister, -tra,
 -trum, adj. — *left* (of direction)
sī quis — *if any, whoever*
†socius, -ī, m. — *ally*
*sōl, sōlis, m. — *sun*
sollicitō, -āre,
 -āvī, -ātus — *stir up, tempt*
*sōlum, adv. — *only*
*sōlus, -a, -um, adj. — *alone, only*
*solvō, -ere, solvī,
 solūtus — *untie, release, perform*
*somnus, -ī, m. — *sleep*
†soror, -ōris, f. — *sister*
*spatium, -ī, n. — *space*
*speciēs, -ēī, f. — *appearance*
†spectō, -āre, -āvī,
 -ātus — *look at*
†spērō, -āre, -āvī,
 -ātus — *hope*
†spēs, speī, f. — *hope*
sponte suā — *of one's own will, voluntarily*
*statim, adv. — *at once, immediately*
statiō, -ōnis, f. — *outpost, picket*
*statuō, -ere, -uī,
 -ūtus — *set up, fix, determine*
stīpendium, -ī, n. — *payment, tax, campaign*
*stō, stāre, stetī,
 statūrus — *stand*
*studeō, -ēre, -uī — *be eager, desire*
†studium, -ī, n. — *eagerness*
†sub, prep. w. acc.
 and abl. — *under, close to*
subdūcō, -ere,
 -dūxī, -ductus — *lead under, lead up to, draw up, beach*
*subitō, adv. — *suddenly*
sublevō, -āre,
 -āvī, -ātus — *assist*
submittō, -ere,
 -mīsī, -missus — *send under, send to assist, yield*
*subsequor, -ī,
 -secūtus — *follow closely*
*subsidium, -ī, n. — *reserve reinforcement, assistance*

succēdō, -ere,
 -cessī, -cessūrus — *approach, come next*
†suī, sibi, sē (sēsē),
 reflex. pron. — *of himself, herself, itself, themselves*
†sum, esse, fuī,
 futūrus — *be*
summa, -ae, f. — *highest sum, total*
*summus, -a, -um,
 adj. — *highest, greatest*
*sūmō, -ere,
 sūmpsī,
 sūmptus — *take*
*super, adv. — *over, above, besides, moreover*
*superior, -ius, adj. — *higher, former*
†superō, -āre, -āvī,
 -ātus — *overcome, surpass, defeat*
supersum, -esse,
 -fuī — *be over, remain, survive*
*superus, -a, -um,
 adj. — *upper*
supplicium, -ī, n. — *punishment*
supportō, -āre,
 -āvī, -ātus — *carry up*
*suprā, adv. and
 prep. w. acc. — *above, beyond*
*suscipiō, -ere,
 -cēpī, -ceptus — *take up, undertake*
*suspīciō, -ōnis, f. — *suspicion*
suspicor, -ārī,
 -ātus — *suspect*
*sustineō, -ēre,
 -tinuī, -tentus — *uphold, resist*
†suus, -a, -um, adj. — *his, her, its, their (own)*

†tam, adv. — *thus, so*
tamen, adv. — *however, nevertheless*
tangō, -ere, tetigī,
 tāctus — *touch*
†tantus, -a, -um,
 adj. — *so great*

*tardō, -āre, -āvī,
-ātus   *make slow, check*
*tardus, -a, -um,
adj.   *slow*
tegō, -ere, tēxī,
tēctus   *cover, conceal*
†tēlum, -ī, n.   *missile, weapon*
*tempestas,
-tātis, f.   *period of time,
weather, storm*
*templum, -ī, n.   *sacred precinct,
temple*
†temptō, -āre, -āvī,
-ātus   *try, attempt*
†tempus, -poris, n.   *time*
†teneō, -ēre, tenuī   *hold*
*tergum, -ī, n.   *back, rear*
†terra, -ae, f.   *earth, land*
*terror, -ōris, m.   *fright, panic*
*tertius, -a, -um,
num. adj.   *third*
testūdō, -inis, f.   *tortoise, tortoise
shell, testudo*
†timeō, -ēre, timuī   *be afraid, fear*
timidus, -a, -um,
adj.   *fearful,
cowardly*
†timor, -ōris, m.   *fear*
*toga, -ae, f.   *toga*
*tollō, -ere, sustulī,
sublātus   *lift, remove*
tormentum, -ī, n.   *military engine*
*tot, indecl. adj.   *so many*
totidem, indecl.
adj.   *just as many*
†tōtus, -a, -um,
adj.   *whole*
†trādō, -ere, -didī,
-ditus   *hand over,
entrust,
surrender*
*trādūcō, -ere,
-dūxī, -ductus   *lead across*
*trahō, -ere, trāxī,
tractus   *drag, draw*
†trāns, prep. w. acc.   *across*
*trānseō, -īre, -iī,
-itus   *go across, cross*
*trānsportō, -āre,
-āvī, -ātus   *carry across,
transport*
*trēs, tria, num.
adj.   *three*

*tribūnus, -ī, m.   *tribune*
tribuō, -ere, -uī,
-ūtus   *assign, grant*
trīduum, -ī, n.   *three days*
†tū, pers. pron.   *thou, you*
*tuba, -ae, f.   *trumpet*
tueor, -ērī, tūtus   *gaze at, protect*
†tum, adv.   *at that time*
tumulus, -ī, m.   *small hill,
mound*
tunc, adv.   *at that time*
turpis, -e, adj.   *base, disgraceful*
*turris, -is, f.   *tower*
tūtus, -a, -um,
adj.   *protected, safe*
†tuus, -a, -um, adj.   *thy, thine, your,
yours*

†ubi (ubī), adv.
and conj.   *where, when*
*ūllus, -a, -um, adj.   *any*
*ulterior, -ius, adj.   *farther, more
distant*
ultrā, prep. w. acc.   *beyond*
ultrō, adv.   *beyond, unasked,
voluntarily*
*ūnā, adv.   *together*
unde, adv.   *whence*
*undique, adv.   *from all sides,
on all sides*
ūniversus, -a, -um,
adj.   *all together*
*ūnus, -a, -um,
num. adj.   *one*
†urbs, urbis, f.   *city*
ūsque, adv.   *up to*
*ūsus, -ūs, m.   *use, advantage,
experience*
*ut, utī, conj.   *that, so that, in
order that*
uter, utra, utrum,
adj.   *which of two*
*uterque, utraque,
utrumque, adj.   *each of two, both*
*ūtilis, -e, adj.   *useful*
†ūtor, -ī, ūsus   *use, employ*

*vacuus, -a, -um,
adj.   *empty*
vadum, -ī, n.   *shoal, ford*
vagor, -ārī, -ātus   *roam*

*valeō, -ēre, -uī,
 -itūrus   be strong
*validus, -a, -um,
 adj.   strong, healthy,
                              powerful
*vallēs, -is, f.   valley
*vāllum, -ī, n.   rampart
*vāstō, -āre, -āvī,
 -ātus   lay waste
vehementer, adv.   strongly
*vel, conj.   or
†veniō, -īre, vēnī,
 ventūrus   come
*ventus, -ī, m.   wind
†verbum, -ī, n.   word
*vereor, -ērī, -itus   fear, respect
*vērō, adv.   in truth, but
 versor, -ārī, -ātus   turn about,
                              dwell
*vertō, -ere, vertī,
 versus   turn
*vērum, adv.   truly, but
 vērus, -a, -um,
 adj.   true
*vesper, -erī, m.   evening
†vester, -tra, -trum,
 adj.   your, yours
 vetus, -teris, adj.   old, long-
                              standing
 vetustus, -a, -um,
 adj.   old, ancient
†via, -ae, f.   road
 vīcīnus, -a, -um,
 adj.   neighboring
*victor, -ōris, m.   conqueror
†victōria, -ae, f.   victory

†vīcus, -ī, m.   village
†videō, -ēre, vīdī,
 vīsus   see
†vigilia, -ae, f.   night watch,
                              guard
*vigilō, -āre, -āvī,
 -ātus   watch
*vīgintī, num. adj.   twenty
†vīlla, -ae, f.   farmhouse
†vincō, -ere, vīcī,
 victus   conquer
 vinculum, -ī, n.   bond, fetter
 vīnea, -ae, f.   vinea, a movable
                              shed
†vir, virī, m.   man
†virtūs, -tūtis, f.   manliness,
                              bravery
*vīs, vim (acc.), f.   force, violence
†vīta, -ae, f.   life
 vītō, -āre, -āvī,
 -ātus   avoid
*vīvus, -a, -um,
 adj.   alive
 vix, adv.   barely, scarcely
†vocō, -āre, -āvī,
 -ātus   call
†volō, velle, voluī   be willing, wish
*voluntās, -tātis, f.   willingness,
                              good will
*vōx, vōcis, f.   voice, word
 vulgus, -ī, n.   common crowd
†vulnerō, -āre, -āvī,
 -ātus   wound
†vulnus, -neris, n.   wound

CHAPTER X*

SELECTIONS FOR TRANSLATION AT SIGHT

1

Roman soldiers of three cohorts are terrified and make for the ships.

Simul, qui in navibus longis remanserant, scalas [1] rapere navesque a terra repellere properabant, ne hostes navibus potirentur. Quibus omnibus rebus perturbati milites nostri cohortium trium, quae in ponte constiterant, cum post se clamorem exaudirent, fugam suorum viderent, magnam vim telorum adversi sustinerent, veriti ne ab tergo circumvenirentur et discessu navium omnino reditu intercluderentur, munitionem in ponte institutam reliquerunt et magno cursu incitati ad naves contenderunt. Quorum pars proximas nacta naves multitudine hominum atque onere depressa est, pars resistens et dubitans, quid esset capiendum consili, ab Alexandrinis [2] interfecta est.

De Bello Alexandrino, 20 (adapted)

2

The carelessness of a Rhodian shipmaster forces Caesar to fight.

Erat una navis Rhodia in dextro cornu longe ab reliquis collocata. Hanc conspicati hostes non tenuerunt sese magnoque impetu ad eam contenderunt. Cui coactus est Caesar ferre subsidium ne turpem in conspectu hostium contumeliam acciperet. Proelium commissum est magna contentione Rhodiorum, qui cum in omnibus dimicationibus et scientia et virtute praestitissent, tum maxime illo tempore totum onus sustinere non recusabant ne quod detrimentum suorum culpa acceptum videretur. Ita proelium secundissimum est factum; magna multitudo propugnatorum [3] est interfecta. Quod nisi nox proeli finem fecisset, tota classe hostium Caesar potitus esset. Hac calamitate perterritis hostibus, adverso vento leniter flante,[4] naves onerarias Caesar remulco [5] Alexandriam [6] deducit.

De Bello Alexandrino, 11 (adapted)

---

[1] scala, -ae f., *a ladder*   [2] Alexandrinus, -a, -um, *of* or *belonging to Alexandria*   [3] *fighting men*   [4] flare, *to blow*   [5] *tow-line*   [6] Alexandria, -ae f., a city in Egypt

---

* This chapter was prepared by John K. Colby, Head of Latin Department, Country Day School, Newton, Mass.

3

Regulus refuses to remain at Rome.

Post haec Carthaginienses a Regulo duce, quem ceperant, petiverunt, ut Romam proficisceretur et pacem a Romanis obtineret ac permutationem[1] captivorum faceret. Ille Romam cum venisset, inductus in senatum nihil egit quod Romani exspectabant sed dixit se ex illa die, qua in potestatem hostium venisset, Romanum esse destitisse. Itaque senatui persuasit, ne pax cum Poenis[2] fieret; illos enim fractos multis casibus spem nullam habere; atque oravit ne tot milia captivorum propter se redderentur. Ipse Carthaginem rediit, offerentibusque Romanis, ut eum Romae tenerent, negavit se in ea urbe mansurum, in qua, postquam hostibus servierat, dignitatem honesti civis habere non posset. Regressus ad Africam omnibus suppliciis interfectus est.

EUTROPIUS, *Breviarium*, II, 25 (adapted)

4

Cassius and Marcellus maneuver against each other.

Cassius fidei magis quam virtuti legionum confidebat. Itaque cum castra castris conlata essent et Marcellus locum idoneum castello cepisset quo prohibere aqua Cassianos posset, Cassius veritus ne genere quodam obsidionis clauderetur in regionibus alienis sibique infestis noctu silentio ex castris proficiscitur celerique itinere Uliam contendit, quod sibi fidele esse oppidum credebat. Hunc Marcellus insequitur et castellis idoneis locis collocatis operibusque in circuitu oppidi continuatis[3] Uliam Cassiumque munitionibus clausit. Quae priusquam perficerentur, Cassius omnem suum equitatum emisit; quem magno sibi usui fore credebat si pabulari frumentarique Marcellum non pateretur, magno autem fore impedimento si clausus obsidione et inutilis necessarium consumeret frumentum.

De Bello Alexandrino, 61 (adapted)

---

[1] *exchange*   [2] **Poeni, -orum** m., *Carthaginians*
[3] **continuare,** *to make continuous*

5

Caesar summons aid to the help of Africa.

Interim nobiles homines ex suis oppidis profugere et in castra Caesaris devenire et de adversariorum eius crudelitate commemorare coeperunt. Quorum lacrimis [1] Caesar maxime commotus, cum antea constituisset e castris aestate inita cunctis copiis auxiliisque accitis [2] bellum cum suis adversariis gerere, hieme proficisci instituit litterisque celeriter in Siciliam ad Alienum missis imperavit ut sine mora ac nulla excusatione hiemis ventorumque quam primum exercitus sibi transportaretur: Africam provinciam perire funditusque [3] everti ab suis inimicis; quod nisi celeriter sociis esset subventum, praeter ipsam Africam terram nihil, ne tectum [4] quidem, quo se reciperent ab illorum scelere insidiisque reliquum futurum.

De Bello Africano, 26 (adapted)

6

Caesar plans to shut off Pompey.

Quibus rebus cognitis Caesar consilium capit ex loci natura.   Erant enim circum castra Pompei permulti colles.   Hos primum praesidiis tenuit castellaque ibi communiit.   Inde, ut loci cuiusque natura ferebat, ex castello in castellum perducta munitione circumvallare Pompeium instituit haec spectans, quod angusta re frumentaria utebatur, quodque Pompeius multitudine equitum valebat, quo minore periculo undique frumentum commeatumque exercitui supportare posset, simul ut pabulatione [5] Pompeium prohiberet equitatumque eius ad rem gerendam inutilem efficeret, tertio ut auctoritatem, qua ille maxime apud exteras [6] nationes niti [7] videbatur, minueret, cum fama per orbem terrarum percrebuisset [8] illum a Caesare obsideri neque audere proelio dimicare.

De Bello Civili, 3, 43

---

[1] lacrima, -ae f., *tear*	[2] *summoned*	[3] funditus, *utterly*
[4] tectum, -ī n., *roof, house*	[5] *foraging*	[6] *foreign*
[7] *to depend*	[8] *had become widespread*	

7

Domitius baffles a crafty enemy.

Haec cum administraret, numquam tamen intermittebat legatos de pace atque amicitia mittere ad Domitium, cum hoc ipso crederet facilius eum decipi[1] posse. At contra spes pacis Domitio in eisdem castris morandi attulit causam. Ita Pharnaces,[2] amissa proximi temporis occasione, cum vereretur ne cognoscerentur insidiae, suos in castra revocavit. Proxima nocte Pharnaces, interceptis tabellariis[3] qui de Alexandrinis[4] rebus litteras ad Domitium ferebant, cognoscit Caesarem magno in periculo versari atque flagitare[5] ab Domitio ut quam primum sibi subsidia mitteret propiusque ipse Alexandriam per Syriam accederet. Qua cognita re, Pharnaces fore victoriae loco credebat, si trahere tempus posset, cum discedendum Domitio celeriter putaret. Domitius autem cum se non tuto discessurum arbitraretur, si sine certamine[6] discederet, ex propinquis castris in aciem exercitum eduxit.

De Bello Alexandrino, 37, 38, 39 (adapted)

8

Caesar's forces strive to reach the hills before those of Afranius. Slaughter of four of Afranius' cohorts.

Erat in celeritate omne positum certamen,[7] utri prius angustias montesque occuparent; sed exercitum Caesaris viarum difficultates tardabant, Afranii copias equitatus Caesaris insequens morabatur. Res tamen ab Afranianis huc erat deducta, ut, si prius montes, quos petebant, attigissent, ipsi periculum vitarent, impedimenta totius exercitus cohortesque in castris relictas servare non possent; quibus interclusis exercitu Caesaris auxilium ferri nulla ratione poterat. Confecit prior iter Caesar atque ex magnis saxis nactus planitiem in hac contra hostem aciem instruit. Afranius, cum ab equitatu novissimum agmen premeretur, ante se hostem videret, collem quendam nactus ibi constitit. Ex eo loco IIII cohortes in montem, qui erat in

---

[1] **decipio, -ere,** *deceive*　　　　　[2] **Pharnaces -is** m., a king of Pontus
[3] *couriers*　　[4] **Alexandrinus, -a, -um,** *of or belonging to Alexandria*
[5] *demand*　　[6] *struggle*　　[7] **certamen** n., *contest*

conspectu omnium altissimus, mittit. Hunc cohortes magno cursu iubet occupare, eo consilio, uti ipse eodem omnibus copiis contenderet et mutato itinere iugis Octogesam [1] perveniret. Hunc cum obliquo itinere peterent, conspicatus equitatus Caesaris in cohortes impetum fecit; nec minimam partem temporis equitum vim cohortes sustinere potuerunt omnesque in conspectu utriusque exercitus interficiuntur.

De Bello Civili, I, 70 (adapted)

9

Libo arrives at Brundisium, terrifies Caesar's men, and notifies Pompey that he does not need the rest of the fleet.

Libo profectus ab Orico [2] cum classe, cui praeerat, navium L, Brundisium [3] venit insulamque quae contra portum Brundisinum est, occupavit, quod melius esse arbitrabatur unum locum, qua necessarius nostris erat egressus, quam omnia litora ac portus custodia clausos teneri. Hic repentino adventu naves onerarias quasdam nactus incendit et unam frumento onustam abduxit magnumque nostris terrorem iniecit et noctu militibus ac sagittariis in terram expositis praesidium equitum deiecit et adeo loci opportunitate profecit [4] uti Pompeium litteris moneret ut naves reliquas, si vellet subduceret et reficeret: sua classe auxilia sese Caesaris prohibiturum.

De Bello Civili, III, 23 (adapted)

10

A battle is interrupted by the appearance of two legions.

Quo cognito, celeriter suo ponte Afranius, quem oppido castrisque coniunctum habebat, legiones IIII equitatumque omnem traiecit duabusque Fabianis occurrit legionibus. Cuius adventu nuntiato L. Plancus, qui legionibus praeerat, necessaria re coactus locum capit superiorem diversamque aciem in duas partes constituit, ne ab equitatu circumveniri posset. Ita congressus impari numero magnos impetus legionum equitatusque sustinet. Commisso ab equitibus proelio signa

---

[1] **Octogesa -ae** f., a city
[3] **Brundisium -i** n., a town
[2] **Oricus, -i** f., a town
[4] **proficio, -ere,** *profit*

legionum duarum procul ab utrisque conspiciuntur, quas C. Fabius ulteriore ponte subsidio nostris miserat suspicatus fore id, quod accidit, ut duces adversariorum occasione et beneficio fortunae ad nostros opprimendos uterentur. Quarum adventu proelium dirimitur,[1] ac suas uterque legiones reducit in castra.

De Bello Civili, I, 40 (adapted)

11

The arrival of two legions under Sulla routs the Pompeians.

Interim certior factus P. Sulla, quem discedens castris praefecerat Caesar, auxilio cohorti venit cum legionibus duabus; cuius adventu facile sunt repulsi Pompeiani. Neque vero conspectum aut impetum nostrorum tulerunt, primisque deiectis reliqui se verterunt et loco cesserunt. Sed insequentes nostros, ne longius prosequerentur, Sulla revocavit. At plerique existimant, si acrius insequi voluisset, bellum eo die potuisse finire. Pompeiani ex iniquo progressi loco in summo constiterant; si per declive [2] sese reciperent, nostros ex superiore insequentes loco verebantur; neque multum ad solis occasum temporis supererat; spe enim conficiendi negotii prope in noctem rem duxerant. Ita Pompeius tumulum quendam occupavit, qui tantum aberat a nostro castello, ut telum tormento missum adigi non posset. Hoc consedit loco atque eum communivit omnesque ibi copias continuit.

De Bello Civili, III, 51 (adapted)

12

Pompey refuses to fight at Asparagium. Caesar fools Pompey by leading his forces to Dyrrachium by a circuitous route, and cuts Pompey off from Dyrrachium.

Caesar, postquam Pompeium ad Asparagium [3] esse cognovit, eodem cum exercitu profectus, expugnato in itinere oppido Parthinorum in quo Pompeius praesidium habebat, tertio die ad Pompeium pervenit iuxtaque [4] eum castra posuit et postridie eductis omnibus copiis acie

---

[1] dirimo, -ere, *break off*　　[2] declive, -is n., *a steep* or *sloping place*
[3] a town of Illyria　　[4] iuxta (prep.) *near*

instructa decernendi potestatem Pompeio fecit.   Ubi illum suis locis
se tenere animadvertit, reducto in castra exercitu aliud sibi consilium
capiendum existimavit.   Itaque postero die omnibus copiis magno
circuito difficili angustoque itinere Dyrrachium[1] profectus est sperans
Pompeium aut Dyrrachium compelli aut ab eo intercludi posse, quod
omnem commeatum totiusque belli apparatum eo contulisset; ut
accidit.   Pompeius enim primo ignorans eius consilium, quod diverso
ab ea regione itinere profectum videbat, angustiis rei frumentariae
compulsum discessisse existimabat; postea per exploratores certior
factus postero die castra movit, breviore itinere se occurrere ei posse
sperans.   Quod fore suspicatus Caesar militesque hortatus ut aequo
animo laborem ferrent, parvam partem noctis itinere intermisso
Dyrrachium venit, cum primum agmen Pompei procul cerneretur,
atque ibi castra posuit.

De Bello Civili, III, 41 (adapted)

13

Labienus crushes a gallant foe.

Prima luce et nostri omnes erant flumen transportati et hostium acies
cernebatur.   Labienus milites cohortatus ut suae pristinae virtutis
retinerent memoriam atque ipsum Caesarem, cuius ductu saepe hostis
tam facile fudissent, praesentem adesse existimarent, dat signum
proeli.   Primo concursu ab dextro cornu, ubi septima legio constiterat,
hostes ita pelluntur ut statim conversi omnem spem salutis in celeritate
fugiendi ponerent; ab sinistro, quem locum duodecima legio tenebat,
cum primi ordines hostium transfixi telis concidissent, tamen acerrime
reliqui resistebant ne quis suspicionem fugae daret.   Ipse dux hostium
Camulogenus suis aderat atque eos firmo animo cohortabatur.   At
incerto etiam nunc exitu victoriae, cum septimae legionis tribunis
esset nuntiatum quae in sinistro cornu gererentur, post tergum hostium
legionem ostenderunt signaque intulerunt.   Ne eo quidem tempore
quisquam loco cessit, sed circumventi omnes interfectique sunt.

De Bello Gallico, VII, 62 (adapted)

[1] **Dyrrachium, -i** n., a town

14

Vercingetorix exerts himself to make good the injury done to his cause by the disaster at Avaricum.

Vercingetorix, ut erat pollicitus, animo laborabat ut reliquas civitates prius donis pollicitationibusque adiungeret quam sibi diffiderent. Huic rei idoneos homines deligebat quorum quisque aut oratione subdola [1] aut amicitia facillime capi [2] posset. Qui Avarico expugnato refugerant, armandos vestiendosque curat; simul, quo celerius deminutae copiae redintegrarentur, imperat certum numerum militum civitatibus, easque certiores facit quam ante diem in castra illos adduci vellet, sagittariosque omnis, quorum erat permagnus numerus in Gallia, conquiri et ad se mitti iubet. His rebus brevi tempore id quod Avarici perierat expletur. Interim Teutomatus, Olloviconis [3] filius, rex Nitiobrigum, [4] cuius pater ab senatu nostro amicus erat appellatus, cum magno equitum suorum numero et quos ex Aquitania conduxerat ad eum pervenit.

De Bello Gallico, VII, 31 (adapted)

15

The Romans scorn the offer of Pyrrhus.

Pyrrhus unum ex legatis Romanorum, Fabricium,[5] sic admiratus est, cum eum pauperem [6] esse cognovisset, ut quarta parte regni promissa sollicitare vellet, ut ad se transiret, atque a Fabricio contemptus est. Quare cum Pyrrhus Romanorum ingenti admiratione teneretur, legatum, Cineam [7] nomine, Romam misit, qui pacem aequis condicionibus peteret. Sed pax illis maxime displicuit renuntiatumque Pyrrho est a senatu eum cum Romanis, nisi ex Italia recessisset, pacem habere non posse. Tum Romani iusserunt captivos omnes, quos Pyrrhus reddiderat, infames [8] haberi, quod armati capi potuissent, nec eos ad veterem statum reverti, priusquam duorum hostium occisorum arma rettulissent. Ita legatus Pyrrhi reversus est.

---

[1] **subdolus, -a, -um,** *wily*
[2] **capi,** from capere, *win over*
[3] **Ollovico, -onis** m.
[4] **Nitiobriges, -um** m., an Aquitanian tribe

[5] **Fabricius, -i** m.
[6] **pauper, -eris** m., *a poor man*
[7] **Cineas, -ae** m.
[8] **infamis, -e,** *disgraced*

16

Because of Caesar's defeat, the town of Gomphi decides not to admit him.

Coniuncto exercitu Caesar Gomphos pervenit, quod est oppidum primum Thessaliae [1] venientibus ab Epiro; [2] quae gens paucis ante mensibus ultro ad Caesarem legatos miserat qui ab eo peterent ut suis omnibus facultatibus uteretur, praesidiumque ab eo militum petierat. Sed eo fama iam praecurrerat de calamitate illa quam Caesar apud Dyrrachium [3] acceperat. Itaque Androsthenes, qui Thessaliae erat praepositus, cum se victoriae Pompei [4] comitem [5] esse mallet quam socium Caesaris in rebus adversis, et portas oppidi praecludit et ad Scipionem [6] Pompeiumque nuntios mittit ut sibi subsidio veniant: se confidere munitionibus oppidi si celeriter succurratur; oppugnationem sustinere non diu posse. Caesar castris munitis suos docuit quantum iis prodesset ad sublevandam omnium rerum inopiam potiri hoc oppido pleno atque opulento.

De Bello Civili, III, 80 (adapted)

17

King Pharnaces tries to avoid a battle, first by friendly phrases, afterwards by delay.

Cum Caesar in Pontum [7] venisset, legati a Pharnace missi ad eum adeunt atque orant ne eius adventus hostilis esset: facturum enim omnia Pharnacem quae imperata essent. Maxime commemorabant nulla Pharnacem auxilia contra Caesarem Pompeio [8] dare voluisse, cum Deiotarus, qui dedisset, tamen amicitia eius uteretur. Caesar respondit se fore aequissimum Pharnaci si quae polliceretur exsecuturus esset. Monuit autem lenibus verbis legatos ne nimis [9] eo gloriarentur [10] beneficio quod auxilia ad Pompeium non misissent; imperavit ut ex

[1] Thessalia, -ae f., *Thessaly*, a country in Greece
[2] Epirus, -i f., a province in Greece   [3] Dyrrachium, -i n., a town
[4] Pompeius, -i m., *Pompey*, a Roman
[5] comitem, equivalent to socium   [6] Scipio, -onis m., a Roman
[7] Pontus, -i m., *the Pontus* (region about the Black Sea)
[8] Pompeius, -i m., *Pompey*, a Roman   [9] nimis (adv.) *too much*
[10] glorior, 1, *boast*

Ponto rex decederet omniaque restitueret sociis civibusque Romanis quae iis eripuisset. Sed Pharnaces liberaliter omnia pollicitus, cum Romam contendentem Caesarem speraret facilius crediturum suis promissis quo celerius ad res magis necessarias proficisceretur, decedendi diem postulare longiorem coepit. Caesar cognita calliditate [1] hominis celerius omnium opinione proelium commisit.

De Bello Alexandrino, 69–71 (adapted)

18

Miltiades urges Darius' Greek guards to destroy a bridge which Darius had built for his Scythian expedition.

Eisdem temporibus Persarum rex Dareus ex Asia in Europam exercitu traiecto Scythis bellum inferre decrevit. Pontem fecit in Histro [2] flumine, qua copias traduceret. Eius pontis dum ipse abesset, custodes reliquit principes quos secum ex Ionia duxerat; quibus singulis illarum urbium perpetua dederat imperia. Sic enim facillime putavit se Graeca lingua [3] loquentes qui Asiam incolerent sub sua retenturum potestate, si amicis suis oppida tuenda tradidisset; quibus se oppresso nulla spes salutis relinqueretur. In hoc fuit tum numero Miltiades. Hic, cum crebri adferrent nuntii male rem gerere Dareum premique a Scythis, hortatus est pontis custodes ne a fortuna datam occasionem liberandae Graeciae dimitterent. Nam si cum eis copiis quas secum transportaverat interisset Dareus, non solum Europam fore tutam, sed etiam eos qui Asiam incolerent Graeci genere liberos a Persarum futuros dominatione et periculo. Id facile effici posse: ponte enim deleto, regem vel hostium ferro vel inopia paucis diebus interiturum esse.

Nepos, *Miltiades*, III (adapted)

19

Hannibal finds out by a trick which is the ship of King Eumenes.

Hannibal socios convocavit iisque praecepit omnes ut in unam Eumenis regis concurrerent navem. Dixit autem se facturum esse ut socii scirent in qua nave rex Eumenes veheretur. Quem si aut

[1] calliditas, -atis f., *cunning*   [2] *the lower Danube*   [3] *tongue, language*

cepissent aut interfecissent, magno eis pollicetur praemio fore. Cohor-tatione militum facta classis ab utrisque in proelium deducitur. Quarum acie constituta, priusquam signum pugnae daretur, Hannibal ut demonstraret suis quo loco Eumenes esset, nuntium in scapha [1] cum litteris mittit. Qui ubi ad navis adversariorum pervenit, litte-rasque ostendens se regem quaerere dixit, statim ad Eumenem deductus est, quod nemo dubitabat quin aliquid de pace esset scrip-tum. Nuntius ducis nave declarata suis, eodem unde erat egressus se recepit. At Eumenes solutis [2] litteris nihil in eis repperit nisi quae ad inridendum [3] eum pertinerent.

Nepos, Hannibal, X, XI (adapted)

20

A sally made by Caesar's German auxiliaries dismays the Gauls.

Interim crebro [4] paucis utrimque [5] procurrentibus inter bina castra [6] palude interiecta contendebatur; quam tamen paludem non numquam aut nostra auxilia Germanorum transibant acriusque hostis inseque-bantur, aut hostes pari cum virtute transgressi nostros longius summovebant.[7] Dum haec geruntur, Germani, quos eo consilio Caesar transduxerat Rhenum [8] ut suis equitibus interpositi proelia-rentur, audacius universi paludem transierunt paucisque in resistendo interfectis contineri non potuerunt quominus [9] reliquam multitudinem hostium pertinaciter [10] insequerentur. Quo impetu repentino factum est ut non solum ii qui aut gladiis opprimebantur aut telis vulnera-bantur timore perterrerentur sed etiam ii qui suis laborantibus sub-sidium ferre consueverant turpiter refugerent. Neque vero prius finem fugiendi fecerunt quam se in castra suorum receperunt. Quorum periculo sic omnes copiae Gallorum sunt perturbatae ut vix iudicari posset utrum [11] secundis rebus insolentiores an adverso casu timidiores essent.

Hirtius, De Bello Gallico, VIII, 10 and 13 (adapted)

[1] scapha, -ae f., *boat*
[2] solvo, -ere, solvi, solutus, *open*
[3] inrideo, -ere, *ridicule*
[4] crebro (adv.)
[5] utrimque (adv.) *on both sides*
[6] bina castra, *i.e.*, of Caesar and the Gauls

[7] summoveo, -ere, *drive off*
[8] Rhenus, -i, m., *the Rhine* (river)
[9] quominus (conj.) *from*
[10] pertinaciter (adv.) *persistently*
[11] utrum (interrog.) *whether*

CHAPTER XI*

ROMAN BACKGROUND

I. OUTLINE SURVEY OF ROMAN HISTORY

The Roman kingdom. No one knows when or how Rome was founded. The Romans told many fascinating stories about their origin, and reckoned their dates from 753 B.C. We do know that Rome was for a long time a city-nation with a king (*rex*), and that a senate (*senatus*) of nobles and an assembly (*comitia*) of freemen helped the king rule. The Roman kings waged many wars and won control of about one third of their home district (*Latium*) in Italy. The last of the kings was overthrown by the nobles about 510 B.C.

The early republic. Rome then became a republic, ruled by representatives of the people. Two officers (*consules*), elected yearly, headed the state, and others were added gradually. The senate and assembly were retained. A bitter struggle between the common people (*plebs*) and the nobles (*patricii*) for power ended about 367 B.C. by a recognition of equal rights for all free citizens. No great conquests were made during this period.

The middle republic. From 367 through 266 B.C. the Romans continued and completed the conquest of Italy north to the Po River, and organized and ruled splendidly the entire peninsula almost as a single nation. A series of wars against outside nations (264–146 B.C.) made Rome the one great power of the Mediterranean world. The fiercest and most important of these (the Punic Wars) were waged against Carthage of North Africa, whose general, Hannibal, very nearly succeeded in crushing Rome. Most of the newly conquered territory was divided into provinces under the absolute rule of governors appointed at Rome.

The later republic. The Romans were unable for a while to deal successfully with the many new and difficult problems of government and social changes that arose from their conquests. They became so corrupt that a virtuous, honorable citizen was an exception. Civil wars and fierce class-strife between the poor and the rich, the slaves and

* This chapter was prepared by W. D. Pearson, Head of Latin Department, Milford School, Milford, Conn.

the free, the Romans and their subjects, marked the period from 146 B.C. to 31 B.C. Julius Caesar fought his way to a dictatorship and made many needed reforms (46–44 B.C.). His heir and grandnephew, Octavius, made himself master of the Roman world in 31 B.C.

The early empire. Octavius, better known as Augustus (*the Majestic*), is usually regarded as the first Roman emperor. He established internal peace, harmony and order, and directed extensive foreign conquests. Ancient civilization reached its height during the first two centuries of the empire (31 B.C.–180 A.D.). Government was efficient; prosperity prevailed; morality improved. Among the ablest emperors of this period were Vespasian, Trajan (under whom the empire reached its greatest extent in 117 A.D.), Hadrian, Antoninus Pius and Marcus Aurelius.

The middle empire. The empire almost broke up in the third century because of a lack of a definite method of succession to the throne and the need of new methods in government to fit changed conditions. There were constant civil wars and a rapid succession of emperors, most of whom were weak or evil.

The later empire. Diocletian (reigned 284–305 A.D.) made such thorough and statesmanlike changes in government that the empire regained for a time some of its old vigor. The most famous of his many reforms was dividing the empire into two main parts (west and east) with two emperors, supposed to rule as partners. The empire continued, however, to decline. It had become wornout from many causes, the greatest of which were probably a decline in population and heavy taxation. The two most outstanding emperors after Diocletian were Constantine the Great (312–337 A.D.) and Theodosius the Great (379–395 A.D.).

The barbarian occupation. After 395 A.D. the Eastern and Western empires were really separate states. The Eastern empire, with its capital at Constantinople, endured more than a thousand years longer. Early in the fifth century Germanic invaders began to occupy permanently different sections of the Western empire and to establish in it kingdoms of their own. In 476 A.D. a German chief, Odovaker, dethroned Romulus Augustulus, the last Western Roman emperor.

Rome's position in history. Rome stands in history chiefly for government, law and organization — definite political and social order. Her genius was revealed at its best during the middle republic and the early empire.

THE ROMAN EMPIRE AT ITS GREATEST EXTENT

The northern boundary of the empire at its greatest extent was the Rhine and the Danube, except for Britain, and a bit of Germany between the middle Rhine and upper Danube, and Dacia. The Tigris-Euphrates valley was held a very short time. Won by Trajan, it was given up by his successor, Hadrian.

II. ROMAN CHARACTER

No description of Roman character can, of course, fit every period or all Romans within any one period. But the Romans did possess certain typical qualities. On the whole, unless corrupted by outside influences, they were industrious, home-loving, simple and frugal in their habits, patient, orderly, reverent of the gods, courageous, honorable privately and publicly, stern in discipline, and patriotic. They were brilliant organizers.

On the other hand (although many exceptions must be made), they were crude and stubborn, and scorned learning, the fine arts, and many of the niceties of civilized life. Certain of their defects were the result of virtues carried to an extreme. Frugal habits, for example, led sometimes to miserliness, and patriotism to cruelty.

Roman history is full of stories that illustrate Roman characteristics. Even if many of these stories are not true, they all reveal either what foreigners thought of the Romans or what the Romans admired or blamed in themselves.*

III. ROMAN DAILY LIFE

The Roman family. Domestic ties meant much to the Romans. At the head of each household (*familia*) was the father (*pater familias*), who was supreme master over the lives and fortunes of every other member of his household as long as he lived. Only his own free will or loss of citizenship might break a father's authority. His wife (*mater familias*), in spite of her husband's legal authority over her, enjoyed in the average household full freedom of action, and held a position of dignity and influence. She managed all the ordinary affairs of the household. The sons (*filii*), the unmarried daughters (*filiae familias*),

---

*The student should become acquainted with the following especially striking stories. Others can readily be found:

The founding of Rome by Romulus; the theft of the Sabine women; the Curiatii and Horatii; Horatius at the bridge; Junius Brutus punishes his sons; Marcus Manlius and the Gauls; Cincinnatus; the career of Spurius Cassius; the Samnite Pontius and the Romans; Manius Curio and the Samnite ambassadors; Pyrrhus and Fabricius; Regulus and the Carthaginians; Maximus the Delayer; the defeat of Hannibal; the career of Cato the Censor; the struggle of the Gracchi.

the households of the married sons, and the slaves, composed the rest of the household. Roman good-sense and family affection, public opinion, and religious feeling, made extremely harsh paternal punishments more and more uncommon after a very early period. Priests might pronounce a cruel father accursed, so that he would be shunned by most people.

The education of children. Educational methods varied naturally according to the period. In early times the parents were the sole teachers, and even much later most parents helped actively in educating the children. The chief qualities taught were obedience, reverence, modesty, respect for authority, self-control, self-reliance, a practical outlook upon life, and patriotism. A chief aim was the development of a strong, healthy body. Boys engaged in many kinds of athletic contests, and learned the art of war; girls were trained in household arts. Until about 200 B.C., the only "book" subjects taught were reading, writing and very elementary arithmetic, and almost the only text was the twelve tables of the laws, which were committed to memory. The rich and fairly well-to-do employed private tutors (usually slaves or freedmen), while the middle class sent their children to private schools. Here boys and girls were instructed together in small classes, although girls more frequently than boys received their entire education at home. There was no compulsory public education. But education was "public," in that a school was often conducted on an open porch facing a public street, and much time was spent in oral drill in unison. Many children were accompanied to school by special slaves (pedagogues), who supervised their conduct and acted as special tutors. There were a number of holidays and a very long summer vacation from school and tutoring. Formal education ended about the seventeenth year. After 200 B.C. the course of study became broader, as there was an influx of Greek teachers, who opened many new schools. The study of the Greek language and literature became more and more popular. Still later Latin literature was added to the course. Also after 200 B.C., more and more stress was laid upon higher education, either under learned lecturers, or in schools that might fairly be called "colleges" or "universities."

Houses. Roman houses were originally small huts, usually of one room, with a hole in the roof for chimney and skylight, and a single door. Rooms, varying in number, and openings for windows were added later; while the former hut became a central hall (*atrium*).

Furniture was very simple — wooden couches, tables and stools; and crude lamps and braziers gave heat and light when necessary. After about 200 B.C., those who could afford it built and lived much more sumptuously. The *atrium* was retained as a front hall, while to the rear of it was the large central hall (*peristylum*), in great part open to the sky, flanked by beautiful columns, and often containing a pool, fountain and gardens. There were two stories, and many rooms for a great variety of purposes. All decorations and appointments were luxurious. The poor lived in frail, crowded tenements of several stories. It became fashionable for the wealthy to maintain country homes (*villae*), with all the comforts of city homes, and extensive, splendidly adorned grounds.

AN EARLY ROMAN HUT

Servants. Practically all servants were slaves, who became more numerous and cheaper as Roman conquests were extended. A slave might be freed by his master and become a freedman (*libertus*), but he was still obligated in a number of ways to his former master. Since most slaves were prisoners of war, they were sometimes the equals or superiors of their masters, socially and intellectually. These were, in general, well cared for, and accorded positions of responsibility. Their very cheapness, however, helped subject the majority of common slaves to very harsh treatment, and horrible slave insurrections occurred during the last days of the republic. As people became kinder under the empire, a number of laws were passed for the protection of slaves.

Meals. The Roman meals were:

(1) **Ientaculum:** A very light breakfast upon arising. This consisted of a bit of bread and wine, and possibly some cheese, an olive or so, etc.

(2) **Cena:** The dinner or principal meal. Any variety of dishes of fish, fowl, meat, vegetables, porridge, bread, fruit, etc. might be served. In early times it was taken at noon. It was finally postponed as the evening meal by all, except manual laborers.

(3) **Vesperna:** A fairly substantial supper, taken toward evening by those who took dinner at noon.

INSIDE A ROMAN HOUSE

A ROMAN VILLA

(4) **Prandium:** A luncheon around noon, for those who took dinner later.

(5) **Merenda:** A late prandium.

Most people took three meals a day, although many took only two (*ientaculum* and *cena*). Early Romans sat at their meals, but reclining became almost universal later among the middle and upper classes.

Dress. Roman dress was marked by its simplicity. A man wore a linen loin cloth, a short-sleeved woolen shirt (*tunica*), reaching to the knees, and in public a white woolen blanket (*toga*) thrown gracefully about him. He had an outer cloak for inclement weather. A woman wore either one or two tunics and a robe (*palla*), the material, style and color of which might be greatly varied. A man usually wore a signet-ring, and women displayed bracelets, chains and other jewelry in great profusion. Although hats were not unknown, they were very seldom worn, but women arranged their hair in artistic coiffures. Both sandals and shoes were worn. There were no stockings. Children of both sexes wore a special toga with a purple stripe (*toga praetexta*).

ROMAN MATRON

Games and amusements. Amusements, although at first very simple and few, played a great part in Roman life after about 250 B.C. Some of the chief amusements were competitive games of skill, chance and physical prowess, carnivals, theatrical performances,

AMPHITHEATER

A CHARIOT RACE IN THE CIRCUS MAXIMUS

gambling, dinner-parties, bathing, traveling, hunting, fishing, boat-ing, and studying and reading. For children there were many toys, such as dolls, tops, etc., and numerous games, some of which were very similar to those played by children to-day. Toward the end of the republic and throughout the empire, the principal amusements were brutal spectacles in amphitheaters, where men, armed vari-ously (*gladiatores*), fought to the death, in different combinations. Often men fought beasts, or beasts fought each other. The greatest amphitheater at Rome was the *Colosseum*, which held about ninety thousand spectators. Chariot races were second in popularity only

A ROMAN AQUEDUCT

to gladiatorial shows. At Rome these were run in the *Circus Maximus*, which was also used for other spectacles, and which accommodated about one hundred fifty thousand.

Water supply. Water from wells and the Tiber River was so unwholesome that about 300 B.C. the Romans began to bring water to their city from distant hills through magnificent aqueducts. There were finally about a dozen of these, one of which was sixty miles long. They were covered channels of stone or brick, and were run under-ground through hills and on imposing arches across valleys and plains. Reservoirs at Rome sent the water through clay or leaden pipes to public fountains, public baths and private houses. Owners of houses paid a water-tax. Ancient Rome was much better supplied with water

HALL OF THE BATHS OF CARACALLA

than modern Rome, with many times the quantity necessary for ordinary purposes. Several of the ancient aqueducts are still in use. In the same way the Romans brought water to many other cities.

Public baths. The Romans borrowed the idea of public baths (*balneae* or *thermae*) from the Greeks, and they became a chief source of diversion. The Romans, however, far surpassed the Greeks in the size and splendor of their baths and the many attractions they offered. They were huge buildings, open from sunrise to sunset, most luxuriously equipped and decorated, where it was possible to enjoy any kind of

A ROMAN SHOP

bath — hot, cold, tepid, vapor, or a plunge, rub-down, etc. They contained lounging-rooms, exercise-rooms, and often gardens, art-galleries, and libraries. The fees were negligible, and children were admitted free of charge. Rich and poor, high and low, bathed together, and even emperors bathed at times with their subjects. Among a certain leisure class it became common to spend many hours a day at the baths, to take lengthy "courses of baths," or to bathe many times a day. Among the most famous baths at Rome were those built by Titus, Trajan, Caracalla, and Diocletian.

Streets and roads. Most city-streets were narrow and dingy, and ran between rows of houses, or tenements of several stories, built wall to wall, the front ground-floors of which were occupied by shops.

Streets were usually paved with slabs of stone, and some were provided with sidewalks. Streets in well-to-do sections were wider, and the buildings less crowded. Traffic, except on foot, was impossible in many streets, and forbidden in others. As might be expected from a great conquering and governing people, the Romans constructed an extensive system of highways, connecting the chief cities and towns under their sway. These were all smoothly graded and heavily paved. Some are in use to-day, while great modern highways are laid over the

ALONG THE APPIAN WAY

original beds of others. The most celebrated Roman road was the Appian Way, connecting Rome with the southeastern Italian seaport, Brundisium.

Police and fire protection. The first regular Roman police and fire-fighting force was created in the first days of the empire. Watchmen, called *vigiles*, acted as both policemen and firemen. There were a number of companies (*cohortes*) of about one thousand each, each under its own captain (*tribunus*). Above the captains was the "commissioner" (*praefectus vigilum*). Scattered about Rome were a number of station-houses. As policemen, the *vigiles* were detailed to duty in public places, much as our own policemen, and they possessed much authority. In the station-houses were kept buckets, ropes, axes, etc., for them to use when they turned firemen. Sometimes they used also a rude "fire-engine," worked by hand. They were much more efficient as policemen than as firemen. Fires were very common, and, when once under way, were seldom extinguished.

IV. GEOGRAPHY

Parts of Gaul were already under Roman dominion before Caesar's conquests. These were (1) *Gallia Citerior* (Hither Gaul), also called *Gallia Cisalpina* (Gaul this side of the Alps), and (2) *Gallia Ulterior* (Further Gaul), also called *Gallia Transalpina* (Gaul beyond the Alps) or simply *Provincia*. Even to-day this latter district is known as *Provence*. Hither Gaul, comprising the part of North Italy drained by the Po River, was won by the Romans in a series of campaigns (266–222 B.C.), and made a province in 81 B.C. Further Gaul was gradually "appropriated" as a connecting link with Spain in the seventy-five years or so after the winning of Spain from Carthage (202 B.C.), and was finally conquered and annexed as a province (125–121 B.C.).

The part of Gaul conquered by Caesar was the territory between the Pyrenees Mountains and the Rhine River, approximately the greater part of modern France, and all of modern Belgium.

V. CAUSES OF THE GALLIC WARS

Conquest by northern barbarians was an ever-present danger to the Romans. Tribes of Gauls despoiled Italy at will and captured and burned Rome itself in 390 B.C. The Teutones and Cimbri, German tribes, shortly before 100 B.C., plundered much of Gaul and Spain, defeated a number of Roman armies, and threatened Rome. Marius, the "Savior of Rome," almost annihilated them in two great battles. In the years following, both Gauls and Germans became more and more restless. Gaul was torn by political factions and the feuds of disorderly chiefs, and great numbers of Germans were crossing into Gaul, often at the invitation of Gauls themselves, who wished their help against other Gauls. All this menaced not only Italy itself eventually, but immediately the Roman province in South Gaul, where many Romans had settled and other Romans had heavy financial interests at stake.

LOCATE:
Gallia Cisalpina
Provincia
Aquitania
Belgium
Britannia
Germania
Mountains:
Alpes (Alps)
Pyrenaei (Pyrenees)
Iura (Jura)
Rivers:
Rhenus (Rhine)
Axona (Aisne)
Sequana (Seine)
Matrona (Marne)
Liger (Loire)
Towns:
Noviodunum (Soissons)
Bibrax (Bièvre, near Rheims)
Cenabum (Orleans)
Narbo (Narbonne)
Bibracte (Autun on Mont Beuvray)
Alesia(Alise Ste. Reine)
Tribes:
Helvetii
Nervii
Veneti
Venelli
Morini
Menapii
Usipetes
Tencteri
Treveri
Suebi
Eburones
Carnutes   Haedui
Arverni   Mandubii

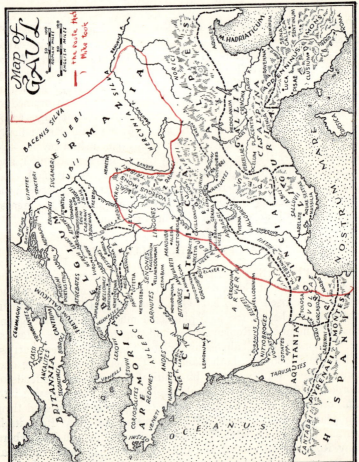

VI. SUMMARY OF CAESAR'S GALLIC WARS

Book I (58 B.C.). A brief, clear description of the geography of Gaul is followed by a lively account of Caesar's first Gallic campaign. The Helvetii, cramped for territory, attempt a huge migration from East Gaul into West Gaul, threatening the Roman province to the south and also threatening Gallic friends of the Romans. Caesar pursues them, defeats them in battle and forces the survivors to return home. He then attacks Ariovistus, an arrogant and powerful German chief, who has settled with many of his people in East Gaul. After a crushing defeat, the Germans flee across the Rhine.

Book II (57 B.C.). The northern tribes of the Belgae ally themselves against the Romans and begin to concentrate their forces. Swift movements by Caesar cause the Belgae to fear for their supplies and to disband. After forcing separately the submission of several tribes, Caesar marches against the Nervii and their allies. A surprise attack by the Nervii results in a decisive Roman victory after a desperate battle. Meanwhile a number of tribes along the coast of Northwest Gaul promise obedience. Caesar scatters his forces for the winter in such a way as to prevent a successful uprising.

Book III (57–56 B.C.). Alpine tribes attack the winter quarters of a Roman legion, that fights its way out and retreats successfully. A victory of Caesar's fleet over the Veneti of Northwest Gaul is followed by the surrender of that district. Meanwhile lieutenant Q. Titurius Sabinus routs the forces of the Venelli and other tribes friendly to the Veneti. Lieutenant Publius Crassus wins for the Romans most of Aquitania. Caesar attacks two unconquered Belgian tribes, the Morini and Menapii, compels them to retreat, but leaves off pursuit because of bad weather.

Book IV (55 B.C.). Caesar expels from North Gaul across the Rhine the German Usipetes and Tencteri, after a shameful massacre of men, women and children. He bridges the Rhine and invades Germany, in order to strike terror into the Germans, but returns to Gaul after eighteen days. An expedition to Britain, with many sensational features, does little more than acquaint the Romans with the land and the people.

Book V (54 B.C.). Invading Britain with a larger force than before, Caesar is opposed especially by the chieftain, Cassivellaunus, who annoys the Romans with his war-chariots. In spite of many successes,

Caesar makes no lasting conquests in the island. Revolting Gauls draw from their winter quarters into ambush two of Caesar's lieutenants, Q. Titurius Sabinus and L. Aurunculeius Cotta, and kill them and most of their men. Reënforced, the Gauls then storm the camp of another lieutenant, Q. Cicero, who gallantly resists them until the arrival of Caesar with an army. A foremost rebel, Indutiomarus, is finally killed by Roman cavalry.

Book VI (53 B.C.). Caesar strengthens his army to make up the losses sustained the previous year, forcefully checks a number of revolts in North Gaul, and conquers the Menapii. Meanwhile lieutenant T. Làbienus vanquishes the Treveri. Caesar now joins with Labienus, invades Germany a second time, and forces the German Suebi to retreat before him. There follows a description and comparison of the customs of Gauls and Germans, and a description of the geography and animals of Germany. Returning to Gaul, Caesar stamps out insurrections, and vainly attempts the capture of Ambiorix, a chief of the Eburones, his greatest enemy in North Gaul.

Book VII (52 B.C.). After a massacre of Roman citizens at Cenabum of the Carnutes, the Gauls arise against the Romans in one final, gigantic rebellion under the heroic chief, Vercingetorix, of the Arverni. Almost every Gallic tribe, even former sturdy friends, such as the Haedui, eventually lines up with Vercingetorix. A brutal war, with varied fortune, is waged by both sides. Caesar suffers some serious reverses. Vercingetorix is driven at last to take refuge with an army of almost one hundred thousand in Alesia, a town of the Mandubii. Caesar invests the town with mighty works, wrecks every attempt at relief, and compels its surrender after a fearful siege. (Vercingetorix was taken a prisoner to Rome, where he was executed in 45 B.C., after adorning Caesar's triumphal procession.)

VII. CHARACTERS IN SELECTIONS PRESCRIBED

Orgetorix: A powerful Helvetian. He plotted to seize supreme power in his state, and instigated two other Gauls to join him in an effort to control all Gaul. The Helvetians attempted to bring him to trial, but Orgetorix probably committed suicide to escape condemnation.

Casticus: A Sequanian who joined Orgetorix in an attempt to control Gaul.

Dumnorix: A prominent, ambitious Haeduan. He hated the Romans, constantly opposed them, and was finally killed at Caesar's order.

Diviciacus: (1) An influential Haeduan, brother of Dumnorix, and friendly to Caesar. (2) A king of the Suessiones before Caesar came to Gaul.

Nammeius and **Verucloetius:** Envoys sent by the Helvetii to Caesar.

Titus Labienus: Caesar's chief lieutenant in the Gallic Wars. (He deserted Caesar, and fought most bitterly against him in the Civil War, in the last battle of which he was killed.)

Lucius Cassius: A Roman consul, defeated by the Helvetii before Caesar went to Gaul.

Lucius Aemilius: One of Caesar's Gallic cavalry officers.

Quintus Pedius: One of Caesar's lieutenants.

Iccius: A chief of the Remi, who was sent to Caesar as an envoy, and who acted as his friend during the Belgian campaign.

Andebrogius: A leader of the Remi, who accompanied Iccius as an envoy to Caesar.

Galba: King of the Suessiones.

Quintus Titurius Sabinus and **Lucius Aurunculeius Cotta:** Lieutenants of Caesar. They were slain by the Eburones.

Gaius Volusenus: One of Caesar's officers. He was sent to Britain in charge of a scouting expedition.

Commius: King of the Atrebates, friendly to Caesar. Sent to Britain by Caesar as an ambassador of good will, he was thrown into chains by the natives. Later he was returned to Caesar.

Publius Sulpicius Rufus: One of Caesar's lieutenants.

Qui decimae legionis aquilam ferebat (*He who bore the eagle of the tenth legion*): The leader of the first Roman charge against the Britons.

Ambiorix: A chief of the Eburones. He led a re___ against Caesar, and successfully avoided capture.

Quintus Tullius Cicero: Brother of the great orator, Cicero. He was one of Caesar's lieutenants, and distinguished himself by resisting a siege of his camp.

Titus Pullo and **Lucius Vorenus:** Brave centurions, who won especial distinction at the siege of Cicero's camp.

Vertico: A Nervian noble, friendly to the Romans.

Ariovistus: A German king, defeated and driven from Gaul by Caesar.

Vercingetorix: An Arvernian chief, commander of the Gauls in their last great uprising against Caesar.

Eporedorix: (1) A noble of the Haedui, one of the leaders of the Gallic army sent to break Caesar's siege of Alesia. (2) A noble of the Haedui, captured by Caesar.

Viridomarus: A leader of the Haedui in the final Gallic rebellion.

Gaius Valerius Domnotaurus: A prominent Gallic citizen of the province, slain in battle.

Cotus and **Cavarillus:** Nobles of the Haedui, captured by Caesar.

Convictolitavis: A noble of the Haedui, whose claim to the chief magistracy of his state Ceasar supported.

Litaviccus: A noble youth of the Haedui, whom Convictolitavis turned against Caesar.

VIII. RESULTS OF CAESAR'S GALLIC CAMPAIGNS

Caesar's wars in Gaul gave him a firm basis of prestige, party strength, military experience, and resources for the Civil War that was to result in his dictatorship.

Gaul itself was thoroughly civilized under the empire and became a chief seat of ancient culture. For hundreds of years it served as a "shock-absorber" and bulwark against invasions of barbarian Germans.

In later centuries Gaul was one of the leading countries that handed down to the modern world the legacies of the ancient world.

SUGGESTIONS FOR COLLATERAL READING

The following books have been selected from among those listed in the New York State Regents Syllabus in Latin.

Biography, History, and Social Life

Abbott, F. F. History and description of Roman political institutions; 3d ed. 1911. Harvard Univ. Press

Bailey, Cyril, *ed.* The legacy of Rome. Oxford. 1923.

Boissier, Gaston. Cicero and his friends. Putnam. 1925.

Brady, Lt. Col. S. G. Caesar's Gallic campaigns. The Military Service Publ. Co., Telegraph Press Bldg., Harrisburg, Pa. 1947.

Breasted, J. H. Conquest of civilization; rev. ed. Harper. 1938.

Carcopino, Jerome. Cicero; the secrets of his correspondence. 2v. Yale Univ. Press. 1951.

———— Daily life in ancient Rome. Yale Univ. Press. 1940.

Collingwood, R. G. Roman Britain; new ed. Oxford. 1932.

Davis, W. S. Day in old Rome. Allyn. 1925.

Duggan, Alfred. Julius Caesar. Knopf. 1955.

Durant, Will. Caesar and Christ. Simon & Schuster. 1944.

Ferrero, Guglielmo. The life of Julius Caesar. Putnam 1933.

Finley, M. J. The world of Odysseus. Viking. 1954.

Foster, Genevieve. Augustus Caesar's world. Scribner. 1947.

Geer, R. M. Classical civilization; Rome; 2d ed. Prentice-Hall. 1950.

Halliburton, R. M. The glorious adventure. Grosset.

Hamilton, Edith. Roman way. Norton. 1932.

Haskell, H. J. New deal in old Rome. Knopf. 1947.

———— This was Cicero. Knopf. 1942.

Hayes, C. J. H. & Moon, P. T. Ancient and medieval history. Macmillan. 1929.

Hill, Herbert. The Roman middle class in the republican period. Macmillan. 1952.

Holmes, T. R. E. Caesar's conquest of Gaul; 2d rev. ed. Oxford. 1911.

Katz, Solomon. Decline of Rome and the rise of medieval Europe. Cornell Univ. Press. 1955.

Kieran, John, & Daley, Arthur. The story of the Olympic games. Lippincott. 1952.

Lewis, Naphtali, & Reinhold, Meyer.   Roman civilization. v. 1
The Republic. Columbia Univ. Press. 1955.

Loane, H. J. Industry and commerce of the city of Rome. Johns Hopkins
Press. 1938.

Mills, Dorothy. The book of the ancient Romans. Putnam. 1927.

Moore, F. G. The Roman's world. Columbia Univ. Press. 1936.

National Geographic Magazine. Everyday life in ancient times. National
Geographic Society. 1951.

Pahlow, E. W. & Stearns, R. P. Man's great adventure; new rev. ed.
Ginn. 1949.

Quennell, Marjorie, & Quennell, C. H. B. Everyday life in Roman
Britain. British Bk. Centre. 1925.

Robinson, C. A. Ancient history: from prehistoric times to the death of
Justinian. Macmillan. 1951.

Robinson, J. H. & others. History of civilization; earlier ages. Ginn.
1937.

Rostovtzeff, M. I. Out of the past of Greece and Rome. Yale Univ.
Press. 1932.

Rothery, A. E. Rome today. Dodd. 1950.

Scullard, H. H. Roman politics, 220-150 B. C. Oxford Univ. Press, 1951.

Showerman, Grant. Eternal Rome. Yale Univ. Press. 1925.

————— Rome and the Romans. Macmillan. 1931.

Starr, C. G., Jr. The emergence of Rome as ruler of the western world.
Cornell Univ. Press. 1950.

Stobart, J. C. The grandeur that was Rome; 3d ed. rev. British Bk.
Centre.

Tanzer, H. H. Common people of Pompeii. Johns Hopkins Press. 1939.

Treble, H. A. & King, K. M. Everyday life in Rome at the time of
Caesar and Cicero. Oxford Univ. Press. 1930.

Walter, Gerard. Caesar; a biography. Scribner. 1952.

Wolff, H. J. Roman law. Oklahoma Univ. Press. 1951

Mythology and Legends

Benson, Sally. Stories of the gods and heroes. Dial. 1940.

Bulfinch, Thomas. The age of fable. Dutton.

————— Mythology. Crowell. 1947.

Church, A. J. Aeneid for boys and girls. Macmillan. 1948.

————— Iliad for boys and girls. Macmillan. 1949.

————— Odyssey for boys and girls. Macmillan.

Colum, Padraic. Children's Homer; adventures of Odysseus and the tale of Troy. Macmillan.

———— The golden fleece and the heroes who lived before Achilles. Macmillan. 1921.

Coolidge, O. E. Greek myths. Houghton. 1949.

———— Trojan war. Houghton. 1952.

Gayley, C. M., *ed.* Classical myths in English literature and art; ed. rev. & enl. Ginn. 1939.

Guerber, H. A. Myths of Greece and Rome. British Bk. Centre. 1921.

Hamilton, Edith. Mythology. Little. 1942.

Hawthorne, Nathaniel. Wonder book and Tanglewood tales. Houghton. 1923.

Herzberg, M. J. Classical myths. Allyn. 1935.

Kingsley, Charles. Heroes: or, Greek fairy tales for my children. Macmillan.

Lowrey, J. S. In the morning of the world. Harper. 1944.

Lum, Peter. Stars in our heaven: myths and fables. Pantheon. 1948.

Norton, D. S. & Rushton, Peters. Classical myths in English literature. Rinehart. 1952.

Price, M. E. Myths and enchantment tales. Rand. 1950.

Sabin, F. E. Classical myths that live today; rev. & enl. ed. Silver. 1940.

Strong, Jay, *ed.* Treasury of the world's great myths and legends. Hart. 1951.

Tatlock, J. Greek and Roman mythology. Appleton. 1920.

Warner, Rex. Men and gods. Farrar, Straus. 1951.

Fiction and Poetry with Classical Background

Atherton, Gertrude. Dido, queen of hearts. Liveright. 1929.

Baker, George. Paris of Troy. Penguin Books.

Bryher, Winifred. Roman wall. Pantheon Books. 1954.

Coles, Manning. Great Caesar's ghost. Doubleday. 1948.

Costain, T. B. The silver chalice. Garden City. 1952.

Davis, W. S. A friend of Caesar. Macmillan. 1925.

DeWohl, Louis. Living wood. Lippincott. 1947.

———— The spear. Lippincott. 1955.

Dolan, M. M. Hannibal of Carthage. Macmillan. 1955.

Douglas, L. C. The robe. Houghton. 1942.

Duggan, Alfred. The little emperors. Coward-McCann. 1953.

Dunscomb, Charles. Bond and the free. Musson. 1955.

Gale, Elizabeth. Julia Valeria. Putnam. 1951.

Godwin, S. A. & Godwin, E. F. Out of the strong. Oxford. 1955.

———— Roman eagle. Oxford. 1951.

Graves, Ralph. Lost eagles. Knopf. 1955.

Hawthorne, Nathaniel. The marble faun. Houghton.

Ingles, J. W. Test of valor. Westminster. 1953.

Kipling, Rudyard. Puck of Pook's Hill. Doubleday.

Koestler, Arthur. The gladiators. Macmillan. 1939.

Lawrence, Isabelle. Gift of the golden cup. Bobbs. 1946.

———— Theft of the golden ring. Bobbs. 1948.

Llewellyn, Richard. The flame of Hercules. Doubleday. 1955.

Lytton, E. G. E. L. Last days of Pompeii. Dutton.

Macaulay, T. B. Lays of ancient Rome. Cambridge Univ. Press.

McLeish, Archibald. The Trojan horse, in Collected Poems 1917-1952.
Houghton. 1952.

Morley, Christopher. The Trojan horse. Lippincott. 1937.

Powers, Alfred. Hannibal's elephants. Longmans. 1944.

Schmitt, Gladys. Confessors of the name. Dial. 1952.

Seton, Anya. Mistletoe and sword. Doubleday. 1955.

Shakespeare, W. Anthony and Cleopatra; Coriolanus; Julius Caesar.
Cambridge Univ. Press.

Shore, Maxine. Captive princess. Longmans. 1952.

Sienkiewicz, Henryk. Quo vadis. Little. 1943.

Slaughter, F. G. Road to Bithynia. Doubleday. 1951.

———— The forgotten daughter. Doubleday. 1933.

Snedelker, C. D. Luke's quest. Doubleday. 1947.

———— Triumph for Flavius. Lothrop. 1955.

———— White Isle. Doubleday. 1940.

Sutcliff, Rosemary. Eagle of the Ninth. Oxford. 1954.

Trease, Geoffrey. Web of traitors. Vanguard. 1952.

Treece, Henry. Dark island. Random House. 1953.

Wallace, Lew. Ben Hur; special large-type ed. Harper.

———— The boy's Ben Hur; abridged ed. Harper. 1928.

White, E. L. The unwilling Vestal. Dutton. 1918.

White, H. C. Four rivers of Paradise. Macmillan. 1955.

Wilder, T. N. Ides of March. Harper. 1948.

Williams, Jay. Counterfeit African. Oxford. 1944.

———— Roman moon mystery. Oxford. 1948.

Yourcenar, Marguerite. Hadrian's memoirs. Farrar, Straus. 1954.

QUESTIONS OF CONTEMPORARY INTEREST

1. Give several reasons why even our great modern highways are not as durable as the Roman roads.

2. State the term that would have been applied, in Caesar's army, to each of the following: "man-of-war" ship, artillery, banner, cavalry, infantry, auxiliaries, captain, quartermaster, colonel, van, rear guard.

3. After what two famous Romans are two of our months still named?

4. Name the countries that are now included within the former boundaries of the Roman Empire at its greatest extent (117 A.D.).

5. Name the modern *Romance* languages. Why are they so called?

6. State the present meaning, and explain the historical origin of each of the following words and expressions: *forum; rostrum; plebeian; patrician; client; Lucullan banquet; veto; Pyrrhic victory; All roads lead to Rome; arena; carrying the war into Africa; Carthage must be destroyed; crossing the Rubicon; I came, I saw, I conquered; Fabian policy; emperor; thou too, Brutus?*

7. Compare Julius Caesar's methods of dealing with the following problems with the methods employed by the present administration in the United States: unemployment; farm-relief; direct relief; concentration of wealth; economy in administration; taxes.

8. Compare the methods used by the Romans in their "winning of the West"—Northwest Africa, Spain, Gaul, etc.—with the methods used by the United States in the "winning of the West."

9. State the meaning of each of the following Latin words and expressions that are commonly used in modern English: *vice versa, nota bene, per se, gratis, bona fide, e pluribus unum, in statu quo, inter nos, modus operandi, post scriptum, alumni, Anno Domini, ante meridiem, post meridiem, ante mortem, post mortem, casus belli, mirabile dictu, sine die, habeas corpus, verbatim, per diem, alter ego, in medias res, memorandum, modus vivendi, versus, deo volente, finis, onus, lapsus linguae, fiat.*

10. Compare several chief amusements or games of today with several to which the Romans were devoted.

CHAPTER XII *

PASSAGES FOR SIGHT COMPREHENSION

(These passages have no titles, since each passage contains the answer to each question asked about it.)

1

Caesar, postquam per *Ubiōs* [1] explōrātōrēs comperit *Suēbōs* [1] sēsē in silvās recēpisse, inopiam frūmentī veritus, quod, ut suprā dēmōnstrāvimus, minimē hominēs Germānī agrīcultūrae student, cōnstituit nōn prōgredi longius; sed nē omnīnō metum *reditūs* [2] suī barbarīs tolleret, atque ut eōrum auxilia tardāret, reductō exercitū, partem ultimam pontis in longitūdinem pedum CC dēlēvit. In extrēmō ponte turrim *tabulātōrum* [3] quattuor cōnstituit praesidiumque cohortium XII pontis tuendī causā pōnit magnīsque eum locum mūnītiōnibus fīrmat. Eī locō praesidiōque C. Volcācium Tullum adulēscentem praefēcit. Ipse profectus est per *Arduennam* [4] silvam, quae est tōtīus Galliae maxima. L. Minucium Basilum cum omnī equitātū praemittit.

CAESAR, *dē Bellō Gallicō*, VI, 29 (adapted)

[1] the name of a tribe.   [3] *stories*
[2] *return*   [4] the *Ardennes*

1. Whom did Caesar send ahead? With whom?
2. Comment on the size of the Ardennes.
3. Comment on the age of C. Volcacius Tullus. What was his task?
4. What did Caesar learn from scouts of the Ubii?
5. What did Caesar fear? Why should he have feared it? What did he decide to do?
6. How much of the bridge and what part of it did Caesar destroy? State *two* of his purposes in doing this.
7. What *three* defenses did Caesar place at the end of the bridge?

* This chapter was prepared by W. D. Pearson, Head of Latin Department, Milford School, Milford, Conn.

2

Magnus bellō Themistoclēs fuit neque minor in pāce. Cum enim portū neque magnō neque bonō Athēniēnsēs ūterentur, hūius cōnsiliō *triplex*[1] *Pīraeī*[2] portus cōnstitūtus est tantīsque mūrīs circumdatus, ut ipsam urbem dignitāte aequāret, *ūtilitāte*[3] superāret. Īdem mūrōs Athēniēnsium restituit suō perīculō. Namque *Lacedaemoniī*[4] causam idōneam nactī propter barbarōrum excursiōnēs, quā negārent oportēre extrā *Peloponnēsum*[5] ūllam urbem mūrōs habēre, nē essent loca mūnīta, quae hostēs possīdērent, Athēniēnsēs *aedificantēs*[6] prohibēre sunt cōnātī. Athēniēnsēs enim duābus victōriīs tantam glōriam apud omnēs gentēs erant cōnsecūtī, ut intellegerent Lacedaemoniī dē prīncipātū sibi cum eīs bellum futūrum esse. Itaque eōs quam īnfirmissimōs esse volēbant.

NEPOS, *Themistoclēs*, VI (adapted)

[1] *triple*
[2] *the Piraeus*
[3] Compare the adjective, **ūtilis**.
[4] *the Spartans*
[5] *the Peloponnesus*
[6] Compare the noun, **aedificium**.

1. By what means had the Athenians won great glory?
2. Why did the Spartans really not wish the Athenians to be strong?
3. What reason did the Spartans give for trying to prevent the Athenians from building walls?
4. State *two* directions in which Themistocles was great.
5. What did the Athenians do at Themistocles' advice? Why? What was the result?
6. What words tell you that Themistocles risked his personal safety in fortifying Athens?

3

Cum Lābiēnus Caesaris cōpiās dēspiceret, Pompeī cōnsilium summīs laudibus efferret, *"Nōlī,"*[1] inquit, *"exīstimāre,*[1] Pompeī, hunc esse exercitum Caesaris, quī Galliam Germāniamque vīcerit. Omnibus interfuī proeliīs, neque incognitam rem prōnūntiō. *Perexigua*[2] pars illīus exercitūs superest; magna pars periit, quod accidere tot proeliīs fuit necesse, multōs *autumnī pestilentia*[3] in Italiā cōnsūmpsit, multī domum discessērunt, multī sunt relictī in Italiā. Hae cōpiae, quās vidētis, ex *dīlēctibus*[4] *hōrum*[5] annōrum in citeriōre Galliā sunt refectae, et plērīque sunt ex colōniīs *Trānspadānīs.*[6] Ac tamen, quod fuit *rōboris,*[7] duōbus proeliīs *Dyrrachī*[8] interiit." Haec cum dīxisset, iūrāvit, sē nisi victōrem in castra nōn reversūrum, reliquōsque, ut idem facerent, hortātus est.

CAESAR, *dē Bellō Cīvīlī,* III, 87 (adapted)

[1] **Nōlī   exīstimāre** = *Do   not suppose.*
[2] The prefix, **per** = *very.*
[3] *autumn fever*
[4] *levies*
[5] *these recent*
[6] *across the Po*
[7] *strength*
[8] The nominative is **Dyrrachium** (a town).

1. Give a good title for the passage.
2. How did Labienus feel in general toward Pompey? Toward Caesar?
3. What did Labienus finally swear? What oath did the rest take?
4. To whom was the speech of Labienus directed? What word tells you this?
5. What was the main point of the speech of Labienus? Why did Labienus think he should be believed?
6. State *four* causes that, according to Labienus, had diminished Caesar's veteran army.
7. What did Labienus state as the chief source of Caesar's present army? Why, in Labienus' opinion, was even this army not as strong as it had been?

4

Simul atque Agēsilāus imperiī potītus est, persuāsit *Lacedae-*
moniīs[1] ut cum exercitū sē mitterent in Asiam bellumque *rēgī*[2]
facerent, docēns *satius*[3] esse in Asiā quam in Eurōpā dīmicārī.
Namque fāma exierat *Artaxerxēn*[4] comparāre classēs pedestrēsque
exercitūs, quōs in Graeciam mitteret. Datā potestāte, tantā celeritāte ūsus est, ut prius in Asiam cum cōpiīs pervēnerit quam
satrapae[5] eum scīrent profectum esse. Quō factum est ut omnēs
imparātōs invenīret. Id ut cognōvit Tissaphernēs, quī summum
imperium tum inter *praefectōs*[6] rēgis habēbat, *indūtiās*[7] ab
Agēsilāō petīvit; eāsque impetrāvit *trimēnstrēs.*[8] Iūrāvit autem
uterque sē sine *dolō*[9] indūtiās cōnservātūrum. In quā *pactiōne*[10]
summā fidē mānsit Agēsilāus; contrā ea Tissaphernēs nihil aliud
quam bellum comparāvit.

NEPOS, *Agēsilāus,* II (adapted)

[1] *the Spartans*
[2] i.e. the king of Persia.
[3] *better*
[4] accusative of the name of the king of Persia— nominative **Artaxerxēs.**
[5] *satraps* (governors of Persian provinces).
[6] *commanders*
[7] *truce*
[8] *for three months*
[9] *trickery*
[10] *agreement*

1. How did Agesilaus observe the truce? How did Tissaphernes observe it?
2. Who was Tissaphernes? What did he seek? In how far did he obtain his desire?
3. What did Agesilaus persuade the Spartans to do? When did he persuade them? What reason for his desire did he give?
4. What had Agesilaus heard Artaxerxes was doing? For what was Artaxerxes doing this?
5. When did Agesilaus arrive in Asia?
6. In what condition were the satraps upon the arrival of Agesilaus in Asia?

5

Erant apud Caesarem in equitum numerō *Allobrogēs*[1] duo frātrēs, Raucillus et Egus, Abducillī fīliī, quī prīncipātum in cīvitāte obtinuerat, *singulārī*[2] virtūte hominēs, quōrum operā Caesar omnibus Gallicīs bellīs optimā fortissimāque erat ūsus. Hīs domī ob hās causās amplissimōs magistrātūs mandāverat, atque eōs senātōrēs dēlēgerat, agrōsque in Galliā ex hostibus captōs praemiaque pecūniae magna tribuerat, *locuplētēsque*[3] ex *egentibus*[4] fēcerat. Hī propter virtūtem nōn sōlum apud Caesarem in honōre erant, sed etiam apud exercitum *cārī*[5] habēbantur; sed *frētī*[6] amīcitiā Caesaris et *stultā*[7] ac barbarā arrogantiā ēlātī, dēspiciēbant suōs stīpendiumque equitum *fraudābant*[8] et praedam omnem domum āvertēbant.

CAESAR, *dē Bellō Cīvilī*, III, 59 (adapted)

[1] the name of a Gallic tribe.	[5] *dear*
[2] Compare the English word.	[6] *relying*
[3] *wealthy*	[7] *stupid*
[4] from **egeō** = *need*.	[8] *stole*

1. Why did Caesar honor Raucillus and Egus? What did the army think of them?
2. What *three* unworthy things did Raucillus and Egus do? How did the author explain these?
3. Of what tribe were Raucillus and Egus? Whose sons were they? What position had their father held?
4. State a number of ways in which Caesar showed his regard for Raucillus and Egus.

6

Caesar legiōnēs equitātumque revocārī atque in itinere resistere iubet, ipse ad nāvēs revertitur; eadem ferē, quae ex nūntiīs litterīsque cognōverat, *cōram*[1] perspicit, sīc ut, āmissīs circiter XL nāvibus, reliquae tamen reficī posse magnō negōtiō vidērentur. Itaque ex legiōnibus *fabrōs*[2] dēligit et ex *continentī*[3] aliōs arcessī iubet; Labiēnō scrībit ut quam plūrimās possit eīs legiōnibus, quae sint apud eum, nāvēs īnstituat. Ipse, etsī rēs erat multae operae ac labōris, tamen commodissimum esse statuit omnēs nāvēs *subdūcī*[4] et cum castrīs ūnā mūnītiōne coniungī. In hīs rēbus circiter diēs decem cōnsūmit, nē nocturnīs quidem temporibus ad labōrem mīlitum intermissīs. Subductīs nāvibus castrīsque ēgregiē mūnītīs, eāsdem cōpiās quās ante praesidiō nāvibus relinquit; ipse *eōdem*[5] unde redierat proficīscitur.

Caesar, *dē Bellō Gallicō,* V, 11

[1] *in person*
[2] *workmen*
[3] *the mainland*

[4] *to be drawn up on land*
[5] an adverb.

1. What order did Caesar give in regard to the legions and cavalry? What did Caesar himself do then?
2. State exactly what Caesar saw had happened to his fleet. How had he previously heard about this?
3. State *two* sources from which Caesar obtained workmen.
4. What was Caesar's message to Labienus?
5. What decision did Caesar make in regard to the fleet? Was it difficult or easy to carry this out? Support your opinion.
6. How long did it take to carry out Caesar's decision? Why was it possible to do this in such a short time?
7. What *two* things did Caesar do after he had accomplished the task he had set for himself?

7

Prīmum Cīmōn imperātor apud flūmen *Strȳmona*[1] magnās copiās *Thraecum*[2] vīcit, oppidum *Amphipolim*[3] cōnstituit eōque decem mīlia Athēniēnsium in colōniam mīsit. Īdem rūrsus imperātor Cypriōrum et Phoenīcum *ducentārum*[4] nāvium classem cēpit eōdemque diē parī fōrtūnā in terrā ūsus est. Namque hostium nāvibus captīs statim ex classe cōpiās suās ēdūxit barbarōrumque māximam vim ūnō impetū reppulit. Quā victōriā magna praedā potītus, cum domum reverterētur, quod iam nōnnūllae īnsulae propter *acerbitātem*[5] imperiī dēfēcerant, bene *animātās*[6] cōnfīrmāvit, *aliēnātās*[7] ad officium redīre coēgit. *Scȳrum,*[8] quam eō tempore Dolopes incolēbant, quod male sē gesserant, vacuēfēcit, possessōrēs veterēs urbe īnsulāque ēiēcit, agrōs civibus dīvīsit.

NEPOS, *Cīmōn,* II (adapted)

[1] accusative of **Strȳmōn.**
[2] genitive plural.
[3] accusative of **Amphipolis.**
[4] *two hundred*
[5] *severity*

[6] perfect participle of a verb allied with **animus.**
[7] Compare the adjective, **aliēnus.**
[8] **Scȳrus,** an island.

1. What did Cimon do to Scyrus? Why? Who lived there?
2. State *three* things that Cimon did among the Thracians.
3. Over whom did Cimon win a naval victory? How great a victory was it? Why was the day of this victory especially remarkable?
4. State precisely what Cimon did after he captured the enemy's fleet.
5. What did Cimon win by his victory over the barbarians (Persians)? For what place did he set out?
6. What had some islands done? Why? State *two* methods pursued by Cimon in dealing with the islands.

8

Caesar *īnfīrmitātem* [1] Gallōrum veritus, quod sunt in cōnsiliīs capiendīs *mōbilēs* [2] et novīs plērumque rēbus student, nihil hīs committendum exīstimāvit. Est enim hōc Gallicae cōnsuētūdinis, ut et *viātōrēs* [3] etiam invītōs cōnsistere cōgant, et quid quisque eōrum dē quāque rē audierit aut cognōverit, quaerant, et mercātōrēs in oppidīs vulgus circumsistat, quibusque ex regiōnibus veniant quāsque ibi rēs cognōverint, prōnūntiāre cōgat. Hīs rēbus atque *audītiōnibus* [4] permōtī, dē summīs saepe rēbus cōnsilia ineunt, quōrum eōs in *vēstīgiō* [5] *paenitēre* [6] necesse est, cum incertīs rūmōribus *serviant,* [7] et plērīque ad voluntātem eōrum *fīcta* [8] respondeant. Quā cōnsuētūdine cognitā, Caesar, nē graviōrī bellō occurreret, *mātūrius* [9] quam cōnsuērat ad exercitum proficīscitur.

Caesar, *dē Bellō Gallicō,* IV, 5–6 (adapted)

[1] *fickleness*
[2] *changeable*
[3] *travelers*
[4] *hearsay*
[5] *on the spot*

[6] *repent*
[7] *pay heed*
[8] *lies*
[9] *earlier*

1. What did Caesar fear? Why did he fear it? What did he think?
2. State exactly how travelers and merchants were connected with a Gallic custom.
3. What can you gather from the passage about the importance the Gauls attached to the tales of travelers and merchants?
4. For what *two* reasons were the Gauls often sorry they had adopted new plans?
5. When did Caesar leave for the army? For what purpose?

9

Equitēs nostium *essedāriīque* [1] ācriter proeliō cum equitātū nostrō in itinere cōnflīxērunt, ita tamen ut nostrī omnibus partibus superiōrēs fuerint atque eōs in silvās collēsque compulerint; sed complūribus interfectīs cupidius īnsecūtī nōnnūllōs ex suīs āmīsērunt. At illī intermissō spatiō, imprūdentibus nostrīs atque occupātīs in *mūnītiōne* [2] castrōrum subitō sē ex silvīs ēiēcērunt, impetūque in eōs factō quī erant in statiōne prō castrīs conlocātī ācriter pugnāvērunt, duābusque missīs subsidiō cohortibus ā Caesare, atque hīs prīmīs legiōnum duārum, cum eae perexiguō intermissō locī spatiō inter sē cōnstitissent, novō genere pugnae perterritīs nostrīs per mediōs audācissimē perrūpērunt sēque inde incolumēs recēpērunt. Eō diē Q. Laberius Dūrus, tribūnus mīlitum, interficitur. Illī, plūribus submissīs cohortibus, repelluntur.

CAESAR, *dē Bellō Gallicō*, V, 15

[1] *charioteers*　　　　　[2] Compare the verb, **mūniō.**

1. Who was killed in the engagements described above?
2. What finally happened to the enemy?
3. Against whom did the Romans (*nostrī*) fight? To what extent were they successful at first?
4. What mistake did the Romans make? What happened because of this?
5. How did the enemy try to outwit the Romans? What aid did Caesar send?
6. What frightened the Romans?

10

Partītō [1] exercitū, Caesar T. Labiēnum cum legiōnibus tribus ad Ōceanum in eās partēs quae *Menapiōs* [2] attingunt proficīscī iubet; C. Trebōnium cum parī legiōnum numerō ad eam regiōnem quae *Atuatucīs* [2] *adiacet* [3] populandam mittit; ipse cum reliquīs tribus ad flūmen *Sabim,* [4] quod īnfluit in *Mosam,* [5] extrēmāsque *Arduennae* [6] partēs īre cōnstituit, quō cum paucīs equitibus profectum *Ambiorīgem* [7] audiēbat. *Discēdēns* [8] post diem septimum sēsē reversūrum cōnfīrmat, quam ad diem eī legiōnī quae in praesidiō relinquēbātur frūmentum dēbērī sciēbat. Labiēnum Trebōniumque hortātur, sī reī pūblicae *commodō* [9] facere possint, ad eam diem revertantur, ut rūrsus commūnicātō cōnsiliō explōrātīsque hostium ratiōnibus aliud initium bellī capere possint.

CAESAR, *dē Bellō Gallicō,* VI, 33 (adapted)

[1] from **partior,** *divide.* The perfect participle of this verb may be used passively.
[2] the name of a tribe.
[3] *lies next*

[4] **Sabis,** the name of a river.
[5] the name of a river.
[6] the name of a forest.
[7] a Gallic chief.
[8] *departing*
[9] *with profit*

1. State Caesar's instructions to T. Labienus.
2. What was C. Trebonius to do? How many legions did he take with him?
3. Where did Caesar decide to go? With how many legions?
4. What report had reached Caesar about Ambiorix?
5. When did Caesar state he would return? Why?
6. When were Labienus and Trebonius to return? On what condition?
7. What did Caesar plan to do after the return of Labienus and Trebonius?

ENGLISH-LATIN VOCABULARY

A

able (be)	*possum, posse, potuī*
absent (be)	*absum, -esse, āfuī, āfutūrus.*
accept	*accipiō, 3 -cēpī, -ceptus.*
accomplish	*perficiō, 3, fēcī, fectus; consequor, ī, secūtus.*
account, on	
account of	*propter* (with acc.)
accordingly	*itaque.*
across	*trāns* (with acc.)
advance	*prōgredior, ī, gressus.*
afraid,	
be afraid	*timeō, 2, -uī.*
Africa	*Africa, -ae* (f.).
after	*post* (prep. with acc.); *postquam* (conj.)
afterward	*posteā.*
against	*in, ad, contrā* (prepos. with acc.).
aid (verb)	*iuvō, 1, iūvī, iūtus.*
aid (noun)	*auxilium, -ī, n.; subsidium, -ī, n.*
alarm	*permoveō, 2, mōvī, mōtus; perturbō* 1.
Alexandria	*Alexandrīa, -ae* (f.)
all	*omnis, -e*
ally	*socius, -ī,* m.
already	*iam.*
although	*cum.*
always	*semper.*
ambassador	*lēgātus, -ī* (m).
among	*apud, inter,* (prepos. with acc.)
and	*et, atque, -que*
announce	*nūntiō,* 1.
another	*alius, -a, -ud.*

answer	*respondeō, 2, -spondī, -spōnsus.*
any (adj.)	*ūllus, -a, -um.*
appoint	*cōnstituō, 3; -uī, -ūtus.*
approach	*appropinquō,* 1.
Ariovistus,	*Ariovistus, -ī* (m).
arms	*arma, -ōrum* (n.).
army	*exercitus, -ūs* (m.).
arrival	*adventus, -ūs* (m.).
arrive	*perveniō, 4, -vēnī, -ventūrus.*
ask	*rogō, 1; petō, 3, -īvī, ītus; quaerō, 3, -sīvī, -sītus.*
assault	
(noun)	*oppugnātiō, -ōnis* (f.).
at	*ad* (with acc.) *in* (with abl.)
attack (verb)	*oppugnō, 1; aggredior, -ī, -gressus; impetum faciō.*
attack (noun)	*impetus, -ūs* (m.).
attempt	*cōnor, 1, cōnātus.*
auxiliaries	*auxilia, -ōrum* (n.).
await	*exspectō,* 1.
away,	
be away	*absum, abesse, āfuī, āfutūrus.*

B

baggage	*impedīmenta, -ōrum* (n. plu.).
bank	*rīpa, -ae* (f.).
barbarian	*barbarus, -ī* (m.).
battle	*proelium, -ī* (n.); *pugna, -ae* (f.).
be	*sum, esse, fuī, futūrus.*
be distant	*absum, -esse, āfuī, āfutūrus.*

bear *ferō, ferre, tulī, lātus.*

because *quod:* **because of,** *propter* (with acc.)

become *fīō, fierī, factus.*

before (adv.) *ante, anteā,*

before (conj.) *priusquam, antequam.*

before (prep.) *ante* (with acc.); *prō* (with abl.).

beg *ōrō,* 1; *obsecrō,* 1.

began *coepī, coepisse, coeptus.*

begin *incipiō,* 3, *-cēpī, -ceptus.*

Belgians *Belgae, -ārum* (m.).

Bellovaci *Bellovacī, -ōrum* (m).

besiege *obsideō,* 2, *-sēdī, -sessus.*

boat *linter, -tris* (f.).

Boii *Boiī, -ōrum* (m.).

both . . and *et . . et.*

brave *fortis, -e.*

bravely *fortiter.*

bravery *fortitūdō, -inis* (f.).

bridge *pōns, pontis* (m.).

bring *ferō, ferre, tulī, lātus; addūco,* 3, *-dūxī, ductus.*

bring forward *agō,* 3, *ēgī, āctus.*

bring together *comportō,* 1; *addūco,* 3, *-dūxī, ductus.*

Britain *Britannia, -ae* (f.).

broad *lātus, -a, -um.*

brother *frāter, frātris* (m.).

Brundisium *Brundisium, -ī* (n.).

Brutus *Brūtus, -ī* (m.).

build *aedificō,* 1; *mūniō,* 4, *-īvī, -ītus; faciō,* 3, *fēcī, factus.*

but *sed, at.*

by *ā, ab* (abl. of agent).

C

Caesar *Caesar, -aris* (m.).

call *vocō,* 1.

camp *castra, -ōrum* (n.).

can *possum, posse, potuī.*

capture *capiō,* 3, *cēpī, captus; expugnō,* 1.

cavalry *equitātus, -ūs* (m.); *equitēs, -um* (m.).

chief *prīnceps, -cipis* (m.).

choose *dēligō,* 3, *lēgī, -lēctus.*

city *urbs, urbis* (f.).

coast *ōra, -ae* (f.).

cohort *cohors, -hortis* (f.).

collect *cōgō,* 3, *-ēgī, -āctus; cōnferō, -ferre, -tulī, -lātus.*

come *veniō,* 4, *vēnī, ventūrus.*

coming *adventus, ūs* (m.).

command (verb) *imperō,* 1; *iubeō,* 2, *iussī, iussus.*

command (noun) *imperātum, -ī* (n.).

command, be in command *praesum, -esse, -fuī, -futūrus.*

commander *imperātor, -ōris* (m.).

Commius *Commius, -ī* (m.).

compel *cōgō,* 3, *-ēgī, -āctus.*

complain *queror, -ī, questus.*

complete *faciō,* 3, *fēcī, factus.*

confederacy *foedus, -eris* (n.).

confer *colloquor, -loquī, locūtus.*

conference *colloquium, -ī* (n.).

conquer *superō,* 1; *vincō,* 3, *vīcī, victus.*

conspiracy *coniūrātiō, -ōnis* (f.).

consul *cōnsul, -ulis* (m.).

council *concilium, -ī* (n.).

country *patria, -ae* (f.).

courage *virtūs, -ūtis* (f.).; *animus. -ī* (m.).

Crassus	*Crassus, -ī* (m.).
cross	*trānseō, īre, -iī, -itus; trānsgredior, -ī, -gressus.*

D

daily	*cotidiānus, -a, -um.*
danger	*perīculum, -ī* (n.).
dare	*audeō, -ēre, ausus.*
daring	*audācia, -ae* (f.).
dawn	*prīma lūx, prīmae lūcis.*
dawn (at)	*prīmā lūce.*
day	*diēs, -ēī* (m.).
daybreak	*prīma (ae), lūx (lūcis).*
decide	*cōnstituō, 3, -uī, -ūtus.*
deep	*altus, -a, -um.*
defeat	*superō, 1.*
defend	*dēfendō, 3, -dī, -sus.*
defender	*dēfēnsor, ōris* (m.).
delay	*moror, 1, -ātus.*
demand	*imperō, 1; postulō, 1.*
depart	*discēdō, 2, -cessī, -cessūrus.*
depth	*altitūdō, -inis* (f.).
desert	*dēserō, 3, -seruī, -sertus.*
desire	*cupiō, 3, īvī,-ītus.*
despair of	*dēspērō, 1 (dē* with abl.).
determine	*cōnstituō, 3, -uī, ūtus; statuō, 3, -uī, -ūtus.*
difficult	*difficilis -e.*
direction	*pars, partis* (f.).
distant (be)	*absum, -esse, āfuī, āfutūrus.*
ditch	*fossa, -ae* (f.).
do	*faciō, 3, fēcī, factus.*
be done	
(go on)	*geror, gerī, gestus.*
doubt	*dubitō, 1.*
draw up	*īnstruō, 3, -strūxī, -strūctus.*
drive	*pellō, 3, pepulī, pulsus.*
drive back	*repellō, 3, reppulī, repulsus.*
Dumnorix	*Dumnorīx, -īgis* (m.).

E

eager	*cupidus, -a, -um.*
early	*māne.*
easily	*facile.*
easy	*facilis, -e.*
else	*reliquus, -a, -um.*
nothing	
else	*nihil aliud.*
encourage	*hortor, -ārī, -ātus; cohortor, 1.*
enemy	*hostis, -is* (m.); *hostēs, -ium* (m.).
enough	*satis.*
envoy	*lēgātus, -ī* (m.).
everything	*omnia, omnēs rēs.*

F

far	*longē.*
farm	*ager, agrī* (m.).
fear (verb)	*timeō, 2, timuī; vereor, verērī, veritus.*
fertility	*bonitās, -tātis* (f.).
few	*paucī, -ae, -a.*
field	*ager, agrī* (m.).
fiercely	*ācriter.*
fight (verb)	*pugnō, 1; contendō, 3, -tendī, -tentus.*
fight (noun)	*pugna, -ae* (f.); *proelium, 4* (n.).
find	*inveniō, 4, -vēnī, -ventus; nancīscor, -ī, nactus.*
find out	*reperiō, 4, repperī, repertus.*
five	*quīnque.*
flee	*fugiō, 3, fūgī, fugitūrus*
fleet	*classis, -is* (f.).
flight	*fuga, -ae* (f.).
put to	
flight	*in fugam dō, dare, dedī, datus.*
foe	*hostis, -is* (m.).
follow	*sequor, sequī, secūtus.*
following	*posterus, -a, -um.*
food	*cibus, -ī* (m.).

foot   *pēs, pedis* (m.).
foot soldier   *pedes, peditis* (m.).
for (in be-
  half of)   *prō* (with abl.).
forced
  march   *magnum iter.*
forces   *cōpiae, -ārum* (f.).
ford   *vadum, -ī* (n.).
form
  (draw up)   *īnstruō, 3, -strūxī,*
                   -strūctus.
form
  (a plan)   *ineō, -īre, -iī, -itus.*
fortified   *mūnītus, -a, -um.*
fortify   *mūniō, 4, -īvī, -ītus.*
fourth   *quārtus, -a, -um.*
friend   *amīcus, -ī* (m.).
friendship   *amīcitia, -ae* (f.).
from   *ā, ab, dē, ē, ex* (prepos.
                   wĭth abl.); (conj.);
                   quōminus.
furnish   *praebeō, 2, -uī, -itus.*

G

gate   *porta, -ae* (f.).
Gaul (the
  country)   *Gallia, -ae* (f.)
  a Gaul   *Gallus, -ī* (m.).
general   *dux, ducis* (m.).;
                   imperātor, -ōris (m.).
Geneva   *Genava, -ae* (f.).
Germans   *Germānī, -ōrum* (m.).
  get posses-
  sion of   *occupō, 1; potior, -īrī,*
                   ītus.
give   *dō, dare, dedī, datus.*
give back   *reddō, 3, -didī, -ditus.*
give up   *dēdō, 3, dēdidī, dēditus.*
go   *eō, īre, iī, itūrus.*
go off   *abeō, -īre, -iī, -itūrus.*
go on   *geror, gerī, gestus.*
go out   *exeō, -īre, -iī, -itum.*
good   *bonus, -a, -um.*
grain   *frūmentum, -ī* (n.).
great   *magnus, -a, -um.*
guard   *praesidium, -ī* (n.).

H

Haedui   *Haeduī, -ōrum* (m.).
halt   *cōnsistō, 3, -stitī.*
happen   *accidō, 3, -cidī; fīō,*
                   fierī, factus.
harbor   *portus, -ūs,* (m.).
Harudes   *Harūdēs, -um* (m.).
haste, in
  great
  haste   *celeriter.*
hasten   *contendō, 3, -tendī,*
                   -tentus; properō, 1;
                   mātūrō, 1.
have   *habeō, 2, -uī, -itus.*
he   *is, ille.*
hear   *audiō, 4, -īvī, -ītus.*
Helvetians   *Helvētiī, -ōrum* (m.).
hill   *collis, -is* (m.).
himself   *ipse, -a, -um.*
his (reflexive) *suus, -a, -um;*
                   (not reflexive), *eius.*
hold   *teneō, 2, -uī; obtineō, 2*
                   -tinuī, -tentus.
home   *domus, -ūs* (f.).
  at home   *domī.*
  home (to-
  wards)   *domum.*
hope (verb)   *spērō, 1.*
hope (noun)   *spēs, -eī* (f.).
horseman   *eques, -itis* (m.).
hostage   *obses, -idis* (c.).
hour   *hōra, -ae* (f.).
how large   *quantus, -a, -um.*
hurl   *coniciō, 3, -iēcī, -iectus.*
hurry   *contendō, 3, -tendī,*
                   -tentus.

I

I   *ego.*
if   *sī; if not, nisi.*
immediately   *statim; prōtinus.*
in   *in* (with abl.).
in order that *ut.*
in order that
  not   *nē.*

in order that nothing	*nē quid.*
inform	*certiōrem (-ēs) faciō,* 3, *fēcī, factus.*
inquire	*quaerō,* 3, *-sīvī, -sītus.*
in regard to	*dē* (with abl.).
instruction	*mandātum, -ī* (n.).
into	*in* (with acc.).
its (reflexive)	*suus, -a, -um;* (not reflexive), *eius.*

J

join battle	*proelium committō,* 3, *-mīsī, -missus.*

K

kill	*interficiō,* 3, *-fēcī, fectus; necō,* 1; *occīdō,* 3, *-cīdī, -cīsus.*
king	*rēx, rēgis* (m.).
know	*sciō,* 4, *scīvī, scītus; intellegō,* 3, *-lēxī, lēctus.*

L

Labienus	*Labiēnus, -ī* (m.).
land (verb)	*ēgredior, -ī, -gressus.*
land (noun)	*ager, agrī* (m.); *terra, -ae* (f.).
large	*magnus, -a, -um.*
lead	*dūcō,* 3, *dūxī, ductus.*
lead back	*redūcō,* 3, *-dūxī, -ductus.*
lead over	*trādūcō,* 3, *-dūxī, -ductus.*
leader	*dux, ducis* (m.).
learn	*cognōscō,* 3, *-gnōvī, -gnitus; intellegō,* 3, *-lēxī, -lēctus; reperiō,* 4, *repperī, repertus.*
leave	*relinquō,* 3, *līquī, -lictus.*
left	*sinister, -tra, -trum.*
legate	*lēgātus, -ī* (m.).
legion	*legiō, -ōnis* (f.).

letter (of alphabet)	*littera, -ae* (f.); (epistle), *litterae, -ārum* (f.); *epistula, -ae* (f.).
liberty	*lībertās, -ātis* (f.).
lieutenant	*lēgātus, -ī* (m.).
line of battle	*aciēs, -ēī* (f.).
Lingones	*Lingonēs, -um* (m.).
listen to	*audiō,* 4, *-īvī, -ītus.*
loyal	*fidēlis, -e.*

M

machine	*māchinātiō, -ōnis* (f.).
make	*faciō,* 3, *fēcī, factus.*
make a march	*iter faciō,* 3, *fēcī. factus.*
make preparation	*comparō,* 1.
make use of	*ūtor, -ī, ūsus.*
make war	*bellum faciō; bellum īnferō, -ferre, intulī, illātus.*
man	*homō, hominis* (c.).; *vir, -ī* (m.).
many	*multī, -ae, -a.*
march (noun)	*iter, itineris* (n.).
march (verb)	*iter faciō.*
marsh	*palūs, -ūdis* (f.).
message	*nūntius, -ī* (m.).
messenger	*nūntius, -ī* (m.).
Metius	*Metius, -ī* (m.).
midst (of)	*medius, -a, -um.*
might	*vīs* (f.).
mile	*mīlle passūs.*
miles	*mīlia passuum.*
Mithridates	*Mithridātēs, is* (m.).
moon	*lūna, -ae* (f.).
mound	*tumulus, -ī* (m.).
more	*plūs, plūris.*
mountain	*mōns, montis* (m.).
move	*moveō,* 2, *mōvī, mōtus.*
much	*multus, -a, -um;*
by much	*multō.*

multitude *multitūdō, -inis* (f.).
my *meus, -a, -um.*

N

nation *nātiō, -ōnis* (f.).
near *propinquus, -a, -um.*
very near *proximus, -a, um-.*
neglect *neglegō, 3, -lēxī, -lēctus; omittō, 3, -mīsī, -missus.*
neighbor *fīnitimus, -ī* (m.).
neighboring *fīnitimus, -a, -um.*
Nervii *Nerviī, -ōrum* (m.).
nevertheless *tamen.*
new *novus, -a, -um.*
news *nūntius,-ī* (m.).
next *proximus, -a, -um.*
  on the
  next day *posterō diē.*
night *nox, noctis* (f.).
no longer *nōn iam.*
no one *nēmō.*
not *nōn.*
noted *cognitus, -a, -um.*
nothing *nihil.*
now *nunc.*
number *numerus, -ī* (m.).

O

obtain *obtineō, 2, -tinuī, -tentus.*
Octavius *Octāvius, -ī* (m.).
old *vetus, -eris.*
on *in* (with abl.).
on account
  of *ob, propter* (prepos. with acc.).
once,
  at once *statim.*
one *ūnus, -a, -um.*
only one *sōlus, -a, -um.*
order *imperō, 1; iubeō, 2, iussī, iussus.*
Orgetorix *Orgetorīx, -īgis* (m.).

other *alius, -a, -ud; the* **other** (of two), *alter, -a, -um;* **the other** (the rest), *reliquus, -a, -um.*
ought *dēbeō, 2, -uī, -itus; oportet, tēre, -tuit.*
our *noster, -tra, -trum.*
out from *ē or ex* (with abl.).
outside *extrā* (with acc.).

P

part *pars, partis* (f.).
peace *pāx, pācis* (f.).
persuade *persuādeō, 2, -suāsī, suāsum.*
permit *permittō, 3, -mīsī, -missus; patior, -ī, passus.*
pillage *praedor, -ārī, -ātus; dīripiō, 3, -ripuī, -reptus*
people *populus, -ī* (m.).
pitch camp *castra pōnō, 3, posuī, positus.*
place *locus, -ī* (m.).
place in
  charge of *praeficiō, 3, -fēcī, fectus.*
plan *cōnsilium, -ī* (n.).
powerful, be
  powerful *valeō, 2, -uī, -itūrus.*
  be most
  powerful *plūrimum valeō, plūrimum possum.*
prevent *prohibeō, 2, -uī, -itus.*
Procillus *Prōcillus, -ī* (m.).
promise *polliceor, -ērī, -itus.*
province *prōvincia, -ae* (f.).
put *pōnō, 3, posuī, positus.*
put at the
  head of *praeficiō, 3, -fēcī, -fectus.*
put to flight *fugō, 1.*

Q

quickly	*celeriter.*
as quickly	
as possible	*quam celerrimē.*

R

reach	*perveniō, 4, -vēnī, -ventum.*
ready	*parātus, -a, -um.*
reason	*causa, -ae* (f.).
for this	
reason	*quā dē causā.*
recall	*revocō, 1.*
receive	*accipiō, 3, -cēpī, ceptus.*
refrain	*abstineō, 2, -tinuī, -tentus.*
regard, in	
regard to	*dē* (with abl.).
remain	*maneō, 2, mānsī, mānsūrus.*
Remi	*Rēmī, -ōrum* (m.).
reply	*respondeō, 2, -spondī, -spōnsus.*
report (verb)	*nūntiō, 1.*
report (noun)	*fāma, -ae* (f.).
resist	*resistō, 3, -stitī.*
rest of	*reliquus, -a, -um.*
retreat	*mē recipiō, 3, -cēpī, -ceptus.*
return	*redeō, -īre, -iī, -itum; revertor, -ī, reversus.*
reward	*praemium,-ī* (n.).
Rhine	*Rhēnus, -ī* (m.).
river	*flūmen, -inis* (n.).
road	*via, -ae* (f.); *iter, itineris* (n.).
Roman (adj.)	*Rōmānus, -a, -um.*
Romans	*Rōmānī, -ōrum* (m.).
Rome	*Rōma, -ae* (f.).
route	*via, -ae* (f.); *iter, itineris* (n).*
run	*currō, 3, cucurrī, cursus.*

S

safety	*salūs, · ūtis* (f.).
sail	*nāvigō, 1.*
same	*īdem, eadem, idem.*
say	*dīcō, 3, dīxī, dictus.*
scout	*explōrātor, -ōris* (m.); *speculātor, -ōris* (m.)
see	*videō, 2, -vīdī, vīsus.*
seek	*petō, 3, -īvī, -ītus.*
seem	*videor, -ērī, visus.*
seize	*occupō, 1; comprehendō, 3,-hendī, -hēnsus.*
senate	*senātus, -ūs* (m.).
senator	*senātor -ōris* (m.).
send	*mittō, 3, mīsī, missus.*
send ahead	*praemittō, 3, -mīsī, -missus.*
Senones	*Senonēs, -um* (m.).
Sequani	*Sēquanī, -ōrum* (m.).
set forth,	
set out	*proficīscor, -ī, -fectus.*
seven	*septem.*
ship	*nāvis -is* (f.).
short	*brevis, -e.*
signal	*signum, -ī* (n.).
since	*cum.*
slay	*occīdō, 3, -cīdī, -cīsus.*
slowly	*tardē.*
small	*parvus, -a, -um.*
so (with	
verbs)	*ita, sīc;* (with adj. and adv.), *tam.*
so great	*tantus, -a, -um.*
soldier	*mīles, -itis* (m.).
some	*aliquī, -quae, -qua; nōnnullī, -ae, -a.*
son	*fīlius, -ī* (m.).
Sontiates	*Sontiātēs, -um* (m.).
soon	*mox.*
soon, as	
soon as	*simul atque.*
as soon as	
possible	*quam prīmum.*
spare	*parcō, 3, pepercī, parsūrus.*

speech	*ōrātiō, -ōnis* (f.).	**thanks**	*grātiae, -ārum* (f.).
speed	*celeritās, -ātis* (f.).	**give**	
spot	*locus, -ī* (m.).	**thanks**	*grātiās agō,* 3, *-ēgī, āctus.*
spring	*vēr, vēris* (n.).	**that** (conj.)	*ut;* (with comparatives)
state	*cīvitās, -ātis* (f.).		*quō;* (with verbs of
station	*cōnstituō,* 3, *-stitui, -stitūtus; pōnō,* 3, *posuī, positus; collocō,* 1.		fearing) *nē.*
		that not	*nē; ut nōn.*
		that (dem. pro.)	*is, ea, id; ille, -a, -ud.*
stay	*maneō,* 2, *mānsī, mānsūrus.*	**that** (rel. pro.)	*quī, quae, quod.*
stone	*lapis, -idis* (m.).	**their** (reflexive)	*suus, -a, -um;* (not reflexive) *eōrum.*
strong, be			
strong	*valeō,* 2, *-uī, -itūrus.*	**there**	*ibi.*
strongly		**there is**	*est.*
fortified	*commūnītus, -a, -um.*	**there was**	*erat.*
Suebi	*Suēbī, -ōrum* (m.).	**thing**	*rēs, reī* (f.).
suitable	*idōneus, -a, -um.*	**think**	*putō,* 1; *exīstimō,* 1;
summer	*aestās, -tātis* (f.).		*arbitror, -ārī, -ātus.*
sunset	*sōlis occāsus, -ūs* (m.).	**third**	*tertius, -a, -um.*
supply	*praebeō,* 2, *-buī, -bitus.*	**this**	*hīc, haec, hoc; is, ea, ıa.*
supply	*rēs frūmentāria, reī frūmentāriae; commeātus, -ūs* (m.).	**though**	*cum.*
		three	*trēs, tria.*
		throne	*rēgnum, -ī* (n.).
surrender	*dēdō,* 3, *dēdidī, dēditus.*	**through**	*per* (with acc.).
		throw	*iaciō,* 3, *-iēcī, iactus.*
surround	*circumdō,* 1, *-dedī, -datus.*	**throw**	
		around	*circumiciō,* 3, *-iēcī, -iectus.*
swiftly	*celeriter.*		
swiftness	*celeritās, -ātis* (f.).	**throw into**	
Syria	*Syria, -ae* (f.).	**confusion**	*perturbō,* 1.
		time	*tempus, -oris* (n.).
		time, for a	
T		**long time**	*diū.*
take	*capiō,* 3, *cēpī, captus*	**to**	*ad, in* (prepos. with acc.).
take by			
assault	*expugnō,* 1.	**top of**	
take posses-		**mountain**	*summus mōns, summī montis.*
sion of	*potior, -īrī, -ītus.*		
tell	*dīcō,* 3, *dīxī, dictus.*	**tower**	*turris, -is* (f.).
ten	*decem.*	**town**	*oppidum, -ī* (n.).
terrify	*perterreō,* 2, *-uī, -itus.*	**tribe**	*gēns, gentis* (f.).
territory	*fīnēs, -ium* (m.).	**troops**	*cōpiae, -ārum* (f.).
than	*quam.*	**try**	*cōnor, -ārī, -ātus.*
		two	*duo, duae, duo.*

U

undertake	*suscipiō, 3, -cēpī, -ceptus.*
until	*dum; priusquam.*
unwilling (be)	*nōlō, nōlle, nōluī.*
urge	*hortor, -ārī, -ātus; cohortor, 1.*
use	*ūtor, -ī, ūsus*

V

valor	*virtūs, -ūtis* (f.).
Varus	*Vārus, -ī* (m.).
Vatinius	*Vatīnius, -ī* (m.).
Veneti	*Venetī, -ōrum* (m.).
very (adj.)	*ipse, -a, -um.*
victory	*victōria, ae* (f.).
violence	*vīs, vīs* (f.).
Volusenus	*Volusēnus, -ī* (m.).

W

wage war	*bellum gerō, 3, gessī, gestus.*
wagon	*carrus, -ī* (m.).
wait for	*exspectō, 1.*
wall	*mūrus, -ī* (m.).
war	*bellum, -ī,* (n.).
weapon	*tēlum, -ī* (n.).
well	*bene.*
what (inter. adj.)	*quī, quae, quod.*
what (inter. pro.)	*quid.*

when	*ubi, cum.*
where	*ubi.*
which	*quī, quae, quod.*
while	*dum.*
who (inter. pro.)	*quis, quid.*
who (rel. pro.)	*quī, quae, quod.*
whole	*tōlus, -a, -um.*
why	*cūr.*
wide	*lātus, -a, -um.*
willing, be willing	*volō, velle, voluī.*
win	*reportō, 1; potior, īrī, ītus.*
wing	*cornū, -ūs* (n.).
winter	*hiems, hiemis* (f.).
winter quarters	*hīberna, -ōrum* (n.).
wish	*volō, velle, voluā.*
not wish	*nōlō, nōlle, nōluā.*
with	*cum* (with abl.).
withstand	*sustineō, 2, -uī, -lentus.*
witness	*testis, -is* (c.).
woods	*silva, -ae* (f.).
wound	*vulnerō, 1.*
write	*scrībō, 3, scrīpsī, scrīptus.*

Y

year	*annus,-ī* (m.).
yet	*tamen.*
yield	*cēdō, 3, cessī, cessūrus.*

ELEMENTARY LATIN MASTERY LIST
(Reprinted from the latest New York State Syllabus)

The definitions of the following words will be found in the alphabetical lists on pages 63-82.

a, ab	cohors	filia	itaque
accipio	conficio	filius	iter
acer	consilium	finis	iubeo
acies	constituo	finitimus	laboro
ad	contendo	flumen	liber (adj.)
adventus	contra	fortis	laudo
aestas	convenio	frater	legatus
ager	convoco	frumentum	legio
ago	copia	fuga	lex
agricola	corpus	fugio	liber (adj.)
altus	cum (prep.)	gero	libero
amicitia	cum (conj.)	gladius	littera
amicus (n. and adj.)	cupio	gloria	loco
amo	cur	habeo	locus
animus	de	hic (pro.)	longus
annus	debeo	hiems	lux
ante	defendo	homo	magnus
appello	deligo	hora	malus
aqua	dico	hostis	maneo
arbitror	dies	iacio	manus
arma	discedo	ibi	mare
audio	diu	idem	mater
auxilium	do	ille	medius
bellum	domus	impedimentum	memoria
bonus	duco	imperator	meus
brevis	dux	imperium	miles
capio	e, ex	impero	milia
caput	ego	impetus	miser
castra	eo (verb)	in	mitto
causa (n.)	eques	incipio	modus
celer	et	infero	moneo
celeritas	exercitus	intellego	mons
certus	existimo	inter	mors
circum	facilis	interficio	moveo
civis	facio	insula	multitudo
civitas	femina	ipse	multus
clarus	fero	is	munio
cognosco	fides	ita	murus

natio	poena	res	totus
natura	pono	respondeo	trado
nauta	pons	rex	trans
navigo	populus	rogo	tu
navis	porta	saepe	tum
ne	porto	salus	tuus
-ne	possum	scio	ubi
nomen	post	scribo	urbs
non	postquam	sed	ut
noster	potens	semper	utor
notus	praemium	senator	venio
novus	praesidium	senatus	verbum
nox	princeps	sequor	vester
nullus	pro	servo	via
numerus	proelium	servus	victoria
nunc	proficiscor	signum	vicus
nuntio	progredior	silva	video
nuntius	prohibeo	sine	vigilia
ob	prope	socius	villa
occupo	propero	soror	vinco
omnis	propter	specto	vir
oppidum	provincia	spero	virtus
oppugno	puella	spes	vita
paro	puer	studium	voco
pars	pugno	sub	volo (velle)
parvus	puto	sui	vulnero
passus	quantus	sum	vulnus
pater	-que	supero	
patria	qui	suus	
pauci	quis	tam	(Also cardinal and
pax	quod	tantus	ordinal numerals: 1-
pecunia	recipio	telum	10, 20, 100, 1,000;
per	redeo	tempto	Roman numerals: I,
periculum	regio	tempus	V, X, L, C, D, M;
persuadeo	regnum	teneo	names of places and
pervenio	rego	terra	persons commonly
pes	relinquo	timeo	met in reading)
peto	retineo	timor	

LATIN—Two Years

Monday, June 17, 1957—1:15 to 4:15 p.m., only

Answer all seven questions.

I. Translate the following passages into English:

[Crassus meets determined foes in the Vocates and the Tarusates.]

Armīs obsidibusque acceptīs, Crassus in fīnēs Vocātium et Tarusātium profectus est. Tum vērō barbarī commōtī sunt quod oppidum mūnītissimum paucīs diēbus expugnātum esse cognōverant. Itaque lēgātōs in omnēs partēs mittere, obsidēs inter sē dare, cōpiās parāre coepērunt. Mittuntur etiam ad cīvitātēs fīnitimās lēgātī et ibi auxilia ducēsque convocantur. Eōrum adventū magnā cum auctōritāte et magnā cum multitūdine hominum bellum gerere cōnantur.

Ducēs dēliguntur quī cum Q. Sertōriō multōs annōs fuerant et summam scientiam reī mīlitāris habēbant. Hī loca capere, castra mūnīre, et commeātibus nostrōs prohibēre cōnstituunt. Ubi Crassus eās rēs animadvertit et numerum hostium augērī vīdit, posterō diē pugnāre cōnstituit.

—Caesar, *Dē Bellō Gallicō*, III, 23 (adapted) [20]

[Caesar finds Pompey difficult to deal with.]

Cum Roscius ea quae Caesar iubēret cognōvisset, cum Lūciō Caesare Capuam pervenit ibique cōnsulēs Pompeiumque invenit. Eīs renūntiat quid Caesar iubeat. Postquam dē eīs rēbus inter sē collocūtī erant, Roscium cum litterīs ad Caesarem remittunt. In hīs Caesarī imperāvērunt ut in Galliam reverterētur, Arīminō excēderet exercitumque dīmitteret. Sī Caesar haec fēcisset, Pompeius dīxit sē in Hispāniam itūrum esse.

Haec condiciō inīqua erat. Cum Pompeius tempus ad colloquendum nōn daret, Caesar exīstimāvit nūllam spem pācis esse. Itaque Caesar ab Arīminō M. Antōnium cum cohortibus quīnque Arrētium mittit; ipse ibi cum duābus cohortibus manet.

—Caesar, *Dē Bellō Cīvīlī*, I, 10-11 (adapted) [20]

Arīminum—town in Umbria

II. Translate into Latin *four* of the following sentences: [16]
   a. After the province was captured, the general sent the so into winter quarters without delay.
   b. When the farmers had hastened out of the fields, they saw that their friends had been killed by the enemy.
   c. The king asked why the allies had not given grain to the troops that summer.
   d. The river was so wide that they were unable to cross it before night.
   e. The Helvetians had set out with their families to find new lands.
   f. Since the army was not fighting, Caesar decided to remain in the camp.

III. Do *not* write a translation of this passage; read it through carefully and then answer in English *each* of the questions below.

[Cassivellaunus, leader of the Britons, prevents Caesar from advancing farther than the Thames.]

Caesar cognitō Britannōrum cōnsiliō ad flūmen Tamesim in fīnēs Cassivellaunī exercitum dūxit. Hoc flūmen ūnō omnīnō locō pedibus aegrē trānsīrī potest. Eō cum vēnisset, animadvertit ad alteram flūminis rīpam magnās cōpiās hostium īnstrūctās esse. Caesar ā captīvīs rīpam mūnītam esse cognōvit. Caesar igitur equitātum praemīsit legiōnēsque statim subsequī iussit. Sed tantā celeritāte prōcessērunt ut hostēs impetum legiōnum atque equitum sustinēre nōn possent atque sē fugae mandārent.

Cassivellaunus, omnī dēpositā spē pugnae, ex viā paulum excēdēbat. In silvīs eius regiōnis mansit quod nostrōs eō iter factūrōs esse cognōverat. Cum Caesar equitātum mīsit quī agrōs vāstāret, Cassivellaunus mīlia circiter quattuor *essedāriōrum* ex silvīs ēmittēbat atque eōs hōc facere prohibēbat.

—Caesar, *Dē Bellō Gallicō,* V, 18-19 (adapted)

essedārius—charioteer

    a. When Caesar learned of the Britons' plans, what did he do? [1]
    b. What did Caesar notice near one bank of the river? [1]
    c. From whom did Caesar learn that the bank was fortified? [1]
    d. As a result, what two things did Caesar do? [2]
    e. What two effects did the speed of our soldiers have upon the enemy? [2]
    f. What did Cassivellaunus do in despair? [1]
    g. Why did he remain in the forests? [1]
    h. What did Cassivellaunus prevent Caesar's cavalry from doing? [1]

IV. On the line at the right of *each* sentence below, write the word or expression, chosen from those in the parentheses, that is grammatically correct. [6]

    a. Mīlitēs (ā duce, duce) convocātī sunt.   *a*..............
    b. Caesar (nāvēs, nāvibus) in hōc bellō ūsus est.   *b*..............
    c. In Galliā (multōs annōs, multīs annīs) mansērunt.   *c*..............
    d. Perīculum erat tantum ut populus (timēbat, timēret).   *d*..............
    e. Rogāvit ubi flūmen (erat, esset).   *e*..............
    f. Legiō auxilium (ferre, ut ferrent) nōn potuit.   *f*..............
    g. Labiēnus (virōs, virīs) ut castra servārent persuāsit.   *g*..............
    h. Nostrī (ā gladiīs, gladiīs) pugnābant.   *h*..............
    i. Caesar equitātum (auxiliō, auxilium) eī legiōnī mīsit.   *i*..............
    j. Virōs (convenīre, ut convenīrent) intellēxit.   *j*..............
    k. Lēgātum optimum (castra, castrīs) praefēcit.   *k*..............
    l. Equōs (in agrōs, in agrīs) relīquērunt.   *l*..............

V. Write *all* the specified forms, placing your answers on the lines at the right: [10]

    a-b. genitive singular of *ille fīlius*   *a-b*..............
    c-d. ablative singular of *omnis diēs*   *c-d*..............
    e-f. nominative plural of *bellum magnum*   *e-f*..............
    g-h. dative singular of *ūnus dux*   *g-h*..............
    i. superlative nominative singular masculine of *celer*   *i*..............

j.	the positive of the adverb from *altus*	*j*...............
k-l.	imperfect subjunctive third plural of *possum*	*k*...............
	arbitror	*l*...............
m.	pluperfect indicative third singular passive of *parō*	*m*...............
n-o.	present subjunctive first plural active of *moveō*	*n*...............
	audiō	*o*...............
p-q.	future active and passive participles of *interficiō*	*p*...............
		q...............
r-s-t.	the active infinitives of *ferō*	*r*...............
		s...............
		t...............

VI. For *each* sentence below, write in Column I a Latin word with which the italicized word is associated by derivation. Then, in Column II, write the *number* preceding the word or expression below each sentence that best expresses the meaning of the italicized word. [8]

	Column I	Column II
[Illustration: The explanation was made in a very *amicable* manner.	amicus	3
(1) angry (2) belligerent (3) friendly (4) verbose	....	........]

	Column I	Column II
a. The surgeon performed several *major* operations. (1) important (2) slight (3) inferior (4) novel	*a*...............	*a*.........
b. The typist worked with *facility*. (1) drudgery (2) enthusiasm (3) indifference (4) ease	*b*...............	*b*.........
c. *Subsequent* experiences proved that John was right. (1) Former (2) Later (3) Recent (4) Ordinary	*c*...............	*c*.........
d. It is *imperative* to finish this assignment. (1) impossible (2) useless (3) urgent (4) difficult	*d*...............	*d*.........
e. There was a *copious* supply of fruit at the exhibition. (1) a pretty (2) an insufficient (3) a varied (4) an abundant	*e*...............	*e*.........
f. No one wished to *relinquish* his ticket. (1) exchange (2) give up (3) keep (4) sign	*f*...............	*f*.........
g. The students were *perturbed* by the report. (1) pleased (2) pacified (3) upset (4) rewarded	*g*...............	*g*.........
h. He was *incensed* at the procedure. (1) angered (2) appalled (3) delighted (4) surprised	*h*...............	*h*.........

VII. On the line at the right of each of *ten* of the statements below, write the *number* preceding the word or expression that best completes the statement. [10]

a. If Caesar led his men out of camp at 5 a.m., this would be during the (1) *prīmā vigiliā* (2) *secundā vigiliā* (3) *tertiā vigiliā* (4) *quārtā vigiliā* a........

b. The officers who were usually in charge of the legions were the (1) *quaestōrēs* (2) *lēgātī* (3) *tribūnī* (4) *centuriōnēs* b........

c. Caesar's wife, Cornelia, was the daughter of the popular party leader, (1) Cinna (2) Sulla (3) Octavius (4) Antony c........

d. A noble Helvetian who formed a conspiracy was (1) Dumnorix (2) Diviciacus (3) Orgetorix (4) Ariovistus d........

e. An important Roman financier who aided Caesar was (1) Crassus (2) Pompey (3) Brutus (4) Cicero e........

f. When Caesar made his momentous decision to cross the Rubicon, he uttered these words: (1) *Vēnī, vīdī, vīcī.* (2) *Alea iacta est.* (3) *Divide et imperā.* (4) *Tempus fugit.* f........

g. In the Civil War Caesar was bitterly opposed by one of his former loyal lieutenants, (1) Quintus Cicero (2) Quintus Pedius (3) Titus Labienus (4) Gaius Volusenus g........

h. For outdoor living the Roman family particularly enjoyed the (1) *culīna* (2) *tablīnum* (3) *peristȳlium* (4) *triclīnium* h........

i. The standard of the Roman legion was called the (1) *aquila* (2) *testūdo* (3) *vexillum* (4) *tuba* i........

j. The planet Neptune is named after the (1) king of the gods (2) god of the sea (3) god of fire (4) king of the winds j........

k. The usual port from which the Romans sailed to Greece was (1) Ostia (2) Tarentum (3) Naples (4) Brundisium k........

l. For political purposes Caesar arranged the marriage of his daughter with (1) Pompey (2) Bibulus (3) Cassius (4) Catiline l........

m. The vanguard of the army was known as the (1) *agmen* (2) *prīmum agmen* (3) *novissimum agmen* (4) *aciēs* m........

n. To assure a good grape harvest, the Romans would pray to (1) Jupiter (2) Juno (3) Venus (4) Bacchus n........

LATIN—Two Years

Friday, January 17, 1958—1:15 to 4:15 p.m., only

Answer all seven questions.

1. Translate the following passages into English:

[Ambiorix, after destroying the camp of Sabinus and Cotta, hastens to attack Cicero's camp.]

Post hanc victōriam, Ambiorīx statim cum equitātū in Aduatucōs, fīnitimōs suōs, proficīscitur. Neque noctem neque diem intermittit peditēsque sē subsequī iubet. Aduatucīs incitātīs, posterō diē in Nerviōs pervenit. Dēmōnstrat magnam partem exercitūs interfectam esse et facile esse legiōnem Cicerōnis subitō opprimere. Hāc ōrātiōne Nerviīs persuādet.

Itaque Ambiorīx quam celerrimē nūntiōs ad cēterās nātiōnēs dīmīsit et sine morā omnēs ad hīberna Cicerōnis properant. Nostrī celeriter ad arma concurrunt, vāllum ascendunt. Ācriter eō diē pūgnātum est quod hostēs omnem spem in celeritāte pōnēbant et hāc victōriā sē victōrēs in perpetuum futūrōs esse crēdēbant.

Caesar, Dē Bellō Gallicō, V, 38-39 (adapted) [20]

[The Beginning of the Second Punic War.]

Maximum omnium bellōrum, quae gesta sunt, est bellum quod Carthāginiēnsēs cum populō Rōmānō gessērunt. Nam neque cīvitātēs fortiōrēs arma cēpērunt neque maiōrem potestātem habuērunt.

Dictum est etiam Hannibalem, puerum parvum, ā patre Hamilcare petere ut in Hispāniam dūcerētur. Cōnfirmāvit sē semper hostem populī Rōmānī futūrum esse. Postquam Sicilia Sardiniaque ā Rōmānīs victae sunt, Hannibal adulēscēns tantā cūrā permovēbātur ut in animō habēret bellum in Italiam inferre. Tum Hannibal in Hispāniam missus est atque mīlitēs exīstimābant patrem Hamilcarem ad sē redīsse quod ille auctōritāte et virtūte Hamilcarī similis esset. Paulō post exercitum trāns Alpēs contrā Rōmānōs dūxit. [20]

—Livy, XXI, 1-4 (adapted)

2. Translate into Latin *four* of the following sentences: [16]
   a. After aid had been given, all the soldiers defended the camp with great courage.
   b. The messenger said that the Gauls were attacking neighboring towns at that time.
   c. Caesar made a journey into that territory to wage war with the Germans.
   d. The slaves fled so swiftly that they could not be captured.
   e. When all the lieutenants had come together, the general told his plans to them.
   f. The king asked why horsemen were not following the army of the enemy.

3. Do *not* write a translation of this passage; read it through carefully and then answer in English *each* of the questions below. [10]

[Labienus resists an attack by Indutiomarus.]

Labiēnus, cum in castrīs mūnītissimīs sēsē tenēret, nihil timēbat. Interim cotīdiē cum omnī equitātū Indutiomarus ad castra ēius accēdēbat ut locum castrōrum cognōsceret. Equitēs omnēs tēla intrā vāllum coniciēbant. Labiēnus autem suōs intrā mūnītiōnem continēbat.

Labiēnus ūnā nocte equitēs omnium fīnitimārum cīvitātum in castra tantā dīligentiā arcessīvit ut ea rēs nōn Trēverīs nūntiārī posset. Interim Indutiomarus et equitēs ēius iterum ad castra accessērunt ut nostrōs ad pūgnam ēvocārent. Subitō Labiēnus ex duābus portīs omnem equitātum ēmittit; omnibus imperāvit ut ūnum peterent, Indutiomarum, et eum occīderent. Indutiomarus in flūmine captus interficitur et caput ēius refertur in castra.

—Caesar, *Dē Bellō Gallicō*, V, 57-58 (adapted)

a. Why did Labienus fear nothing?
b. What did Indutiomarus do every day?
c. Why did he do this?
d. What did his horsemen do?
e. How did Labienus react to these actions?
f. What reinforcements did Labienus receive?
g. What did Indutiomarus do again?
h. What action did Labienus take this time?
i. What particular orders did Labienus give?
j. What happened to Indutiomarus finally?

4. Write *all* the specified forms, placing your answers on the lines at the right: [10]

a-b.	dative singular of *aciēs ūna*	*a-b*.............
c-d.	genitive plural of *cīvis līber*	*c-d*.............
e-f.	ablative plural of *eadem manus*	*e-f*.............
g-h.	ablative singular of *flūmen omne*	*g-h*.............
i.	comparative masculine singular nominative of *magnus*	*i*.............
j.	superlative of *lātē*	*j*.............
k-l.	pluperfect indicative active and passive third singular of *pōno*	*k*............. *l*.............
m-n.	active participles of *vincō*	*m*............. *n*.............
o.	future active infinitive of *mūniō*	*o*.............
p-q.	imperfect subjunctive third plural of *possum cōnor*	*p*............. *q*.............
r-s.	present indicative active third plural of *faciō moneō*	*r*............. *s*.............
t.	present active imperative second plural of *agō*	*t*.............

5. On the line at the right of *each* sentence below, write the word or expression, chosen from those in the parentheses, that is grammatically correct. [6]

a. Vir (quī, quem) vīdistī est lēgātus.   *a*.............
b. Vōbīs (manēre, ut maneātis) persuādēbit.   *b*.............
c. Nōn omnēs Rōmānī erant (bonī, bonōs).   *c*.............
d. Tria mīlia (hominēs, hominum) iter faciunt.   *d*.............

e. Mīlitēs (prōcēdere, prōcēdēbant) dīxit.   e................
f. Locus (prō castrīs, castrīs) idōneus erat.   f................
g. Rogat cūr castra (oppugnārent, oppugnent).   g................
h. Helvētiī (patriae suae, ad patriam suam)
   remissī sunt.   h................
i. Nihil (dīxisse, dīcere) potuit.   i................
j. Eō annō (cōnsul, cōnsulem) factus est.   j................
k. Gallī (ā Caesare, Caesarī) vincendī sunt.   k................
l. Mīlitēs audācter (hostēs, hostibus) restitērunt. l................

6. For *each* sentence below, write in Column I a Latin word with which the italicized word is associated by derivation. Then, in Column II, write the *number* preceding the word or expression below each sentence that best expresses the meaning of the italicized word. [8]

[Illustration: The explanation was made in a very *amicable* manner.   *Column*   *Column*
                                                                           I   *II*
(1) angry (2) belligerent (3) friendly (4) verbose

                                                                           amicus   3
                                                                          ....]

                                                                          Column   *Column*
                                                                           I   *II*
a. The corporation had its *annual* meeting in
   May.
   (1) yearly (2) final (3) business (4) organiza-
   ational
b. He believes in *corporal* punishment.   a...............   a........
   (1) capital (2) bodily (3) severe (4) military b...............   b........
c. They saw an exhibit of *marine* life.
   (1) primitive (2) animal (3) sea (4) plant   c...............   c........
d. That country faced *insuperable* difficulties.
   (1) innumerable (2) unconquerable (3) inhu-
   man (4) unforeseen   d...............   d........
e. It is important to acquire good *diction*.
   (1) spelling   (2) reading ability   (3) writing
   habits (4) speaking habits   e...............   e........
f. He did not show *partiality* in his decision.
   (1) wisdom (2) favoritism (3) patriotism (4)
   authority   f...............   f........
g. They kept a *nocturnal* guard over the treasure.
   (1) heavy (2) military (3) secret (4) nightly   g...............   g........
h. He was fond of sending *petitions* to his senator.
   (1) notes (2) commands (3) requests (4) gifts   h...............   h........

7. On the line at the right of each of *ten* of the statements below, write the *number* preceding the word or expression that best completes the statement. [10]

a. Before being consul, a Roman usually held the of-
   fices of quaestor, aedile, and (1) praetor   (2)
   censor (3) pontifex maximus (4) tribune   a........
b. The religion of the Gauls was controlled by (1)
   vestals   (2) druids   (3) a pontifex maximus (4)
   soothsayers   b........
c. In his youth Caesar came under the suspicion of
   (1) Augustus (2) Hannibal (3) Pyrrhus (4) Sulla c........

d. The last king of the Romans was (1) Servius Tullius (2) Numa (3) Tarquinius Superbus (4) Romulus

d. ....

e. Caesar's camp was fortified by a *vāllum* and a (1) *fossa* (2) *testūdō* (3) *vīnea* (4) *ballista*

e. ....

f. A legendary character known for his strength was (1) Pan (2) Orpheus (3) Hercules (4) Oedipus

f. ....

g. A sorceress who aided Jason and later caused his downfall was (1) Ariadne (2) Medea (3) Penelope (4) Circe

g. ....

h. One of the most famous ancient ruins in Rome is (1) Hadrian's villa (2) Pompeii (3) the Colosseum (4) the Acropolis

h. ....

i. The Latin name for Paris was (1) *Bibracte* (2) *Alesia* (3) *Lutetia* (4) *Noviodūnum*

i. ....

j. In Book I of the Gallic Wars, Caesar describes his war with the (1) Sequanians (2) Aquitanians (3) Belgians (4) Helvetians

j. ....

k. The people most feared by the Roman soldiers were the (1) Graecī (2) Germānī (3) Aegyptiī (4) Britannī

k. ....

l. Caesar's greatest political rival was (1) Sulla (2) Alexander (3) Pompey (4) Cicero

l. ....

m. The words *vēnī, vīdī, vīcī,* were said by Caesar in connection with his (1) expedition to Egypt (2) victory at Pharsalus (3) campaign in Britain (4) victory over Pontus

m. ....

n. Among the murderers of Caesar was his friend (1) Brutus (2) Crassus (3) Marius (4) Labienus

n. ....

LATIN—Two Years

Monday, June 16, 1958—1:15 to 4:15 p.m., only

Answer all seven questions.

1. Translate the following passages into English:
[Caesar goes to Port Itius on the English Channel, where he prepares for the invasion of Britain.]

Hīs rēbus cōnstitūtīs, Caesar ad portum Itium cum legiōnibus pervēnit. Ibi cognōscit LX nāvēs tempestāte repulsās esse. Cum cursum tenēre nōn possent, eōdem ā quō profectae erant revertērunt. Caesar reliquās nāvēs ad nāvigandum parātās esse atque omnibus rēbus īnstrūctās esse invenit. Equitātus tōtīus Galliae numerō mīlium quattuor etiam convenit prīncipēsque omnibus ex cīvitātibus. Paucōs ex quibus quī amīcī erant relinquere in Galliā atque reliquōs sēcum dūcere cōnstituit. Id fēcit quod, cum ipse abesset, tumultum Galliae verēbātur.

Erat ūnā cum cēterīs Dumnorīx Haeduus. Cum tempestās esset idōnea, Caesar mīlitēs equitēsque ascendere in nāvēs iubet. At Dumnorīx cum equitibus Haeduōrum ā castrīs discēdere coepit. Hāc rē nūntiātā, statim Caesar eum interficī iubet.

—Caesar, *Dē Bellō Gallicō,* V, 5-7 (adapted)   [20]

[Caesar withdraws from the siege with Pompey following closely.]
Itaque Caesar sine ūllā morā, postquam virōs vulnerātōs servāvit, omnia impedīmenta prīmā nocte ex castrīs Apollōniam praemīsit. Ūna legiō praesidiō hīs missa est. Hōc factō, duās legiōnēs in castrīs retinuit atque eōdem itinere reliquās legiōnēs dē quartā vigiliā praemīsit. Parvō spatiō intermissō signum darī iussit ut eius exitus quam tardissimē cognōscerētur. Tum ipse statim ēgressus et novissimum agmen cōnsecūtus celeriter ex cōnspectū castrōrum discessit. Postquam Pompēius eius cōnsilium cognōvit, nōn morātus est sed suum exercitum ex castrīs ēdūxit atque equitātum quī novissimum agmen morārētur praemīsit. Pompēius, autem, eōs cōnsequī nōn potuit quod Caesar iam longē aberat.

—Caesar, *Dē Bellō Cīvīlī,* III, 75 (adapted)   [20]

2. Translate into Latin *four* of the following sentences: [16]
   a. The Romans heard that the enemy had led a large army into Gaul.
   b. After the town had been captured, many hostages were given to Caesar.
   c. The river was so deep that our men were unable to cross at that time.
   d. When the citizens had seen the danger, they decided to remain in the city a few days.
   e. The senate asked why the Helvetians were coming with their troops.
   f. The soldiers hastened to the province to obtain the aid of the allies.

3. Do *not* write a translation of this passage; read it through carefully and then answer in English *each* of the questions below.

[Darius with Datis and Artaphernes invades Greece.]
Dārīus, autem, rēx Persārum, cum ex Eurōpā in Asiam redīsset, clas-

sem nāvium centum comparāvit ut Graeciam in suam potestātem re-
dūceret. Eī Dātim et Artaphernem praefēcit. Hī virī celeriter urbem
Eretriam cēpērunt omnēsque cīvēs captōs in Asiam ad rēgem misērunt.
Tum ad Atticam accessērunt atque suās cōpiās in campum Marathōna
dēdūxērunt. Is abest ab oppidō mīlia passuum decem. Athēniēnsēs hōc
tumultū permōtī auxilium ā Spartānīs petīvērunt; domī nōminavērunt
decem praetōrēs, quī exercituī praeessent. In hīs erat Miltiadēs, quī eōs
hortābātur ut campum quam celerrimē caperent potius quam moenibus
sē dēfenderent.

—Nepos, *Dē Rēgibus,* I, 4 (adapted)

    a. Who was Darius and where had he been? [1]
    b. What did he do when he returned to Asia? Why? [2]
    c. What two things did Datis and Artaphernes accomplish? [2]
    d. What did they do when they reached Attica? [1]
    e. How far was this plain from the town? [1]
    f. Why did the Athenians ask the Spartans for aid? [1]
    g. What was the duty of the ten praetors? [1]
    h. What did Miltiades urge them to do? [1]

4. On the line at the right of *each* sentence below, write the word
or expression, chosen from those in the parentheses, that is grammatically correct. [6]

    a. Puer (ad vīllam, vīllae) properāvit.   *a*...............
    b. Rēx (ad Rōmānōs, Rōmānīs) grātus erat.   *b*...............
    c. In eō locō (ut manērent, manēre) potuērunt.   *c*...............
    d. Ubi est tuus pater, (Mārcus, Mārce)?   *d*...............
    e. Rogāvī cūr id (facerent, faciēbant).   *e*...............
    f. Omnēs mīlitēs (gladiōs, gladiīs) ūtēbantur.   *f*...............
    g. Dux (mīlitēs convenīre, ut mīlitēs convenīrent) dīxit. *g*...............
    h. Illa est fēmina (quae, quam) vīdī.   *h*...............
    i. Labiēnus (cīvēs, cīvibus) ut oppidum relinquerent
       persuāsit.   *i*...............
    j. Equus (cum celeritāte, celeritāte) cucurrit.   *j*...............
    k. Caesar (imperātor, imperātōrem) exercitūs factus est. *k*...............
    l. Labor (puellīs, ā puellīs) perfectus est.   *l*...............

5. Write *all* the specified forms, placing your answers on the lines
at the right: [10]

    a-b. genitive singular of *hic adventus*   *a-b*...............
    c-d. nominative plural of *ille fīlius*   *c-d*...............
    e-f. ablative singular of *vir fortis*   *e-f*...............
    g-h. accusative singular of *id vulnus*   *g-h*...............
    i-j. dative singular of *ūna rēs*   *i-j*...............
    k. superlative nominative singular masculine of *malus* *k*...............
    l. comparative of *longē*   *l*...............
    m-n. pluperfect subjunctive active third plural of *cōnficiō* *m*...............
                              doceō   *n*...............
    o-p. perfect indicative third singular of *arbitror*   *o*...............
                              possum *p*...............
    q-r. future indicative active first plural of *rogō*   *q*...............
                                regō   *r*...............
    s. present participle of *laudō*   *s*...............
    t. perfect passive infinitive of *vincō*   *t*...............

6. For *each* sentence below, write in Column I a Latin word with which the italicized word is associated by derivation. Then, in Column II, write the *number* preceding the word or expression below each sentence that best expresses the meaning of the italicized word. [8]

	Column I	Column II
[Illustration: The explanation was made in a very *amicable* manner. (1) angry (2) belligerent (3) friendly (4) verbose	amicus	3 ....]

	Column I	Column II
a. The *interrogation* lasted for many hours. (1) interruption (2) audition (3) meeting (4) questioning		
b. We respect men of *vision*. (1) wealth (2) courage (3) foresight (4) ambition	a.................	a........
c. There was no *intervention* at this time. (1) interference (2) threat (3) proposal (4) rejoicing	b.................	b........
d. Illness *retarded* his progress. (1) stopped (2) delayed (3) changed (4) prevented	c.................	c........
e. They did not *contradict* the statement. (1) confirm (2) alter (3) endorse (4) deny	d.................	d........
f. He is a man of great *integrity*. (1) cleverness (2) honesty (3) generosity (4) distinction	e.................	e........
g. He received *vital* information. (1) essential (2) unimportant (3) interesting (4) perplexing	f.................	f........
h. The child's *intelligence* is remarkable. (1) native ability (2) calmness (3) self-confidence (4) loyalty	g.................	g........
	h.................	h........

7. On the line at the right of each of *ten* of the statements below, write the *number* preceding the word or expression that best completes the statement. [10]

a. "These are my jewels," responded Cornelia, referring to her (1) sons (2) daughters (3) slaves (4) rings .... a........

b. The queen of the lower world was (1) Circe (2) Penelope (3) Proserpina (4) Ceres .... b........

c. In Gaul the ruling class consisted of men known as (1) *rēgēs* (2) *praetōrēs* (3) *cōnsulēs* (4) *Druidēs* .... c........

d. The chieftain who annoyed Caesar with his warchariots was (1) Mithridates (2) Vercingetorix (3) Hannibal (4) Cassivellaunus .... d........

e. In offensive warfare Caesar relied primarily on (1) caution (2) speed (3) delay (4) rashness .... e........

f. The business and financial section of Rome was the (1) Campus Martius (2) Forum (3) Palatine (4) Circus Maximus .... f........

g. The Rubicon River formed the boundary between Italy and (1) *Gallia Ulterior* (2) *Helvētia* (3) *Germānia* (4) *Gallia Citerior*

g........

h. A governor of a Roman province usually held the title of (1) proconsul (2) censor (3) quaestor (4) aedile

h........

i. The arrogant German whom Caesar defeated was (1) Galba (2) Ariovistus (3) Orgetorix (4) Diviciacus

i........

j. In 59 B.C. Caesar became consul along with (1) Pompey (2) Crassus (3) Bibulus (4) Catiline

j........

k. The seaport of the city of Rome was (1) Ostia (2) Brundisium (3) Naples (4) Ariminum

k........

l. Caesar left Rome in his youth because he feared (1) Cinna (2) Marius (3) Octavius (4) Sulla

l........

m. The number of cohorts in a Roman legion was (1) 10 (2) 15 (3) 25 (4) 30

m........

n. The sea which the Romans referred to as *Mare Nostrum* was the (1) Aegean (2) Black (3) Mediterranean (4) Caspian

n........

o. The forced march which Caesar employed in emergencies was known as (1) *magnum iter* (2) *longum iter* (3) *breve iter* (4) *optimum iter*

o........

Latin—Two Years

Monday, January 19, 1959—1:15 to 4:15 p.m., only

Answer all seven questions.

1. Translate the following passages into English:

[Hannibal uses strategy against King Eumenes.]

Hannibal, cum magnum numerum nāvium nōn habēret, Eumenem, rēgem *Pergamēnōrum,* insidiīs superāre cōnstituit. Mīlitibus imperāvit igitur ut multās viyās serpentēs in vāsa *fīctilia* colligerent et in nāvibus suīs ea pōnerent. Pollicitus est sē dēmōnstrātūrum esse in quā nāve rēx nāvigāret. Hanc nāvem sōlam ē tōtā classe eōs oppugnāre iussit. Tum Hannibal, cōnfirmāns sē pācem rogāre, lēgātum mīsit quī ad Eumenem epistulam ferret. Hōc modō cognōvit in quā nāve rēx esset. Proeliō commissō, Eumenēs impetum sustinēre nōn potuit et nāve suā effūgit. Sociī eius tamen vehementer restitērunt. Tum Hannibalis mīlitēs serpentēs in reliquās nāvēs iacere coepērunt. Nautae, serpentibus vīvīs perterritī, ad castra sua fūgērunt.

—Nepos, *Hannibal* (adapted)   [20]

Pergamēnōrum—Pergamenians (inhabitants of Pergamum, a city in Asia Minor)
fīctilia—earthen

[Caesar crosses the Cevennes Mountains and gathers troops.]

Etsī mōns Cevenna, quī Arvernōs ab Helviīs dīvidit, hōc tempore annī altissimā *nive,* iter impediēbat, tamen Caesar nīvem removet et viae summō labōre mīlitum apertae sunt. Ad fīnēs Arvernōrum pervēnit et hōs subitō oppressit, etsī sē mūnītōs esse monte Cevennā exīstimābant. Caesar equitibus imperat ut agrōs vāstent quam lātissimē et maximum terrōrem hostibus inferant. Celeriter haec fāma ad Vercingetorīgem fertur. Omnēs perterritī Arvernī eum circumveniunt et implōrant ut eōs dēfendat. Quōrum verbīs incitātus, castra ex Biturīgibus movet et in Arvernōs proficīscitur. Caesar autem in hīs locīs paucōs diēs morātus, ab exercitū discēdit et magnīs itineribus *Viennam* pervenit. Ibi equitātum obtinet.

—Caesar, *Dē Bellō Gallicō* VII, 8-9 (adapted)   [20]

nix, nivis—snow
Vienna—a town on the Rhone

2. Translate into Latin *four* of the following sentences: [16]
   a. Caesar fortified the camp immediately since he feared an attack that night.
   b. After the soldiers had been led out, the general praised their courage.
   c. The Germans were not able to understand why our men had suddenly departed.
   d. The leader sent scouts through the forest in order that he might learn the route.
   e. The water was so deep that the foot soldiers went across by boats.

f. For many days the Romans did not hear that their ambassadors had been seized.

3. Do *not* write a translation of the following passage; read it through carefully and then answer in English *each* of the questions below. [Use everything in the text that will make your answers clear and complete.] [10]

[After the battle of Dyrrachium the citizens of Gomphi consider deserting to Pompey.]

Caesar cum exercitū Gomphōs pervēnit, quod est oppidum prīmum Thessaliae venientibus ab Ēpīrō. Incolae huius oppidī paucīs ante mēnsibus ad Caesarem lēgātōs mīserant ut suīs omnibus commeātibus uterētur praesidiumque ab eō mīlitum petīverant. Sed fāmam iam audīverant dē proeliō Dyrrachīnō. Itaque Androsthenēs, praetor Thessaliae, cum sē esse socium Caesaris in rēbus adversīs nōllet, omnem ex agrīs multitūdinem servōrum ac līberōrum in oppidum coēgit. Tum portās clausit et ad Pompeium nūntiōs mīsit ut ad sē auxilium ferret.

—Caesar, *Dē Bellō Cīvīlī*, III, 80 (adapted)

a. Who accompanied Caesar to Gomphi?
b. Where was Gomphi located for travelers from Epirus?
c. What had the people of Gomphi done a few months previously?
d. What offer had they made to Caesar?
e. What favor had they asked?
f. What report had reached them?
g. Who was Androsthenes?
h. In what situation was he unwilling to be involved?
i. What two classes of men did he collect?
j. What did he request Pompey to do?

4. Write *all* the specified forms, placing your answers on the lines at the right. [10]

a-b.	genitive singular of *decima legiō*	*a-b*...............
c-d.	ablative singular of *gravis impetus*	*c-d*...............
e-f.	accusative singular of *eadem fēmina*	*e-f*...............
g-h.	genitive plural of *magnus portus*	*g-h*...............
i.	superlative masculine singular nominative of *audāx*	*i*...............
j.	positive degree of the adverb from *brevis*	*j*...............
k-l.	future indicative active third singular of *doceō ēripiō*	*k*............... *l*...............
m-n.	active participles of *gerō*	*m-n*...............
o-p.	imperfect subjunctive third plural of *ēō moror*	*o*............... *p*...............
q-r.	perfect indicative active third plural of *agō removeō*	*q*............... *r*...............
s-t.	present passive infinitive of *habeō mittō*	*s*............... *t*...............

5. On the line at the right of *each* sentence below, write the word or expression, chosen from those in the parentheses, that is grammatically correct: [6]

a. (Magnō clāmōre, Magnō cum clāmōre) Gallōs terruērunt.

                a.................

b. Cōnsilia (Labiēnō, ā Labiēnō) capienda sunt.   b.................

c. Hostēs (discesserant, discessisse) putāvērunt.   c.................

d. Cum fortis (esset, erat), in mediōs hostēs prōcessit.

                d.................

e. Castrīs eōrum incēnsīs, victōria erit (nobīs, ad nōs).

f. Intellegimus quid (agerēs, agās).   e.................

g. Domum revertam (ut mātrem videam, mātrem vidēre).   f.................

h. Frūmentum (ad eōs, eīs) nōn dēerat.   g.................

i. Ab senātū (amīcus, amīcum) appellātus est.   h.................

j. Ibi (duābus hōrīs, duās hōrās) manēbunt.   i.................

k. Auxilium (Rōmānīs, ad Rōmānōs) nōn dedimus.   j.................

l. Rēgīna (quī, quae) vēnit pecuniam tulit.   k.................

                l.................

6. For *each* sentence below, write in column I a Latin word with which the italicized word is associated by derivation. Then in column II, write the *number* preceding the word or expression below each sentence that best expresses the meaning of the italicized word.   [8]

	Column I	Column II
[Illustration: The explanation was made in a very *amicable* manner. (1)angry (2)belligerent (3)friendly (4)verbose	amicus	3
	....	........]
	Column I	Column II

a. The speaker attempted in vain to *support* his statement.
(1)withdraw   (2)uphold   (3)deny   (4)improve

          a.................   a........

b. Her *salutation* was gracious and sincere.
(1)greeting   (2)message   (3)compliment   (4)presentation

          b.................   b........

c. At this hour the *solarium* is usually empty.
(1)attic study   (2)swimming pool   (3)rumpus room   (4)sun parlor

          c.................   c........

d. This student did not *participate* in athletics.
(1)lead   (2)take part   (3)succeed   (4)continue

          d.................   d........

e. Our difficulties in planning the picnic were *insuperable*.
(1)challenging (2)discouraging (3)unending   (4)unconquerable

          e.................   e........

f. Because of the sandstorm we could not *ventilate* the room.
(1)air   (2)seal   (3)clean   (4)arrange

          f.................   f........

g. *Silvan* scenes always appeal to him.
  (1) Misty   (2) Romantic   (3) Homely
  (4) Forest

g................   g........

h. The judge's voice had a note of *finality*.
  (1) elegance   (2) loftiness   (3) decisiveness
  (4) scorn

h................   h........

7. On the line at the right of each of *ten* of the statements below, write the *number* preceding the word or expression that best completes the statement. [10]

a. Caesar's final victory over Pompey himself occurred at (1) Rome (2) Pharsalus (3) Thapsus (4) Brundisium

a........

b. The century, nominally 100 men, generally consisted of (1) 120 (2) 80 (3) 60 (4) 40

b........

c. The standard of the Roman legion was the (1) *vēxillum* (2) *aquila* (3) *būcina* (4) *trāgula*

c........

d. The German leader whom Caesar forced to return across the Rhine was (1) Sabinus (2) Ariovistus (3) Galba (4) Cassivellaunus

d........

ɛ. To educate their children the Romans often employed teachers from (1) Egypt (2) Spain (3) Greece (4) Britain

e........

. A Roman kitchen was called (1) *ātrium* (2) *peristȳlum* (3) *vestibulum* (4) *culīna*

f........

g. The god to whom the Romans gave credit for success in war was (1) Jupiter (2) Apollo (3) Mercury (4) Mars

g........

h. Caesar was killed because he (1) oppressed the poor (2) was becoming dangerously powerful (3) changed the calendar (4) made too many grants of land to his veterans

h........

i. A Roman officer charged with supplying food and clothing to soldiers was known as a (1) *mercātor* (2) *praetor* (3) *quaestor* (4) *tribūnus*

i........

ɿ. The Roman legion was composed of (1) Roman citizens (2) conquered barbarians (3) hired troops (4) freed men

j........

k. Most famous of the Seven Hills of Rome for beautiful residences was the (1) Palatine (2) Esquiline (3) Capitoline (4) Quirinal

k........

l. A famous Roman road builder was (1) Lucius Lucullus (2) Quintus Hortensius (3) Appius Claudius (4) Marcus Cato

l........

m. A Roman held the office of praetor (1) for one year (2) for two years (3) until elected consul (4) for life

m........

ɴ. By refusing to divorce his wife, Caesar aroused the the hatred of (1) Pompey (2) Cinna (3) Crassus (4) Sulla

n........

LATIN—Two Years

Answer all seven questions.

1. Translate the following passages into English:

[Alexander and his horse, Bucephalus]

Equus Alexandrī rēgis Bucephalas nōmine fuit. Dē hōc equō hae fabulae sunt nōtae. Ubi *ornātus* erat et armātus ad proelium, nēmō eum ascendere poterat, nisi rēx. Cum Alexander in Bellō *Indicō* rēs fortēs faceret, in aciem hostium cum Bucephalā īvit, sed salūtem suam nōn satis prōvīdit. Cōniectīs undique tēlis, equus in capite et in corpore graviter vulnerātus est. Antequam mortuus est, tamen ex mediīs hostibus rēgem magnā cum celeritāte statim portāvit, atque ubi eum extrā tēla extulit, in terrā *cēcidit* et ē vītā excessit. Tum Alexander, bellō cōnfectō, oppidum in eīsdem locīs posuit atque ob honōrem equī id Bucephalos appellātum est.

—Aulus Gellius, *Noctēs Atticae* (adapted) [20]

> *ornātus*—equipped
> *Indicō*—Indian
> *cēcidit*—from *cadō*, fall

[Deceived by the stratagem of Sabinus, the enemy attacked his camp.]

Sabīnus, ut fāmam timōris suī cōnfirmāret, quendam Gallum dēlēgit ex eīs quōs auxilī causā sēcum habēbat. Huic magnīs praemiīs persuādet ut ad hostēs trānseat et quid fierī velit docet. Ubi Gallus prō *perfugā* ad eōs vēnit, timōrem Rōmānōrum nūntiat. Dēmōnstrat Caesarem ipsum ā Venetīs premī et dīcit proximā nocte Sabīnum ex castrīs exercitum ēductūrum esse ut ad Caesarem auxilium ferat. Hōc audītō, omnēs conclāmant hanc occāsiōnem victōriae nōn āmittendam esse et sē ad castra Sabīnī īre dēbēre. Multae rēs ad hoc cōnsilium Gallōs hortābantur, maximē quod hominēs facile crēdunt id quod volunt. Hīs rēbus adductī arma capiunt et ad castra contendunt.

—Caesar, *Dē Bellō Gallicō*, III, 18 (adapted) [20]

> *perfugā*—deserter

2. Translate into Latin *four* of the following sentences: [16]

    a. When Caesar had hastened into Gaul with his legions, he attacked the enemy.

    b. The messenger knew that the soldiers were marching through the territory of the enemy.

    c. The attack was so great that the Helvetians were not able to hold the town.

    d. The Romans made a bridge across the river in order to defend the province.

    e. After the city had been captured, the general led all the troops back into camp.

    f. The allies asked why Caesar was not sending aid on that day.

3. Do *not* write a translation of this passage; read it through carefully and then answer in English *each* of the questions below. [10]

[Hamilcar makes peace with the Romans.]

Hamilcar, adulēscēns Carthāginiēnsis, prīmō Punicō bellō in Sīciliā exercituī praeesse coepit. Ante ēius adventum et marī et terrā rēs Carthāginiēnsium male gerēbantur. Ubi tamen adfuit saepe oppugnāvit semperque superior discessit. Interim Carthāginiēnsēs, classe ā Rōmānīs superātā, statuērunt bellī fīnem facere eamque rem iūdiciō Hamilcaris permīsērunt. Ille, etsī bellum gerere studēbat, tamen pācem faciendam esse putāvit quod patriam oppressam diūtius calamitātēs bellī ferre nōn posse intellegēbat. Sed Carthāginiēnsēs, sī eīs tempus esset ad rēs *reficiendās*, Rōmānōs armīs secūtī virtūte vincerent. Hōc cōnsiliō pācem effēcit.

—Nepos, *Hamilcar* I (adapted)

reficiendās—from *reficiō*, restore

    a. Who was Hamilcar?
    b. What was his responsibility in the first Punic War?
    c. In what situation were the Carthaginians before his arrival?
    d. How did he conduct himself against the enemy?
    e. What happened to the Carthaginian fleet?
    f. Name one thing which the Carthaginians decided to do.
    g. What did Hamilcar actually wish to do?
    h. Nevertheless, what better course of action did he believe should be pursued?
    i. Why did he think that?
    j. What did Hamilcar think his people might do if given time?

4. On the line at the right of *each* sentence below, write the word or expression, chosen from those in the parentheses, that is grammatically correct. [6]

    a. Caesar iter multa mīlia (passūs, passuum) faciēbat.   *a*.................
    b. Rōmānī (ad Gallōs, Gallīs) fīnitimī erant.   *b*.................
    c. Monuit (nē, ut nōn) fugerent.   *c*.................
    d. Quīnque (diēbus, diēs) mānsērunt.   *d*.................
    e. (Hieme, In hieme) Rōmānī nōn pugnābant.   *e*.................
    f. Nūntius (ab hostibus, hostibus) interfectus est.   *f*.................
    g. Dux exīstimāvit mīlitēs fortiter (pugnāvisse, pugnāvissent).   *g*.................
    h. Servus fūgerat nē (interficiātur, interficerētur).   *h*.................
    i. Nōs omnēs (labōrāre, ut labōrēmus) dēbēmus.   *i*.................
    j. Imperātor (mīlitibus, mīlitēs) ut impetum facerent imperāvit.   *j*.................
    k. Servum (quī, quem) discēdēbat vīdī.   *k*.................
    l. Locus (ad castra, castrīs) idōneus est.   *l*.................

5. Write *all* the specified forms, placing your answers on the lines at the right: [10]

    a-b. accusative plural of *ea manus*   *a-b*.................
    c-d. genitive singular of *īdem vir*   *c-d*.................
    e-f. ablative singular of *prīma aciēs*   *e-f*.................
    g-h. dative and accusative singular of *ego*   *g*.................
                                      h.................
    i. comparative nominative singular masculine of *magnus*   *i*.................

j. superlative of *breviter*   j..............
k-l. future active indicative third plural of *pōnō*   k..............
        timeō   l..............
m-n. perfect indicative third singular of *cōnor*   m..............
        possum   n..............
o-p. pluperfect subjunctive active and passive third sin-   o..............
        gular of *capiō*   p..............
q-r. present active indicative and subjunctive third plur-
        al of *ferō*   q..............
                                                                                  r..............
s. future active infinitive of *dīcō*   s..............
t. future passive participle of *mūniō*   t..............

6. For *each* sentence below, write in Column I a Latin word with which the italicized word is associated by derivation. Then, in column II, write the *number* preceding the word or expression below each sentence that best expresses the meaning of the italicized word. [8]

	Column I	Column II

[Illustration: The explanation was made in a very *amicable* manner.
(1) angry (2) belligerent (3) friendly (4) verbose

	Column I	Column II
	amicus	3
	....	.........]

	Column I	Column II

a. The police were unable to *pacify* the rioting youths.
   (1) intimidate   (2) arrest   (3) disperse   (4) calm
   a..............   a..........

b. He considered those difficulties to be *insuperable.*
   (1) unavoidable   (2) insurmountable   (3) unbearable   (4) unimportant
   b..............   b..........

c. War is a *potential* menace in our time.
   (1) dangerous   (2) serious   (3) possible   (4) continuous
   c..............   c..........

d. The new roads were intended to *facilitate* the movement of traffic.
   (1) make easier   (2) control   (3) reroute   (4) reduce
   d..............   d..........

e. The Gracchi were interested in *agrarian* reforms.
   (1) election   (2) religion   (3) land   (4) tax
   e..............   e..........

f. *Intermittent* sounds came from the loudspeaker.
   (1) Continuous   (2) Periodic   (3) Raucous   (4) Muffled
   f..............   f..........

g. *Linguistic* studies are considered increasingly important.
   (1) Scholarly   (2) Scientific   (3) Language   (4) Advanced
   g..............   g..........

h. We should not *minimize* the danger from
radioactivity.
(1) underestimate   (2) ignore   (3) despair of
(4) exaggerate   *h*................ *h*.........

7. On the line at the right of each of *ten* of the statements below,
write the *number* preceding the word or expression that best completes
the statement. [10]

a. Caesar belonged to the social group called   (1) *pop-
ulārēs*   (2) *optimātēs*   (3) *equitēs*   (4) *lībertīnī*   *a*........

b. As a youth, Caesar went to Rhodes to study   (1)
history   (2) oratory   (3) art   (4) military science   *b*........

c. While praetor, Caesar served as a   (1) judge   (2)
lawyer   (3) treasurer   (4) priest   *c*.......

d. To strengthen his alliance with Pompey, Caesar
(1) gave him his daughter, Julia, in marriage   (2)
offered him wealth   (3) put a fleet at his disposal
(4) made him a senator   *d*.......

e. In his proconsulship, Caesar fought many campaigns
in the conquest of   (1) Greece   (2) Gaul   (3)
Egypt   (4) Asia Minor   *e*........

f. Caesar impressed the Germans by his   (1) oratory
(2) capture of the pirates   (3) bridging of the Rhine
(4) linguistic ability   *f*........

g. Caesar's most trusted lieutenant in charge of the
tenth legion was   (1) Labienus   (2) Antony   (3)
Considius   (4) Diviciacus   *g*........

h. One of the non-military achievements of Caesar was
(1) abolition of slavery   (2) establishment of free
public education   (3) building of the Colosseum
(4) revision of the calendar   *h*........

i. The last office that Caesar held was that of   (1) tribune   (2) censor   (3) dictator   (4) aedile   *i*........

j. An adventurer who gained the Golden Fleece was
(1) Hercules   (2) Perseus   (3) Theseus   (4) Jason   *j*........

k. The Romans enjoyed watching races in the   (1) Circus Maximus   (2) Comitium   (3) Basilica Julia
(4) Roman Forum   *k*.......

l. For its culture, Rome was most indebted to   (1)
(1) Egypt   (2) Britain   (3) Greece   (4) Syria   *l*........

m. A Roman camp was fortified by a *vāllum* and a
(1) *catapulta*   (2) *fossa*   (3) *galea*   (4) *vexillum*   *m*.......

n. The home of all the gods was Mount   (1) Vesuvius
(2) Parnassus   (3) Aetna   (4) Olympus   *n*........

LATIN—Two Years

Monday, June 20, 1960—1:15 to 4:15 p.m., only

Answer all seven questions.

1. Translate the following passages into English:

[The enemy attacks the Roman camp with great violence.]

Cum Rōmānī castra pōnerent, hostēs ex omnibus partibus, signō datō, dēscendere coepērunt et tēla in vāllum iaciēbant. Prīmō nostrī fortiter pugnābant neque frūstrā ullum tēlum mittēbant. Sī pars quaedam castrōrum premī vidēbātur, eō contendēbant et auxilium ferēbant. Cum, autem, hostēs *dēfessī* excēdēbant, aliī quī in proeliō nōn fuerant appropinquābant. Nōn modō Rōmānī *dēfessī* nōn ex pugnā excessērunt, sed etiam vulnerātī ex eō locō ubi steterant excēdere nōn poterant, quod nostrī numerō paucī erant. Itaque P. Sextius Baculus, centuriō Rōmānus, et G. Volusēnus ad Galbam concurrunt atque unam spem salūtis esse celeriter exīre docent. Hoc maximā difficultāte faciunt.

—Caesar, *Dē Bellō Gallicō,* III, 4-5 (adapted) [20]

dēfessī—weary

[The Gauls try to complete the destruction of Rome.]

Gallī, cum inter incendia et ruīnās urbis nihil praeter armātōs hostēs vidērent, impetum facere in *arcem* cōnstituunt. Prīmā lūce, omnis multitūdō in forum dūcitur. Ab eō locō Gallī ad montem Capitōlīnum magnō clāmōre prōgrediuntur. Adventum eōrum Rōmānī nōn timent sed praesidiīs firmīs ad omnēs aditūs contendunt ubi hostēs ascendere possunt. Manent in mediō monte atque ex locō superiōre impetum faciunt et Gallōs tantā caede dēpellunt ut numquam posteā Gallī hoc genus pugnae temptāverint.

Dēspērātā victōriā, Gallī *arcem* obsidēre parant sed frūmentum nōn habent. Igitur pars exercitūs per fīnitimōs populōs ad agrōs vāstandōs missa est.

—Livy, *Ab Urbe Conditā,* V, 43 (adapted) [20]

arx, arcis—citadel

2. Translate into Latin *four* of the following sentences: [16]
   a. The soldiers hastened through the province in order to fortify that town.
   b. The lieutenant was not able to learn what the troops of the enemy were doing in this place.
   c. The general thought that the Romans had sailed from the harbor of the Gauls because of fear.
   d. The horsemen were so swift that they arrived at the camp on the next day.
   e. After the cavalry had been sent ahead, Caesar ordered all the legions to advance.
   f. When the foot soldiers had fled, Caesar followed them across the river with great speed.

3. Do *not* write a translation of this passage; read it through carefully several times and then answer in complete English sentences *each*

of the questions below. Use everything in the text that will make your answers clear and complete.

[The Sotiates attack Crassus on the march.]

P. Crassus, cum in Aquītāniam vēnisset, intellēxit in eīs locīs bellum magnā cum dīligentiā gerendum esse. Itaque rē frūmentāriā prōvīsā, virīs fortibus ēvocātīs, in Sotiātum fīnēs exercitum dūxit.

Cuius adventū cognitō, Sotiātēs in itinere agmen nostrum aggressī sunt; tum equitātū suō pulsō, mīlitēs sē ostendērunt et nostrōs reppulērunt. Pugnātum est diū atque acriter cum Sotiātēs sē suā virtūte lībertātem tōtīus Aquītāniae dēfendere putārent. Nostrī, autem, quid sine imperātōre et sine reliquīs legiōnibus efficere possent dēmōnstrāre cupīvērunt. Hostēs, tandem, vulneribus cōnfectī, terga vertērunt. Quōrum magnō numerō interfectō, Crassus ex itinere oppidum Sotiātum oppugnāvit.

—Caesar, *Dē Bellō Gallicō*, III, 20-21 (adapted)

a. What did P. Crassus realize ought to be done?   [1]
b. What two preparations did he make before leading the army into the territory of the Sotiates?   [2]
c. What did the Sotiates do upon his arrival?   [1]
d. What happened to the cavalry of the Sotiates?   [1]
e. What two things did the enemy's soldiers then do?   [1]
f. Why did the Sotiates fight so fiercely?   [1]
g. What did the Roman soldiers wish to show?   [1]
h. What did the enemy do at last?   [1]
i. What did Crassus do after killing a large number of the enemy?   [1]

4. On the line at the right of *each* sentence below, write the *number* preceding the word or expression that makes the sentence grammatically correct.   [6]

a. Litterae   [(1)ā senātōre   (2)senātōrem   (3)senātōre   (4)senātōrēs]   missae sunt.   *a*........

b. Prīnceps petīvit cūr aciēs nōn instrūcta   (1)erant   (2)esset   (3)esse   (4)erat   *b*........

c. Dux praemium   [(1)equite   (2)ad equitem   (3)ad equitēs   (4)equitī]   dedit.   *c*........

d. Imperātor legiōnem   [(1)ut pugnet   (2)pugnāre   (3)ut pugnāret   (4)quī pugnāret]   iūssit.   *d*........

e. Marcus   [(1)tribūnī   (2)tribūnum   (3)tribūnō   (4)tribūnus]   factus est.   *e*........

f. Properā,   [(1)amīcō   (2)amīcus   (3)amīce   (4)amīcī],   ad auxilium ferendum.   *f*........

g. Duo mīlia   [(1)mīlitum   (2)ex mīlitibus   (3)mīlitēs   (4)mīlitis]   prōgressī sunt.   *g*........

h. Vir auxiliō   [(1)sociī   (2)ad socium   (3)sociō   (4)prō sociō]   erat.   *h*........

i. Lēgātus   [(1)rēgum   (2)rēgī   (3)rēgem   (4)rēge]   persuādēre nōn poterat.   *i*........

j. Gallī   [(1)tēlōrum magnōrum   (2)tēlīs magnīs   (3)tēla magna   (4)tēlum magnum]   ūtuntur.   *j*........

    k. Exercitus   [(1)prō multīs diēbus   (2)in multōs
      diēs   (3)multōs diēs   (4)ad multōs diēs]   fugiē-
      bat.   *k*........

    l. Germānī   [(1)familiam   (2)familiīs   (3)familiās
      (4)cum familiīs]   vēnērunt.   *l*........

5. Write *all* the specified forms, placing your answers on the lines
at the right: [10]

  a-b. accusative plural of *fīlius miser*   *a-b*...............
  c-d. accusative singular of *id flūmen*   *c-d*...............
  e-f. ablative singular of *lēx omnis*   *e-f*...............
  g-h. genitive singular of *spēs ipsa*   *g-h*...............
    i. dative singular of *tū*   *i*...............
  j-k. comparative and superlative of *graviter*   *j*...............
                                                                k...............
    l. perfect active indicative third plural of *accipiō*   *l*...............
  m. pluperfect passive indicative third singular of *laudō*   *m*...............
  n. future indicative active first plural of *moveō*   *n*...............
  o. present subjunctive active third singular of *sciō*   *o*...............
  p. imperfect subjunctive third plural of *eō*   *p*...............
  q-r. perfect infinitives, active and passive, of *scrībō*   *q*...............
                                                                r...............
    s. future active participle of *proficīscor*   *s*...............
    t. present active imperative second plural of *servō*   *t*...............

6. For *each* sentence below, write in column I a Latin word with
which the italicized word is associated by derivation. Then, in column
II, write the *number* preceding the word or expression below each sentence that best expresses the meaning of the italicized word.   [8]

                                                       Column   *Column*
                                                         I   *II*

  [Illustration: The explanation was made in a very
               amicable manner.
     (1)angry   (2)belligerent   (3)friendly   (4)verbose   amicus   3
                                                       ....]

                                                         Column   *Column*
                                                         I   *II*

    a. Owing to its *paucity,* water was at a pre-
       mium.
       (1)abundance   (2)scarcity   (3)pollution
       (4)fluoridation   *a*...............   *a*......

    b. That nation was *invincible* for centuries.
       (1)unconquerable   (2)prosperous   (3)unjust
       (4)aggressive   *b*...............   *b*......

    c. The king's declaration *nullified* the rights
       of the citizens.
       (1)destroyed   (2)multiplied   (3)insured
       (4)legalized   *c*...............   *c*......

    d. In this circumstance *fortitude* is needed.
       (1)help   (2)speed   (3)armament
       (4)courage   *d*...............   *d*......

    e. Black birch will not *ignite* easily.
        (1)bend (2)catch fire (3)grow (4)rot *e*................ *e*......

    f. Lack of money is no *impediment* to good
       living.
        (1)aid   (2)advantage   (3)hindrance
        (4)encouragement   *f*................ *f*......

    g. The President *conferred* with his cabinet.
        (1)agreed   (2)remained   (3)was satis-
       fied   (4)consulted   *g*................ *g*......

    h. The candidate's speech was *audacious.*
        (1)political   (2)brilliant   (3)daring
        (4)unscheduled   *h*................ *h*......

7. On the line at the right of each of *ten* of the statements below, write the *number* preceding the word or expression that best completes the statement. [10]

    a. By marrying Cornelia, Caesar incurred the anger
       of   (1)Brutus (2)Hannibal (3)Scipio (4)Sulla *a.*,......

    b. Caesar showed military prowess in his youth by
       the capture of a group of   (1)rebels (2)pirates
       (3)slaves   (4)deserters   *b*........

    c. In 58 B.C. Caesar was made proconsul of (1)Gaul
       (2)Egypt   (3)Spain   (4)Bithynia   *c*........

    d. Caesar's political rival was   (1)Octavian   (2)
       Pompey (3)Alexander   (4)Cinna   *d*........

    e. The usual commander of a Roman legion was
       called   (1)*quaestor*   (2)*centuriō*   (3)*lictor*
       (4)*lēgātus*   *e*........

    f. The usual battle formation of the Roman army was
       the   (1)*novissimum agmen*   (2)*tormenta*   (3)
       triplex aciēs (4)*impedīmenta*   *f*........

    g. Of all the Gauls, the bravest were the   (1)Bel-
       gians   (2)Helvetians   (3)Aquitanians   (4)Se-
       quanians   *g*........

    h. The Ides of March marks the occasion of Caesar's
       (1)death   (2)birth   (3)victory in Egypt   (4)
       crossing of the Rubicon   *h*........

    i. Caesar uttered the words *"Vēnī, vīdī, vīcī"* on the
       occasion of his   (1)defeat of the Germans   (2)
       victory in Pontus   (3)arrival in Britain   (4)as-
       sassination   *i*........

    j. Much of our knowledge of daily Roman life comes
       from the study of the buried city of   (1)Pompeii
       (2)Naples   (3)Delphi   (4)Milan   *j*........

    k. One of Rome's most dangerous enemies was   (1)
       Alexander   (2)Cato   (3)Hannibal   (4)Marius   *k*........

    l. A Roman contribution to civilization was   (1)silk
       (2)the wheel   (3)glass   (4)good roads   *l*........

    m. An ancient ruin in Rome often visited by tourists
       is   (1)the Parthenon   (2)the Colosseum   (3)the
       Erectheum   (4)Cleopatra's Needle   *m*........

    n. Paris gave the golden apple to   (1)Juno   (2)Diana
       (3)Venus   (4)Psyche   *n*........

LATIN—Two Years

Answer all seven questions.

1. Translate the following passages into English:

[The Gauls turn from besieging the Roman camp to attack Caesar. He is warned of their approach by a messenger from Cicero.]

a. Gallī, rē cognitā per explōrātōrēs, obsidiōnem relinquunt et ad Caesarem omnibus cōpiīs, ad numerum circiter mīlia LX, contendunt. Cicerō, datā facultāte, quendam Gallum ab *Verticōne,* nōbilī virō Nerviōrum, petit, quī litterās ad Caesarem ferat; hunc monet ut iter dīligenter faciat; scrībit in litterīs hostēs ab sē discessisse omnemque multitūdinem ad eum vertisse. Hīs litterīs circiter mediā nocte lātīs, Caesar suōs facit certiōrēs eōsque ad pugnandum animō cōnfirmat. Posterō diē prīmā lūce movet castra et circiter mīlia passuum quattuor prōgressus, trāns vallem et flūmen multitūdinem hostium videt.

—Caesar, *Dē Bellō Gallicō,* V, 49 (adapted) [20]

Verticōne—Verticō is nominative singular

[Hannibal, by a clever stratagem, outwits Fabius near Capua.]

b. Hannibal, hāc pugnā pugnātā, Rōmam profectus est. Nūllō resistente, in propinquis montibus morātus est. Cum Hannibal mīlitēs in castrīs complūrēs diēs tenuisset et Capuam redīret, Q. Fabius Maximus, dictātor Rōmānus, in agrō contrā eum cōpiās īnstrūxit. Hannibal, montibus clausus, sine ūllā difficultāte salūtem per *īnsidiās* invēnit. Nam incendit *sarmenta* quae in cornibus *iuvencōrum dēligāverat* et hōrum multitūdinem magnam ad Rōmānōs mīsit. Rōmānī spectāculō novō ita commōtī sunt ut nēmō extrā vāllum castrōrum ēgredī audēret.

Quamdiū Hannibal in Italiā fuit, nēmō eī in aciē restitit; nēmō post pugnam *Cannēnsem* contrā eum castra in campō posuit.

—C. Nepos, *Hannibal,* 5 (adapted) [20]

īnsidiās—strategy
sarmenta—faggots (bundle of twigs)
iuvencōrum—young bulls
dēligāverat—had tied
quamdiū—as long as
Cannēnsem—of Cannae

2. Translate into Latin *four* of the following sentences: [16]

a. The brave citizens seized arms in order to defend their city.

b. After the town had been conquered, the soldiers killed all the men with swords.

c. The leader said that he would easily drive the enemy from the territory.

d. The horsemen were so swift that they were able to flee from danger.

e. When Caesar had made the journey into the province, he put Labienus in charge of the army.

f. At that time the general asked why the lieutenant and the tenth legion were not making an attack.

3. Do *not* write a translation of this passage; read it through carefully several times and then answer *in complete English sentences each* of the questions below. Use everything in the text that will make your answers clear and complete. [10]

[The Greek Themistocles outwits the Persian Xerxes.]

At Xerxēs, Thermopylīs expugnātis, statim ad urbem Athēnās accessit atque eam incendiō *dēlēvit.* Cum nautae, flammā perterritī, manēre nōn audērent et plūrimī hortārentur ut domōs suās redīrent et mūrō sē dēfenderent, Themistoclēs ūnus restitit et *ūniversōs* vincere posse dīcēbat, sed *dispersōs* cōnfirmābat *peritūrōs esse.* Cum Eurybiadēs, rēx Spartānōrum, quī tum bellō praeerat, verbīs nōn movēbātur, Themistoclēs servum suum fidēlissimum ad Xerxem mīsit ut eī nūntiāret Graecōs in fugā esse atque, sī Graecōs statim aggrederētur brevī tempore eum omnēs oppressūrum esse. Hāc rē audītā, Xerxēs nihil malī crēdēns, postridiē inīquō sibi locō, in tam angustō marī *cōnflixit* ut eius multitūdō nāvium *explicārī* nōn posset. Victus igitur est magis etiam cōnsiliō Themistoclis quam armīs Graeciae.

—Nepos, *Themistoclēs,* 4 (adapted)

dēlēvit=vāstāvit
ūniversōs—if united
dispersōs—if scattered
peritūrōs esse—from *pereō,* perish
cōnflixit=proelium commīsit
explicārī—from *explicō,* spread out

a. What success did Xerxes achieve after the battle of Thermopylae?

b. Name *one* effect of the fire on the sailors.

c. What *two* actions did the majority earnestly recommend?

d. What reason did Themistocles give for objecting to these actions?

e. What post did the Spartan king Eurybiades hold?

f. What was his reaction to Themistocles' advice?

g. According to Themistocles' message, what were the Greeks doing?

h. What did he say Xerxes would gain by attacking at once?

i. What harmful effect did Xerxes suffer in the battle because of his unfavorable position?

j. To what does Nepos attribute Xerxes' defeat?

4. On the line at the right of *each* sentence below, write the *number* preceding the word or expression which, when inserted in the blank, makes the sentence grammatically correct. [6]

a. Dux .... frūmentum dedit.

    (1) nōs   (2) ad nōs   (3) nōbīs   (4) ad nōbīs   *a* ....

    b. Rōmānī multa mīlia .... cēpērunt.
        (1)mīlitum   (2)mīlitēs   (3)ex mīlitibus   (4)mīlitis *b*........

    c. Caesar .... appellātus est.
        (1)imperātōrem   (2)imperātōrī   (3)imperātōre
        (4)imperātor   *c*........

    d. Nūntius .... convēnisse dīxit.
        (1)virī   (2)virō   (3)virōs   (4)virīs   *d*........

    e. Rōmānī .... servōrum nōn ūsī sunt.
        (1)auxilium   (2)auxiliō   (3)auxilī   (4)auxiliōrum *e*........

    f. Puerī .... vocābantur.
        (1)mātre   (2)mātrem   (3)mātris   (4)ā mātre   *f*........

    g. Servī lībertātem .... nōn poterant.
        (1)ut obtineant   (2)ut obtinērent   (3)obtinent
        (4)obtinēre   *g*........

    h. Ego tam timidus eram ut .....
        (1)fūgī   (2)fugerem   (3)fugiam   (4)fūgeram   *h*........

    i. Eques ad ducem prōcessit .....
        (1)ut praemium acciperet   (2)ut praemium accipit
        (3)praemium accipere   (4)praemium accēpisse   *i*........

    j. Imperātor scīvit quis .....
        (1)pervēnit   (2)pervēnerat   (3)pervēnisset   (4)
        perveniat   *j*........

    k. Lēgātus .... imperāvit.
        (1)virīs ut castra ponerent   (2)virīs ut castra po-
        nent   (3)virōs ut castra ponerent   (4)virōs castra
        ponere   *k*........

    l. Rōmānī .... nōn nocuērunt.
        (1)captīvos   (2)captīvīs   (3)captīvus   (4)captī-
        vōrum   *l*........

5. Write *all* the specified forms, placing your answers on the lines at the right: [10]

    a-b.   nominative plural of *id vulnus*   *a-b*...............

    c-d.   genitive singular of *difficile negōtium*   *c-d*...............

    e-f.   accusative plural of *ego*   *e*...............

                tū   *f*...............

    g.   vocative of *Sextus*   *g*...............

    h-i.   superlative nominative singular masculine of *pulcher* *h*...............

                similis   *i*...............

    j-k.   positive degree of the adverbs from *dīligēns* *j*...............

                lātus   *k*...............

    l.   present imperative active second singular of *rogō* *l*...............

    m-n.   future indicative passive third plural of *doceō* *m*...............

                mūniō   *n*...............

    o-p.   present indicative third singular of *adsum* *o*...............

                ūtor   *p*...............

    q-r.   imperfect indicative and subjunctive first plural of *eō* *q*...............

                                          r...............

s-t.   pluperfect subjunctive active and passive third   *s*................
         singular of *dēfendō*   *t*................

6. For *each* sentence below, write in column I a Latin word with which the italicized word is associated by derivation. Then, in column II, write the *number* preceding the word or expression below each sentence that best expresses the meaning of the italicized word. [8]

	Column I	Column II
[Illustration: The explanation was made in a very *amicable* manner.	amīcus	3
(1) angry (2) belligerent (3) friendly (4) verbose	....	........]

	Column I	Column II
a. He is *conserving* his strength for the next encounter. (1) testing (2) increasing (3) keeping (4) measuring	*a*................	*a*.........
b. No further *concessions* will be requested. (1) reasons (2) penalties (3) explanations (4) privileges	*b*................	*b*.........
c. *Exhort* him to leave. (1) Urge (2) Forbid (3) Compel (4) Command	*c*................	*c*.........
d. That nation has made no *notable* contribution to science. (1) enduring (2) original (3) recent (4) outstanding	*d*................	*d*.........
e. The prisoner seems to have a *dual* personality. (1) baffling (2) pleasing (3) double (4) dominant	*e*................	*e*.........
f. *Consequently,* we shall remain here. (1) Therefore (2) Probably (3) Possibly (4) Positively	*f*................	*f*.........
g. Mr. Reed is the *donor* of the new car. (1) winner (2) purchaser (3) driver (4) giver	*g*................	*g*.........
h. She gives the impression of being habitually *frustrated*. (1) suspicious (2) defeated (3) exhausted (4) excited	*h*................	*h*.........

7. On the line at the right of each of *ten* of the statements below, write the *number* preceding the word or expression that best completes the statement. [10]

a. During the Gallic Wars, Caesar invaded   (1) Britain   (2) Spain   (3) Ireland   (4) Egypt   *a*.........

b. The Gauls fought their last war with Caesar under the leadership of (1) Orgetorix (2) Ambiorix (3) Ariovistus (4) Vercingetorix   *b*........

c. In Book I of *Dē Bellō Gallicō* Caesar describes the migration of the Helvetians and the (1) revolt of Aquitania (2) war with the Germans (3) invasion of Germany (4) war with the Belgians   *c*........

d. Caesar's last words were said to have been (1) *Vēnī, vīdī, vīcī* (2) *Alea iacta est* (3) *Carthāgō dēlenda est* (4) *Et tū, Brūte*   *d*........

e. Caesar fought in a civil war against (1) Marius (2) Pompey (3) Octavian (4) Crassus   *e*........

f. The number of men in a legion was generally about (1) 1,000 (2) 2,500 (3) 3,600 (4) 10,000   *f*........

g. The army's marching formation was called (1) *āgmen* (2) *exercitus* (3) *aciēs* (4) *ōrdō*   *g*........

h. Caesar is credited with making improvements in the (1) clock (2) toga (3) sword (4) calendar   *h*........

i. Rome's first government was (1) an oligarchy (2) a dictatorship (3) a monarchy (4) a republic   *i*........

j. As a result of Caesar's wars, Rome left a great cultural heritage to (1) the Far East (2) France (3) Africa (4) Greece   *j*........

k. One of Rome's important institutions was the public (1) bath (2) school system (3) postal system (4) museum   *k*........

l. The Roman schoolboy studied Homer's (1) *Aeneid* (2) *Iliad* (3) *Argonauts* (4) *Anabasis*   *l*........

m. A great inventor in Greek mythology was (1) Hercules (2) Midas (3) Daedalus (4) Mars   *m*........

n. In the Roman Forum was located the (1) *Campus Martius* (2) *Colosseum* (3) *Via Sacra* (4) *Circus Maximus*   *n*........

LATIN—Two Years

Tuesday, June 19, 1962—1:15 to 4:15 p.m., only

Part 1

Translate each of the following passages into English. Write your translation in the space provided on the separate answer sheet.

[The story of the ten prisoners at Cannae.]

a. Post proelium *Cannēnse* Hannibal decem ex nostrīs mīlitibus quōs cēperat, Rōmam mīsit. Imperāvit eīs ut senātōribus Rōmānīs dīcerent Carthāginiēnsēs cum Rōmānīs captīvōs *permūtāre* velle. Priusquam profectī sunt, pollicitī sunt sē reditūrōs esse in castra Hannibalis sī Rōmānī captīvōs nōn *permūtārent.*

Vēnērunt ad urbem Rōmam decem captīvī. Nūntiāvērunt quid Carthāginiēnsēs fierī vellent. Hoc senātōribus Rōmānīs *grātum* nōn erat. Parentēs captīvōrum magnō dolōre *affectī sunt.* Fīliōs implōrābant nē ad hostēs redīrent. Tum octō ex hīs captīvīs respondērunt sē *iūre iūrandō* tenērī, et ad Hannibalem rediērunt. Duo Rōmae mānsērunt et sē *iūre iūrandō* līberātōs esse dīcēbant. Omnēs Rōmānī exīstimābant captīvōs quī mānsissent esse sine honōre et eīs inimīcissimī erant.

—Gellius, *Noctēs Atticae,* VI, 18 (adapted)   [20]

> *Cannēnse*—of Cannae
> *permūtāre*—exchange
> *grātum*—acceptable, pleasing
> *affectī sunt*—from *afficiō*—were afflicted
> *iūre iūrandō*—from *iūs iūrandum*—oath

[The Veneti, a coastal tribe of western Gaul, oppose the Romans.]

b. Auctōritās Venetōrum est longē amplissima omnis *ōrae maritimae,* quod Venetī nāvēs plūrimās habent et in Britanniam saepe nāvigant. Scientiā et ūsū rērum nauticārum cēterōs *antecēdunt.* In marī vāstō paucōs portūs tenent. Venetī etiam paene omnēs eōs quī eō marī prope fīnēs suōs ūtuntur *habent vectīgālēs.*

Prīmō Sīlium et Velānium, lēgātōs Rōmānōs, *retinent* quod per eōs exīstimābant sē obsidēs quōs Crassō dedissent *recuperātūrōs esse.* Auctōritāte Venetōrum adductī, fīnitimī etiam lēgātōs *retinent.* Hī erant lēgātī quōs P. Crassus frūmentī obtinendī causā in complūrēs cīvitātēs dīmīserat. Celeriter prīncipēs reliquārum cīvitātum inter sē *coniūrant* atque cōnfirmant sē Rōmānōrum servitūtem nōn *perlātūrōs esse.*

—Caesar, *Dē Bellō Gallicō,* III, 8 (adapted)   [20]

> *ōrae maritimae*—from *ōra maritima*—coast
> *antecēdunt*—surpass
> *habent vectīgālēs*—hold subject to tribute
> *retinent*—from *retineō*—detain
> *recuperātūrōs esse*—from *recuperō*—get back
> *coniūrant*—conspire
> *perlātūrōs esse*—from *perferō*—submit, endure

Part 2

Directions (1-10): In the space provided on a separate answer sheet, rewrite *each* of the following sentences, substituting for the italicized Latin term the grammatical form called for or the proper form of the expression in parentheses. *Make any other changes in each sentence that are required by the substitution,* but, unless the meaning is changed by the parenthetical instructions, be sure to retain the general idea of the original sentence. [10]

1. Urbs *ā cōnsulibus fortibus* dēfendētur. (mūrus altus)
2. *Cōgō* eum mēcum discēdere. (Persuādeō)
3. *Diū* in castrīs manēbant. (Trēs hōrae)
4. *Dīxit* nāvēs in litore incēnsās esse. (Dēmōnstrō ubi)
5. *Centum* equitēs aderant. (Duo mīlia)
6. *Cum proelium cōnfectum esset,* Caesar suōs in castra redūxit. (ablative absolute)
7. *Domī* labōrābat. (Vīlla)
8. Mīlitēs castra *posuērunt.* (passive voice)
9. Sociī ad Caesarem frūmentum *portāvērunt.* (dō)
10. *Ad oppidum occupandum* hostēs vēnērunt. (*ut* clause)

Part 3

Directions (11-20): Read the following passage carefully, but do *not* write a translation. Below the passage you will find ten questions. For each question, select the alternative that best answers the question on the basis of the information given in the passage and write its *number* in the space provided on the line at the right. You may read the passage as many times as you wish. [20]

[Eporedorix and Viridomarus kill the Roman garrison at Noviodonum, seize and destroy Caesar's stores and burn the town.]

Noviodūnum erat oppidum Haeduōrum ad rīpās *Ligeris* flūminis idōneō locō positum. Ad hunc locum Caesar omnēs obsidēs Galliae, frūmentum, pecūniam pūblicam, impedīmentōrum magnam partem contulerat. Ad eundem locum numerum equōrum comparātum huius bellī causā in Ītaliā et Hispāniā etiam mīserat. Cum Eporedorix Viridomārusque, sociī Caesaris, eō vēnissent cognōvērunt Haeduōs ad Vercingetorīgem lēgātōs dē pāce et amīcitiā mīsisse. Hanc occāsiōnem nōn neglegendam esse exīstimāvērunt.

Itaque interfectīs Noviodūnī praesidiīs, hī virī pecūniam et equōs inter sē dīvīsērunt. Effēcērunt ut obsidēs cīvitātum ad magistrātum in oppidum Bibracte dēdūcerentur. Oppidum Noviodūnum incendērunt quod ā sē tenērī nōn posse iūdicābant. Quam maximum frūmentum nāvibus remōvērunt et reliquum aquā et incendiō dēlēvērunt. Ipsī ex fīnitimīs regiōnibus cōpiās cōgere atque praesidia ad rīpās *Ligeris* pōnere coepērunt. Equitatum omnibus locīs timōris faciendī causā mīsērunt. Spērāvērunt sē ab rē frūmentāriā Rōmānōs exclūdere posse quod flūmen eō tempore altissimum propter tempestātēs hiemis erat.

—Caesar, *Dē Bellō Gallicō,* VII, 55 (adapted)

Ligeris—the Loire river

11. Caesar Noviodūnum iter fēcit quod   (1) erat maximum
(2) locus bonus erat   (3) Haeduōs timuit   (4) frūmentum nōn
habēbat   11........

12. Praeter (*except*) equōs, quot (*how many*) rēs Caesar
Noviodūnum coēgerat? (1) trēs (2) quattuor (3) sex (4) septem   12........

13. Caesar equōs comparāverat ut   (1) bellum gereret
(2) frūmentum portāret   (3) pācem faceret   (4) salūtem quaereret   13........

14. Etsī Eporēdorīx et Viridomārus erant sociī Caesaris, tamen
(1) fidem Caesaris nōn servāvērunt (2) auxilium incolīs Noviodūnī
dedērunt (3) Haeduōs ad Vercingetorīgem mīsērunt (4) Caesarem
interfēcērunt   14........

15. Eporēdorīx et Viridomārus pecūniam inter sē dīvīsērunt
postquam   (1) magistrātūs dēdūxērunt   (2) nāvēs remōvērunt
(3) regiōnēs vāstāvērunt   (4) praesidia occīdērunt   15........

16. Obsidēs Galliae quōs Caesar cēperat ab Eporēdorīge Viri-
domārōque   (1) interfectī sunt   (2) ad magistrātum missī sunt
(3) arma capere coactī sunt   (4) ad nāvēs remōtī sunt   16........

17. Eporēdorix et Viridomārus oppidum incendērunt quod
(1) cīvēs Noviodūnī ipsōs ad Caesarem trādere voluērunt (2) magistrātūs hoc iussērunt (3) auxiliō Caesarī esse voluērunt (4) difficile
id dēfendere erat   17........

18. Hī virī magnam partem frūmentī   (1) Caesarī dedērunt
(2) in nāvibus posuērunt   (3) ad Vercingetorīgem portāvērunt
(4) Bibracte tulērunt   18........

19. Eporēdorīx et Viridomārus cōpiās coēgērunt quās (1) fīnitimī sibi dederant   (2) ex omnibus locīs cēperant   (3) Rōmānī
mīserant   (4) ad rīpās Ligeris vīderant   19........

20. Eporēdorīx et Viridomārus spērāvērunt (1) flūmen Ligerem
altissimum esse   (2) tempestātēs futūrās esse   (3) Rōmānōs rem
frūmentāriam nōn habitūrōs esse (4) Rōmānōs equitātum missūrōs
esse   20........

Part 4

Directions (21-30): On the line at the right, write the *number* of the
word or expression which, when inserted in the blank, makes *each* sentence
grammatically correct.   [10]

21. Gallī rogāvērunt cūr Caesar auxilum nōn ....
    (1) tulisset (2) tulerat (3) tulisse (4) tulit   21........

22. Labiēnus tempestātem .... nūntiāvit.
    (1) ad ducem (2) duce (3) ducī (4) ducis   22........

23. Mīlitēs fugitīvōs .... nōn poterant.
    (1) ut caperent (2) capere (3) cēpisse (4) ad capiendum   23........

24. Lēgātus dīxit legiōnēs pontem fortiter ....
    (1) dēfendisse (2) dēfendēbant (3) dēfenderent (4) dē-
fendissent   24........

25. Haeduī iter .... faciēbant.
    (1) in eō diē (2) eī diēī (3) in eum diem (4) eō diē   25........

26. Imperātor collem mūnīvit .... caperētur.
    (1) nōn (2) nē (3) quīn (4) neque   26........

27. Mīles, cum hostēs ...., cucurrit.
    (1) videat (2) vidēbit (3) vīdisset (4) vidēre   27........

28. Caesar tribūnum .... praefēcit.
    (1) legiōnēs (2) legiōnem (3) legiōne (4) legiōnī   28........

29. Puer ad Graeciam nāvigāvit ad urbēs clārās ....
    (1) videndās (2) vidēret (3) vidēre (4) videnda   29........

30. Rēx .... mihi locūtus est.
    (1) suum (2) ipsum (3) sē (4) ipse   30........

Part 5

Directions (31-40): For *each* sentence below, write in column I a Latin word with which the italicized word is associated by derivation. Then in column II write the *number* preceding the word or expression that best expresses the meaning of the italicized word. [10]

	Column I	Column II
[*Illustration*: The explanation was made in a very *amicable* manner. (1) angry (2) belligerent (3) friendly (4) verbose	amīcus	3 ....]

	Column I	Column II
31. An eagle's nest is usually *inaccessible*. (1) very high (2) difficult to reach (3) difficult to see (4) indestructible	31...............	....
32. The department store allows *deductions* on the customer's bills under certain conditions. (1) increases (2) adjustments (3) discounts (4) postponements	32...............	....
33. The Justice Department *interrogated* the suspected enemy agents. (1) questioned (2) arrested (3) investigated (4) fingerprinted	33...............	....
34. *Conservation* of forest regions will help prevent land erosion. (1) Exploitation (2) Protection (3) Augmentation (4) Restriction	34...............	....
35. The Secretary of State called the ambassador's note a *provocation* to war. (1) commitment (2) deterrent (3) step (4) challenge	35...............	....
36. The facts which you mention are not *pertinent* to this case. (1) prejudicial (2) suitable (3) important (4) related	36...............	....

37. The museum fire caused *irreparable* loss.
    (1) minor   (2) irrelative   (3) irremediable
    (4) much   37................   ....

38. Failure to file the proper papers *invalidated* his
    claim to the estate.
    (1) nullified   (2) strengthened   (3) delayed
    (4) sealed   38................   ....

39. Expansion and *contraction* of concrete roads
    have been engineering problems.
    (1) shrinking (2) surfacing (3) drying (4) erosion   39................   ....

40. A wise man maintains his *composure*.
    (1) wealth (2) reputation (3) power (4) calmness   40................   ....

Part 6

Directions (41-55): In the following passage fifteen words or expressions
are italicized and repeated in the questions below. Choose *ten* questions.
Write on the line at the right the *number* of the alternative that best explains each of these *ten* words or expressions as it is used in the passage.
[10]

Like that of several other nations, the history of Rome began with a
legend. According to that legend, a *great city* in Asia Minor was once
besieged and captured by the Greeks by means of the *now-famous trick*.
A *warrior* of that city escaped and sailed to Italy where he settled. *One of
his descendants,* according to tradition, *eventually* founded Rome and
became its first king.

Under the succeeding line of kings the tiny state flourished, until *one
of the kings* by his tyrannical rule so enraged the citizens that they rose up
and expelled him. At this time the Romans adopted a *new form of government* with *two officials* elected annually holding the highest political office,
and kept this form for nearly five hundred years. At first there were serious
class conflicts. The *aristocrats* bullied the *poorer class,* allowing its members
no share in the government. With the passage of time, however, the poorer
class did win many of the rights and privileges of the richer Roman citizens.

In their external struggles the Roman subdued one neighbor after another;
they completely destroyed their most *formidable enemies* in a series of wars
called the Punic Wars. Great glory now came to the city, and *Jupiter* looked
down from the *Capitoline* upon the yearly Saturnalia. Soon he was to hear
the proclamation *vēnī, vīdī, vīcī* and see the *first emperor* assume the
supreme power of Rome.

41. *great city*
    (1) Miletus   (2) Troy   (3) Ephesus   (4) Damascus   41........

42. *now-famous trick*
    (1) Greek fire   (2) wooden horse   (3) spiked chariot
    (4) smoke screen   42........

43. *warrior*
    (1) Aeneas   (2) Hector   (3) Achilles   (4) Hercules   43........

44. *One of his descendants*
    (1) Ascanius   (2) Romulus   (3) Anchises   (4) Ulysses   44........

45. *eventually*
    (1) 1000 B.C.   (2) 850 B.C.   (3) 753 B.C.   (4) 500 B.C.   45........

46. *one of the kings*
    (1) Midas   (2) Xerxes   (3) Alexander the Great
    (4) Tarquin the Proud   46........

47. *new form of government*
    (1) monarchy (2) fascism   (3) republic   (4) communism   47........

48. *two officials*
    (1) consuls   (2) praetors   (3) tribunes   (4) censors   48........

49. *aristocrats*
    (1) equitēs   (2) patricians   (3) novī hominēs   (4) merchants   49........

50. *poorer class*
    (1) hostages   (2) senators   (3) slaves   (4) plebeians   50........

51. *formidable enemies*
    (1) Greeks (2) Macedonians (3) Germans (4) Carthaginians   51........

52. *Jupiter*
    (1) king of the gods   (2) first king of Rome   (3) god of war
    (4) Roman general   52........

53. *Capitoline*
    (1) one of the temples   (2) senate house   (3) one of the
    hills of Rome   (4) one of the palaces in Rome   53........

54. *vēnī, vīdī, vīcī*
    (1) Brutus's cry after the assassination of Caesar (2) Caesar's
    last words   (3) Caesar's message of victory   (4) Pompey's
    announcement from Pharsalia   54........

55. *first emperor*
    (1) Augustus   (2) Antony   (3) Trajan   (4) Hadrian   55........

LATIN—Two Years

Tuesday, June 18, 1963—1:15 to 4·15 p.m., only

Part I

Translate each of the following passages into English. Write your translation in the space provided on a separate answer sheet.

[Caesar and Pompey contend for supreme power.]

a. Caesar victor ā Galliā rediit et secundum *consulātum* postulāre coepit. Eō accepto sine ūllā pugnā, Mārcellus cōnsul et aliī senātōrēs contrā rem locūtī sunt atque, dīmissīs exercitibus, eum ad urbem redīre iussērunt. Cum mīlitēs suōs cōēgisset, Caesar tamen ā mūnītiōnibus profectus est atque contrā patriam cum exercitū vēnit. Cōnsulēs cum Pompeiō senātōribusque ex urbe in Graeciam fūgērunt. Ad eum locum Caesar properāvit atque, prīmō proeliō commissō, in fugam datus est. Incolumis tamen erat quod Pompeius eum noctū sequī nōluit et Caesar Pompeium potestātem vincendī āmīsisse dīxit. Posteā Pompeius, cum superārētur, petīvit ut ā rēge Aegyptī auxilium acciperet. Ille rēx, fortūnās suās sequēns, Pompeium occīdit et caput eius ad Caesarem mīsit.

—Eutropius, *Historiae Rōmānae Breviārium,* VI, 19-21 (adapted) [20]
cōnsulātum—consulship

[Curio addresses his soldiers in North Africa
and urges them to be loyal to Caesar.]

b. Cūriō, conciliō mīlitum convocātō, nārrat quōmodo Caesar ita ūsus sit eōrum studiō *ad Corfīnium* ut magnam partem Italiae beneficiō atque auctōritāte eōrum ad sē dūxerit. "Omnēs cīvitātēs," inquit, "vōs et vestrum factum secūtae sunt. Propter hoc, Pompeius, nūllō proeliō pulsus, ex Italiā excessit. Caesar, mē, quem sibi *cārissimum* habuit, et prōvinciās, Siciliam atque Āfricam, vestrae fideī commīsit.

"At sunt eī quī vōs moneant ut nōs relinquātis. Quid enim magis cupiunt quam ūnō tempore et nōs circumvenīre et vōs magnō *maleficiō* tenēre? Vōs autem, incertā victōriā, Caesarem secūtī estis; vōsne iam Pompeium bellī fortūnā victum sequēminī?"

Quā ōrātiōne permōtī, mīlitēs Cūriōnem cohortantur nē dubitet impetum facere et suam fidem virtūtemque sentīre.

—Caesar, *Dē Bellō Cīvīlī,* II, 32-33 (adapted) [20]
ad Corfīnium—near Corfīnium
cārissimum—from *cārus,* dear
maleficium—crime

Part II

Directions (1-10): On a separate answer sheet, rewrite *completely each* of the following sentences, substituting for the italicized Latin term the grammatical form called for or the proper form of the expression in parentheses. *Make any other changes in each sentence that are required by the substitution,* but, unless the meaning is changed by the parenthetical instructions, be sure to retain the general idea of the original sentence. [10]

1. Mīlitibus *imperat* ut maneant. (iubeō)
2. Ulixēs ad silvam iit *ad cibum inveniendum.* (*ut* purpose clause)
3. *Mārcus* frātribus parvīs fābulam *nārrat.* (direct address and imperative)
4. Dux respondit, "*Mīlitēs nostrī bene pugnāvērunt.*" (indirect statement)
5. *Fossa* est minima. (Castra)
6. Multitūdō ā Germāniā *Rōmam* vēnerat. (prōvincia)
7. Frūmentum ā sociīs *parātum erat.* (active voice)
8. Hannibal *ibi* morārī nōluit. (eī fīnēs)
9. Caesar, *ubi* legiōnēs īnstrūxit, impetum fēcit. (*cum* circumstantial clause)
10. *Mox* ad Graeciam pervēnit. (Posterus diēs)

Part III

Directions (11-20): Read the following passage carefully, but do *not* write a translation. Below the passage you will find ten incomplete statements. Select the answer that best completes *each* statement *on the basis of the information given in the passage* and write its number in the space provided. [20]

[The rivalry and brave deeds of two centurions]

Erant in eā legiōne fortissimī virī, centuriōnēs, T. Pullō et L. Vorēnus, quī perpetuās contrōversiās habēbant. Ex hīs Pullō, cum ācerrimē ad mūnītiōnēs pugnārētur, "Quid dubitās," inquit, "Vorēne? Quam opportūnitātem probandae tuae virtūtis exspectās? Hic diēs dē nostrīs contrōversiīs iūdicābit."

Haec cum dīxisset prōcēdit extrā mūnītiōnēs et in eam partem hostium quae dēnsa vīsa est currit.

Veritus opīniōnem omnium, Vorēnus in vāllō nōn remanet sed eum statim sequitur. Spatiō relīctō, Pullō pīlum in hostēs conicit atque ūnum ex multitūdine Gallōrum currentem vulnerat: hunc scūtīs dēfendunt hostēs; in illum (Pullōnem) ūniversī tēla coniciunt neque eī facultātem prōgrediendī dant. Trānsfīgitur scūtum Pullōnis et tēlum in *balteum* conicitur. Hic cāsus arma vertit; gladium ēdūcere nōn potest et sīc hostēs eum circumstant. Inimīcus Vorēnus contendit ad auxilium eī dandum. Statim omnis multitūdō ad eum ā Pullōne currit. Illum (Pullōnem) enim tēlō trānsfīxum arbitrantur.

Gladiō pugnat Vorēnus atque, ūnō interfectō, reliquōs paulum pellit; dum persequitur cupidius in locum īnferiōrem dēicitur. Vorēnō circumventō, nunc eī auxilium fert Pullō, atque, duo virī incolumēs, complūribus interfectīs, summā cum laude sēsē intrā mūnītiōnēs recipiunt.

—Caesar, *Dē Bellō Gallicō*, V, 44 (adapted)

balteum—belt

11. T. Pullō et L. Vorēnus erant duo mīlitēs quī (1)oppidum mūniēbant (2)rem frūmentāriam cōnferēbant (3)inter sē pugnābant (4)dē hostibus iūdicābant

11........

12. Pullō rogāvit Vorēnum cūr (1)nōn in vāllō mānsisset (2)aciem hostium explōrāvisset (3)ducem legiōnis exspectāret (4)nōn fortitūdinem ostenderet   12........
13. Pullō sē Vorēnō virtūte praestāre dēmōnstrāre volēbat (1)pugnandō hostēs (2)loquendō magnopere (3)rogandō ducem (4)eum interficiendō   13........
14. Cum Pullō in proelium properāret, Vorēnus eum subitō cōnsecūtus est quod (1)eī pīlum dare volēbat (2)dux ita imperāvit (3)timēbat quid omnēs sentīrent (4)eum amābat   14........
15. Tēlum in hostēs ā Pullōne iactum (1)mīlitēs reppulit (2)virōs terruit (3)Vorēnum vulnerāvit (4)Gallō nocuit   15........
16. Post impetum hostium, Pullō nōn poterat (1)prōcēdere contrā hostēs (2)pedem referre (3)balteum invenīre (4)multitūdinem vidēre   16........
17. Pullō nōn sē dēfendēbat cum (1)vulnerātus esset (2)arma sua āmīsisset (3)territus esset (4)armīs suīs ūtī nōn posset   17........
18. Hostēs Vorēnum persecūtī sunt quod (1)Pullōnem vulnerātum esse crēdēbant (2)Pullō ex multitūdine currēbat (3)ille scūtum Pullōnī dābat (4)ille gladium nōn habēbat   18........
19. Cum Vorēnus in perīculō esset (1)Pullō intrā mūnītiōnēs sē recēpit (2)Pullō eī auxilium dedit (3)mīlitēs Rōmānī ex castrīs cucurrērunt (4)Gallī eum laudāvērunt   19........
20. Postquam duo centuriōnēs in castra rediērunt (1)erant inimīciōrēs quam prius (2)ab omnibus laudātī sunt (3)dona eīs data sunt (4)vulnera eōrum cūrāta sunt   20........

Part IV

Directions (21-30): In the space provided, write the *number* of the word or expression which, when inserted in the blank, makes *each* sentence grammatically correct. [10]

21. Ariovistus .... Germānōrum dēlēctus est. (1)ducem (2)ducis (3)ducī (4)dux   21........
22. Helvētiī mūrum fēcērunt .... (1)sē dēfendere (2)ut sē dēfendant (3)sē dēfendisse (4)ut sē dēfenderent   22........
23. Caesar Labiēnum .... praefēcit. (1)virī (2)virōrum (3)virīs (4)virōs   23........
24. Caesar .... rediit. (1)ad domum (2)domī (3)domum (4)domū   24........
25. Bibulus .... persuāsit ut fortiter pugnārent. (1)nautārum (2)nautīs (3)nautās (4)nautae   25........
26. Explōrātōrēs in castrīs .... remānsērunt. (1)multī diēs (2)multōs diēs (3)multīs diēbus (4)multōrum diērum   26........
27. Sēquanī proximī .... erant. (1)Belgīs (2)ad Belgās (3)Belgārum (4)in Belgās   27........
28. Nōn audīvit urbem .... ab hostibus. (1)captus esse (2)captum esse (3)captam esse (4)capta esse   28........
29. Dominus .... praemia dedit. (1)servī (2)servīs (3)ad servōs (4)servōs   29........
30. Germānī per .... iter fēcērunt. (1)montēs (2)montibus (3)monte (4)montium   30........

Part V

Directions (31-40): For *each* sentence below, write in column I on a separate answer sheet a Latin word with which the italicized word is associated by derivation. Then in column II write the *number* preceding the word or expression that best expresses the meaning of the italicized word. [10]

[*Illustration*: The explanation was made in a very *amicable* manner.
(1)angry   (2)belligerent   (3)friendly   (4)verbose

Column I	Column II
amicus	(3)

31. The members of the school board were convinced that their actions were *legitimate.* (1)lawful   (2)unprecedented   (3)illegal   (4)restricted

32. The *brevity* of the official's reply was cause for concern. (1)extensiveness   (2)indirectness   (3)shortness   (4)effectiveness

33. The lawyer made a *cogent* statement of the facts. (1)lengthy (2)forceful   (3)weak   (4)witty

34. The young research assistant took *copious* notes on the experiments. (1)meager   (2)interesting   (3)abundant   (4)significant

35. The *emissary* disembarked on the evening of August 3. (1)alien (2)envoy   (3)immigrant   (4)emigrant

36. The United Nations *convened* to consider sanctions against several nations. (1)refused   (2)retired   (3)agreed   (4)assembled

37. The serum was declared *impotent* by the scientists. (1)harmful (2)effective   (3)venomous   (4)powerless

38. A disease in its *incipient* stage is often difficult to diagnose. (1)final   (2)initial   (3)secondary   (4)tertiary

39. It is *imperative* for the students to follow directions. (1)necessary (2)proper   (3)impertinent   (4)impossible

40. The astronaut's report *confirmed* many spatial theories. (1)expanded   (2)described   (3)verified   (4)contradicted

Part VI

Directions (41-55): Of the following fifteen italicized words or expressions select *ten.* In the spaces provided write the *number* of the alternative that best explains the italicized word or expression as it is used in the passage. [10]

The Mediterranean Sea, to which the Romans gave a special *name,* reflects in its stories and legends the modes of thought of four great national cultures. Upon entering it through the Strait of Gibraltar, one sees why the ancients associated the Rock of Gibraltar with the notion of a *divinity* supporting the sky. From here Mercury, winged *rod* in hand, is said to have flown from the lofty *mountain* which was the home of the gods, to Carthage, where he urged Aeneas to *accomplish his mission.*

Mercury's flight was over Mediterranean waters on which some boats were carrying grain to the *City of the Caesars;* others, sped by *three banks of oars,* were bringing apes and peacocks from ancient Nineveh. Centuries later there glided over these waters the silver and purple sailboat of an *Oriental queen* whose beauty nearly deprived Rome of all the advantage once gained by Scipio's defeat of his *greatest adversary* and whose story has been given to us in motion pictures. Through these waters the *Greek hero* who struggled for many years to reach his native city and who has become the symbol of all homing travelers and spacemen steered his ships.

The Mediterranean was perilous as well as beautiful, and the lively imagination of the ancients led them to regard the whirlpools and rocks between Sicily and Italy as *monsters* to which mariners fell prey. They saw storms as the work of a *god opening a huge bag of winds,* or of Neptune roughening the waters by a *device* symbolically his own. This imagination led to the conviction that man alone does not shape his own destiny but is partially dependent upon the gods. Such a belief is revealed in the Romans' use of small images representing the *guardian gods of the household.* To these statues the *head of the family* made ceremonial offerings.

41. **name**
    (1)*mare magnum*   (2)*mare nostrum*   (3)*mare rēgāle*
    (4)*mare nāvigābile*   41........

42. **divinity**
    (1)*Iuppiter*   (2)*Mārs*   (3)*Vulcānus*   (4)*Atlās*   42........

43. **rod**
    (1)*cādūceus*   (2)*aquila*   (3)*signum*   (4)*fascēs*   43........

44. **mountain**
    (1)*Vesuvius*   (2)*Aetna*   (3)*Olympus*   (4)*Īda*   44........

45. **accomplish his mission**
    (1)build a fleet   (2)visit the underworld   (3)found a new city   (4)unite with the Carthaginians   45........

46. **City of the Caesars**
    (1)*Rōma*   (2)*Athēnae*   (3)*Tarsus*   (4)*Tyrus*   46........

47. **three banks of oars**
    (1)*nāvēs longae*   (2)*trirēmēs*   (3)*nāvēs plānae*   (4)*quinquerēmēs*   47........

48. **Oriental queen**
    (1)*Dīdō*   (2)*Octāvia*   (3)*Andromachē*   (4)*Cleopātra*   48........

49. **greatest adversary**
    (1)*Cȳrus*   (2)*Alexander*   (3)*Hannibal*   (4)*Pyrrhus*   49........

50. **Greek hero**
    (1)*Ājax*   (2)*Hector*   (3)*Paris*   (4)*Ulixēs*   50........

51. **monsters**
    (1)*Minōtaurus et Thēseus*   (2)*Scylla et Charybdis*
    (3)*Bellerophōn et Pēgasus*   (4)*Charōn et Cerberus*   51........

52. **god opening a huge bag of winds**
    (1)*Orpheus*   (2)*Zephyrus*   (3)*Pān*   (4)*Aeolus*   52........

53. **device**
    (1)trident   (2)thunderbolt   (3)lyre   (4)arrow   53........

54. **guardian gods of the household**
    (1)*Penātēs*   (2)*Cyclōpēs*   (3)*Tītānī*   (4)*Mūsae*   54........

55. **head of the family**
    (1)*pontifex maximus*   (2)*pater familiās*   (3)*pater patriae*   (4)*rēx sacrōrum*   55........